M000249281

Emmanuel

EMMANUEL

Levinas and Variations on God with Us

Donald Wallenfang

CASCADE *Books* · Eugene, Oregon

EMMANUEL
Levinas and Variations on God with Us

Copyright © 2021 Donald Wallenfang. All rights reserved. Except for brief quotations in critical publications or reviews, no part of this book may be reproduced in any manner without prior written permission from the publisher. Write: Permissions, Wipf and Stock Publishers, 199 W. 8th Ave., Suite 3, Eugene, OR 97401.

Cascade Books
An Imprint of Wipf and Stock Publishers
199 W. 8th Ave., Suite 3
Eugene, OR 97401

www.wipfandstock.com

PAPERBACK ISBN: 978-1-6667-0000-8
HARDCOVER ISBN: 978-1-6667-0001-5
EBOOK ISBN: 978-1-6667-0002-2

Cataloguing-in-Publication data:

Names: Wallenfang, Donald, author.

Title: Emmanuel : Levinas and variations on God with us / by Donald Wallenfang.

Description: Eugene, OR : Cascade Books, 2021 | Includes bibliographical references and index.

Identifiers: ISBN 978-1-6667-0000-8 (paperback) | ISBN 978-1-6667-0001-5 (hardcover) | ISBN 978-1-6667-0002-2 (ebook)

Subjects: LCSH: Lévinas, Emmanuel—Criticism and interpretation. | Philosophical theology. | Theology.

Classification: B2430.L484 W34 2021 (print) | B2430.L484 W34 (ebook)

11/10/21

To my anonymous natural mother
who loved me to birth and gave me up for adoption
with great responsibility

CONTENTS

CHAPTER 1

LEVINAS AND MOUNT ZION

גָּדוֹל יְהוָה וּמְהֻלָּל מְאֹד בְּעִיר אֱלֹהֵינוּ
הַר־קָדְשׁוֹ יְפֵה נוֹף מְשׂוֹשׂ כָּל־הָאָרֶץ הַר־צִיּוֹן יַרְכְּתֵי צָפוֹן קִרְיַת מֶלֶךְ רָב

Great is the LORD and highly to be praised
in the city of our God:

His holy mountain, beautiful in elevation,
the joy of all the earth, Mount Zion,

the heights of Zaphon, the city of the great king.

—Ps 48:2–3

וּבְהַר צִיּוֹן תִּהְיֶה פְלֵיטָה וְהָיָה קֹדֶשׁ וְיָרְשׁוּ בֵּית יַעֲקֹב אֵת מוֹרָשֵׁיהֶם

But on Mount Zion there will be some who escape;
the mountain will be holy,

and the house of Jacob will take possession
of those who dispossessed them.

—Obad 1:17

MOUNT ZION. THE MESSIANIC city where only the just can remain. A lofty
ethical height. Based on its Hebrew, Arabic, and Hurrian roots, Zion means
"castle, dry land, citadel, ascend to the top, top of the mountain, river, brook."
It is the very place of transcendence ("trans-ascend") where those who ascend to its summit are changed forever. Mount Zion signifies the highest of
elevations because it is the homeless home of the humblest souls. The great
messianic King lives here because it is the hallowed altitude of responsibility
for the other. There is no more perfect joy. There is no more regal reward. On
Mount Zion, the just escape the slavery of the self, according to the holiness

of self-forgetfulness by orientation toward the other. Through a dispossession of the disobedient self, the call of the other sounds the sentinel on to self-possession in the form of self-donation. *Shema Israel* (Deut 6:4–5).

For those of us who love to pore over texts and more texts and even more texts, we sometimes are met with an author who makes an impression on us that leaves us never the same. It is like finding gold, striking a hidden spring, being met with a truth we have sensed all along but never knew how to say it. And yet this author says it with such eloquence, clarity, and persuasion, that we cannot help but blurt out "This is the truth!" as we close the book, only to open it again as soon as possible. I have had the good fortune of encountering many such authors, but one who stands out above the rest for me is Emmanuel Levinas.

What is it about his life and writing that compels me to compose a book in his honor, for the sake of sharing with even more readers the depth and richness of his thought? Perhaps what I find in his life and work is a penetrating instance of the paradigmatic.[1] When I consider the question of the meaning of being human, I find in Levinas and his work the golden arrow of meaning that pierces through to the heart of the matter. As a Catholic Christian and zealous seeker of truth, I am met with that for which I search in the work of Emmanuel Levinas. Throughout my studies I remained convinced that everything cashes out in ethics. There are so many ideas and testimonies in circulation, but I wonder into those that might influence our lives for the better with greatest effect.

Whether or not you have heard of Emmanuel Levinas before; whether or not you have probed the pages of any of his writings; whether or not you stumbled upon this book by chance or by interest; I would like to introduce you to a friend I never have met in person in the pages to follow. The gist of my argument is that, especially in a post-Holocaust world, Christianity is in desperate need of Judaism. In fact, overcoming the Marcionite heresy once again, the roots of Christianity remain Jewish. As a patently Jewish

---

1. See Tracy, *Analogical Imagination*, 112: "I find myself in another realm of authentic publicness, a realm where 'only the paradigmatic is the real.'" Cf. Wallenfang, *Dialectical Anatomy of the Eucharist*, 233–34: "In a world of radical plurality, cultural diversity, and nauseating ambiguity, one can decide only according to the paradigmatic . . . The freedom of personal decision is my own—granted that it is dependent upon the personal decisions of others—a freedom that is free to decide personally insofar as it is provided with an absolute content upon which to decide absolutely . . . To maintain the notion of truth-content as truth-as-paradigmatic is to suggest that, given the project of human living, insofar as 'human' refers to an inclusive understanding of personhood, that which is paradigmatic appears and proclaims itself as a pattern, a model, and exemplary for all. The paradigmatic as the real, truth as paradigmatic, self-attests to its status as the true one in the midst of its counterfeit competitors. In the fairy tale of Cinderella, the glass slipper fits the foot of only one maiden in the land."

philosopher, Levinas reintroduces we followers of Jesus to who he is as the Jewish God-Man. The Catholic Church cannot understand herself apart from her roots in Judaism. Not just historical, cultural, and archaeological roots, but philosophical, spiritual, and theological roots as well. As Christians, we never must tire of asking again with Tertullian, yet this time in reverse order, "What does Athens have to do with Jerusalem?" Or perhaps another way to put it is: "What does a hyper-Hellenized (and, moreover, secularized) Christianity have to do with a betrayed and forgotten Judaism?" This is the pivotal question for Christian philosophy and theology today. Without an intentional retrieval of its Jewish roots, Christianity never again will be able to understand itself or profit humanity in a way that is not destructive of the other.

One of the premier theological tasks of our day is interreligious dialogue, that is, relating and conversing with the religious other. Most often we attempt to understand the other—if we attempt to understand the other at all—in terms of the self-same self. Why not invert the paradigm and let the other reveal him or herself according to their surprising and irreducible otherness? If we come clean with the history and evolution of the inherent diversity of cultures around the world, we realize how vague and superficial are our categories and oftentimes arbitrary lines of religious demarcation. For instance, at what point do the religious identities diverge between the monotheistic theological intuitions of Zoroaster, Moses, and Muhammed; between the veneration of saints, the veneration of ancestors, and the veneration of various avatars of the divine; between the mythological pantheons of ancient Greece and Rome, and those of the more ancient Vedantic sages; between the wisdom teachings of Solomon, Confucius, and Siddhartha Gautama; between the yearning of salvation in one soul, and that in another?[2]

Certainly, there are precise differences between the creeds, cults, and codes of the splendid variety of religious traditions that span human time and space, and our incessant interaction with divinity. At the same time, we must confess that the lines we draw in the sand between self and other are much more subtle and indiscreet than we may tend to admit. And this is the paradox: that we claim great difference where there is little difference, and that we deny great difference where there is intractable difference. In the former case, we call foul where there is no foul, we lay blame where there is no blame, and we cast doubt where there is no reason to doubt. For example, we think against truth when we do not recognize a common

---

2. See my "Introduction" and "Dialectical Truth between Augustine and Pelagius" in Cavadini and Wallenfang, *Evangelization as Interreligious Dialogue*, xv–xl, 122–39.

humanity across national boundaries, ethnic dissimilarities, and cultural varieties. In the latter case, we confuse the part for the whole, the self for the other, humanity for divinity. For example, we contradict truth when we pretend to reduce the other-than-the-self to the same-as-the-self, whether to assimilate only what conforms to ipseity or to excrete what appears as unassimilable illeity.[3] Again, in the former case, any shade of difference is interpreted as divisiveness. Good diversity is interpreted as bad division, and unity is univocal with uniformity. In the latter case, actual difference is denied in favor of a *reductio ad se* ("reduction to the self"), and diversity is univocal with divisiveness. Any detection of heterogeneity is reduced to homogeneity, whether in the form of assimilation or excretion. When it comes to religious diversity, relativism is too easy a solution, and so is communication breakdown, most often in the form of a violent outburst in attempt to annihilate the unassimilable other.

This book will attempt to sustain the *pas de deux* between unity and plurality as the very signification of truth. Without genuine plurality, there is no possibility of genuine unity; without the bond of real unity, plurality remains irreconcilable and disunified. Emmanuel Levinas is a thinker who invites us again and again to think more than we have thought before by means of an elsewhere that delivers itself to thought, and from thought, in instances of exorbitance. Because there is no way to tame the alterity of the elsewhere—the other-than-the-miserable-solitude-of-the-self—we are ennobled as philosophers to ask fresh questions once again—questions that point to a truth that is neither self-manufacturable nor slumbering away in some remote corner of its half-baked dogmatism. Judaism provokes humanity to ask the question of humanity in the most humane way inasmuch as its covenantal commitment to a radical personal ethical monotheism deflects the facile reductionism of YHWH or the face of the other to a hegemonic aping of the self.[4] For who else has the self to rule (*hegemoneúo*, "reign, rule") save its lonesome self when lacking solicitude for the other? Or to where else has the self to lead (*hegéomai*, "lead") itself other than right back to itself (without ever having left) with no regard for or reliance on the other?

3. See Bataille, "Use Value of D. A. F. de Sade."

4. See Malka, *Emmanuel Levinas*, 84: "To be Jewish. Not the pride or the vanity of being Jewish. That is worth nothing. But an awareness of the extraordinary privilege of undoing the banality of existence, of belonging to a people who are human before humanity" (Malka quoting Levinas); and 299: "The meeting place between Jewish thought and universal thought is none other than the very place that tears us away from every place that is easily found: the face of the Other that carries upon it the imprint of the Creator" (Malka quoting Rabbi Daniel Epstein).

Several different themes will be treated in this book: interreligious dialogue, the contrast between analytic philosophy and continental philosophy, the diverse schools of phenomenology, the relationship between law and freedom, the phenomenality of the Internet, the face of maternity, the face of childhood, and the dialectic between contemplation and ethics. Chapters 2–6 were written originally as conference presentations, especially for the annual meetings of the North American Levinas Society. It should be noted that portions of material of the present book were published previously in the following places:

"Virtual Counterfeit of the Infinite: Emmanuel Levinas and the Temptation of Temptation," in *The Html of Cruciform Love: Toward a Theology of the Internet*, edited by Eric Lewellen and John Frederick, 132–50. Eugene, OR: Pickwick Publications, 2019

"Levinas and Marion on Law and Freedom: Toward a New Dialectical Theology of Justice." *Pacifica* 29.1 (2017) 71–98

"Face Off for Interreligious Dialogue: A *Theo*logy of Childhood in Jean-Luc Marion versus a Theo*logy* of Adulthood in Emmanuel Levinas." *Listening* 50.2 (2015) 106–16

The work of Emmanuel Levinas has sustained my attention over the past ten years and finally the time has come to present the summation of my findings and reflections. In addition to the essays above, Levinas featured prominently in my dissertation, "Trilectic of Testimony: A Phenomenological Construal of the Eucharist as Manifestation–Proclamation–Attestation" (2011), that was substantially revised, updated, and published as *Dialectical Anatomy of the Eucharist: An Étude in Phenomenology* (2017). I provide an abbreviated analysis of his work, along with that of Paul Ricoeur, in chapter 3 of that volume. Further, much of Levinas's thought influenced my presentation of the life and work of Edith Stein in *Human and Divine Being: A Study on the Theological Anthropology of Edith Stein* (2017), as well as the final chapter on phenomenological ethics in *Phenomenology: A Basic Introduction in the Light of Jesus Christ* (2019), and chapter 7 of *Evangelization as Interreligious Dialogue* (2019), entitled "Dialectical Truth between Augustine and Pelagius: Levinas and the Challenge of Responsibility to Superabundant Grace." However, it gives me great joy to bring together the present book, *Emmanuel: Levinas and Variations on God with Us*, as a culmination of my testimony to such an instructive figure for our times and those to come.

The title of this book is not incidental to the book's express intention. *Emmanuel* is in obvious reference to Emmanuel Levinas, as well as to the famous passage from the book of the prophet Isaiah: "Therefore the Lord himself will give you a sign: the young woman, pregnant and about to bear a son, shall name him Emmanuel" (7:14).[5] The subtitle—*Levinas and Variations on God with Us*—is no less meaningful. With reference to the musical composition technique called "variations on a theme," this book seeks to offer variations on the primary theme set forth in my 2017 book *Dialectical Anatomy of the Eucharist: An Étude in Phenomenology.*[6] This theme is precisely the fruitful dialectic between manifestation and proclamation, between sacrament and word, between contemplation and ethics. *Emmanuel: Levinas and Variations on God with Us* will continue to develop this contrapuntal theme between the manifestation-oriented phenomenology of Jean-Luc Marion and the proclamation-oriented phenomenology of Emmanuel Levinas. I intentionally use the musical motif of "variations" with implicit reference to the auditory configuration of the call of the other in the work of Levinas. Though the book will sustain a lively counterpoint between Marion and Levinas, the accent this time will be on the contributions of Levinas.

Once again, my overall aim is to increase awareness of, appreciation of, and devotion to the work of Emmanuel Levinas. His is simply too important of a philosophical voice to let drift to the margins of history, even if one were to do so in the name of the recondite character of his writings. As with many phenomenologists, it is necessary for commentators and teachers to simplify the meaning and message of their works, without diluting the intricacy of their contents too severely. Inevitably, the present book brings its own accessibility issues, but be assured that my intent is to help make Levinas's work more relatable to a wider audience, especially Christian believers who have forgotten the indelible significance of Judaism for Christianity. The reality is that, since the Jewish Holocaust (1941–45) wherein 6 million Jewish men, women, and children were murdered for the sole reason that they were Jewish, Christian theology cannot carry on the same as before. Something went incredibly wrong for thinking during that time, in that particular region of the world. Granted, anti-Semitism has been a fatal error of faulty Christian thinking since its nascent beginnings. Yet, because of this, we followers of Jesus of Nazareth

---

5. Cf. Matt 1:23. The meaning of the Hebrew name עִמָּנוּ אֵל ("Emmanu-el"), namely, "God with us," is of central importance for our study of the life and work of Emmanuel Levinas. Signifying the presence of YHWH to deliver his people from destruction and abandonment, the name Emmanuel lives at the heart of the Judeo-Christian tradition of faith.

6. For the musical form of variations, see, for example, Ludwig von Beethoven's *32 Variations for Piano in C Minor* (1806), Johannes Brahms's *Variations on a Theme of Paganini* (1863), and Johann Sebastian Bach's *Goldberg Variations* (1741).

must be all the more sensitive to the brutal history inscribed in the corpses and ashes of our ancestors' victims. Without further ado, let us turn our attention to the life and work of Emmanuel Levinas.

I. Who Is Emmanuel Levinas?

Emmanuel. A Hebrew name that means "God with us." But what does it really mean to say, "God with us?" Beginning from a purely philosophical standpoint, this is to say that human thought does not cease to concern itself with God. God as a word. God as a concept. God as an answer. But, above all, God as a question. When thinking along with Emmanuel Levinas, the God question accompanies you every step of the way, even when the question is transposed into a visceral and agonizing groping: "Where are you, God?"[7] Within his modest autobiographical account, Levinas admits that his life story "is dominated by the presentiment and the memory of the Nazi horror."[8] Similarly, his final magnum opus, *Otherwise than Being or Beyond Essence*, is dedicated "to the memory of those who were closest among the six million assassinated by the National Socialists, and of the millions on millions of all confessions and all nations, victims of the same hatred of the other man, the same anti-Semitism."[9] As human beings, we share a very bloody history, and Levinas's philosophy is acutely aware of this fact. Even worse, Levinas surmises that those who perpetrated the Shoah, whether of Catholic or Protestant background, "had all probably done their catechism. . . . The world in which pardon is all-powerful becomes inhuman . . . the possibility of infinite pardon tempts us to infinite evil."[10]

Born in Kaunas, Lithuania, on January 12, 1906, as the eldest of three sons (the others named Boris and Aminadav), Levinas and his family knew the horrors of anti-Semitism firsthand. His father, his mother, and his two brothers we murdered by machine-gun fire in Kaunas during the time of the Jewish Holocaust. Levinas himself was spared only because he had become a French citizen in 1931, served as a translator in the French military, and was held captive as a prisoner of war by the Nazi army from 1940–45. Levinas discovered the news of his family's execution only after his release from

7. See Malka, *Emmanuel Levinas*, 296: "In reference to the 'Holocaust,' to say that God is with us in every circumstance is just as odious as the *Gott Mit Uns* that was emblazoned on the executioners' belts" (Malka quoting Levinas).

8. Malka, *Emmanuel Levinas*, xiv. I will refer to Salomon Malka's well-crafted biographical account of Levinas as a constant authority throughout this introduction.

9. Levinas, *Otherwise than Being or Beyond Essence*, v.

10. Robbins, *Is It Righteous to Be?*, 41, and Levinas, *Difficult Freedom*, 139.

prison. During the time of his captivity, Levinas recounts a chilling image
of how, upon returning to the prisoner camp from hard labor in the woods
over the course of a few weeks, a dog named Bobby would welcome the
exhausted inmates with cheerful barks and humane enthusiasm, whereas
the Nazi soldiers only treated their fellow human beings with violent dehumanizing contempt. Later on, Levinas would refer to Bobby as "the last
Kantian in Nazi Germany," meaning that the canine practiced the Kantian
categorical imperative with an instinctive fidelity, in contrast to the Nazi
soldiers who acted more like vicious dogs than men.[11] The prison guards
eventually would drive away the dog as well.

What I find incredible about the life of Levinas is how he continued
to think philosophically through all of the trauma, torture, and tragedy he
experienced. Salomon Malka writes of Levinas that "the heroic effort that
demanded a repudiation of fatalism would, in a sense, remain the silent
source of everything else."[12] He never gave up hope to think, to ponder, to
search for meaning, to search out the face of the other, and to describe the
infinite contours of this incessant encounter with the unmanifest visage
and unflagging voice of his fellow man. His work was built upon the richness of Rabbinic Judaism, Russian literature, the dailiness of common life,
the legacy of his father's bookstore, and rigorous philosophy. Before undergoing the trauma of the Shoah, Levinas moved to France to study philosophy at the University of Strasbourg from 1923–28. He, too, caught wind
of the new movement in philosophy called phenomenology, inaugurated
by Edmund Husserl (1859–1938) at the turn of the twentieth century, and
decided to meet this philosophical pioneer in person. He went to Freiburg
to sit in class with Husserl during his final semester of teaching before his
retirement in 1928. Levinas also would stay and sit in on a seminar taught
by Husserl's heir apparent, Martin Heidegger (1889–1976). Fascinated by
the method of phenomenology, Levinas went on to publish his Strasbourg
doctoral thesis in 1930, *The Theory of Intuition in Husserl's Phenomenology*.
In 1931, Levinas published a French translation of Husserl's Sorbonne lectures, entitled *Cartesian Meditations*. With these two publications, Levinas
successfully helped introduce phenomenology to France. Levinas said of
Husserl, "He gave me eyes to see."[13]

What is it about the method of phenomenology that attracted Levinas? One thing for sure was its power to turn attention away from the self
and toward the other-than-the-self that awakened the self to consciousness.

11. Levinas, *Difficult Freedom*, 153.
12. Malka, *Emmanuel Levinas*, 64.
13. Malka, *Emmanuel Levinas*, 40.

Phenomenology, as a purely descriptive method, demands a bracketing of what Husserl called "the natural attitude."[14] The natural attitude is a biased and calcified attitude that pronounces judgment before an adequate description of a given state of affairs has taken place. In other words, the natural attitude does not permit a phenomenon to give itself by itself. The natural attitude insists on determining a phenomenon rather than letting the phenomenon express itself according to its own sui generis givenness. Levinas observed the gross discrimination against his own people by attitudes that reduced the person to refuse, and, thereby, eclipsed the ethics of being human vis-à-vis other human persons. In phenomenology, Levinas found a compelling philosophical approach to the other that let the other remain other without either reducing the other to more of the same or excreting the other due to her unassimilability to the same. Levinas, by concentrating on Husserl's theory of intuition, traced the accent on the phenomenon that gives itself to the conscious ego rather than emphasizing the theory of intentionality that treats of phenomena by beginning with the self and what it makes of them.

Following the completion of his doctoral program in philosophy, Levinas served in the French military as a translator from 1931–40. This role itself attests to Levinas's competency and gift for negotiating between diverse languages: Yiddish, Russian, German, French, and Hebrew, while of course studying Greek and Latin at the university. With his graduate education complete and having obtained job stability, Levinas married his neighbor's daughter with whom he grew up in Lithuania, Raïssa Levy, on September 11, 1932. We cannot help but wonder into the relationship between Emmanuel and Raïssa, and how she must have inspired his philosophical reflections on the call of the other, the face of the feminine, voluptuosity, erotic desire, and the caress. Four years later, on February 28, 1935, their daughter, Simone, was born.[15] That same year saw the publication of one of Levinas's earliest philosophical essays, De l'evasion, that, even in its brevity, indicates the future trajectory his philosophy would take. While detained as a prisoner of war from 1940–45, Raïssa and Simone were protected in hiding by Emmanuel's

14. For an in-depth description of the method of phenomenology as it has evolved up into the twenty-first century, see Wallenfang, Phenomenology; Wallenfang, Dialectical Anatomy of the Eucharist, especially 5–21; Wallenfang, Human and Divine Being, especially xxiii–xxiv; and Wallenfang, "Pope Francis and His Phenomenology of Encuentro," 57–71.

15. I had the good fortune of meeting Simone, her husband Georges Hansel, and their son David and his wife Joëlle, as well as their sons, at the North American Levinas Society meetings in 2013, 2014, and 2015. Once I asked Simone what it was like to be the daughter of Emmanuel Levinas. She looked at me in the eye and said, "It was very hard to be his daughter." My impression of what she meant by that had to do with his high demands of a responsible ethical life for himself and his family members.

good friend, Maurice Blanchot (who he had met in Strasbourg), and later by the sisters of Saint Vincent de Paul in Prelfort.

Once an armistice was reached at the conclusion of the Second World War, and the prisoners were released from captivity, Levinas served as the director of a Jewish secondary school, the *École Normal Israélite Orientale* (ENIO) in Paris, training French teachers for the schools of the *Alliance Israélite Universelle du Bassin Méditerranéen*. He held this post from 1945–61.[16] The same year he began this directorship, Raïssa and Emmanuel's second daughter, Andrée Éliane, died only a few months after her birth. Two years later, Levinas would publish his first original monograph, *Existence and Existents*, a text he began to write while in prison, and which he dedicated to his deceased daughter. Again, two years later, Raïssa gave birth to their son, Michael, on April 18, 1949.

Thirteen years after beginning his position as the director of the ENIO, Levinas began to give annual Talmudic lectures, and would do so for the next thirty years. In 1961, he completed and published his first magnum opus, which was, at the same time, his *doctorat d'etat* (habilitation thesis): *Totality and Infinity: An Essay on Exteriority*. In this book, Levinas sets forth the itinerary of the self's irrevocable departure from itself toward the other. Completing his *doctorat d'etat* opened the door for Levinas to obtain a university professorship.[17] He became professor of philosophy at the University of Poitiers and would teach there until 1967. During the late 1960s, Levinas also taught at the University of Fribourg in Switzerland. From 1967 to 1973, Levinas taught at the University of Paris-Nanterre alongside Paul Ricoeur, and from 1973 to 1979, Levinas held a post at the prestigious University of Paris-Sorbonne until his retirement. In 1974, Levinas would publish his second and final magnum opus, *Otherwise than Being or Beyond Essence*. In this book we find an even more radicalized and intensified articulation of the self's unrelenting vocation to responsibility for the other to the point

16. See Malka, *Emmanuel Levinas*, 101, 103: "If he took this [directorship at the ENIO] on himself, it was because he wanted to be in the fray, surrounded by Jewish students, hoping to transmit something to them. It wasn't at all because other options were not open to him. . . . This was someone who lived out his philosophy in his life from day to day. He was no different in his attitude. He had a humanism, or a humanity that was quite remarkable. He lived the lives of others" (Malka quoting Levinas's assistant at the school, Thérèse Goldstein). Cf. Malka, *Emmanuel Levinas*, 200, where Malka comments that Paul Ricoeur, Jacques Derrida, and Emmanuel Levinas "were all teachers first."

17. See Malka, *Emmanuel Levinas*, 261: "So much was intense for him: the idea that in the field of philosophy as in the arts only exceptional abilities could justify dedicating oneself to a vocation" (Malka quoting Levinas's son, Michael, speaking about his father).

of obsessive substitution, under the figure of prophecy. Emmanuel's wife would die in Paris in September of 1994, and Emmanuel would die in the early morning hours of December 25, 1995, in Paris on the Christian feast of the Nativity of Emmanuel, "God with us."

This brief silhouette of Levinas assists us in anchoring the following abstractions of thought in the concrete life from which they emerged. In 1977, the year before he was elected to the Chair of Saint Peter, Karol Wojtyła remarked to his goddaughter that "there are two great philosophers in the religious sphere: Levinas and Ricoeur."[18] Wojtyła studied moral philosophy and theology and there was no doubt that Levinas caught his attention by establishing ethics as first philosophy, signified by the language of responsibility for the other. Ricoeur commented that, for Levinas, "there is Husserl, that is to say, a philosophical radicalness that was both for him and for me unjustifiably covered up by Heidegger."[19] Ricoeur sums up Levinas's philosophical oeuvre with two words: "Husserl and the Torah."[20] In a similar way, Jean-Luc Marion, in reference to Levinas's philosophy, said that "when it was declared [by Levinas] that the ethical is the ultimate horizon of philosophy, a current was made to flow backwards." Contra Heidegger, for both Husserl and Levinas, *Dasein* is not at the center of the universe after all. Instead, the original impetus of Husserl's phenomenological conversion (*epoché*) is a reorientation of the self around that which is not identical to the self—a counter-consciousness of the ego that displaces the ego as the featured attraction. Levinas radicalizes the phenomenological reduction by pointing to a prior non-phenomenalized signification that predates all forms of manifest givenness: the ethical call of the other. Corroborated by the Jewish *pièce de résistance*, the Torah, Levinas's philosophy assumed a decentering ethical character that dislocates the self from a position of unassailable privilege vis-à-vis any other. For Levinas, philosophy does not proceed from and return to the self like a boomerang. Rather, faithful to "the things themselves," mature philosophy crashes in upon the self from a personal elsewhere that certifies the self as agent responsible.

At the ENIO, Levinas was known to say to his students often, "You've got to get in the game!"[21] By this expression, he probably meant many things, but one thing he meant for sure was that you have to rise up to your predestined vocation of living in radical responsibility for the other person who faces you. In putting together this book, I hope that this is just one way that I

18. Malka, *Emmanuel Levinas*, 228.
19. Malka, *Emmanuel Levinas*, 196.
20. Malka, *Emmanuel Levinas*, 196.
21. Malka, *Emmanuel Levinas*, xxxiii.

am "getting in the game" in this Levinasian sense. Levinas "once appealed to these words by Rosenzweig from *The New Thinking*: 'The book is not a goal that has been reached, not even a preliminary one. It itself must be answered for, instead of it carrying itself or being carried by others of its kind. This responsibility happens in everyday life.'"[22] It is true that this book, *Emmanuel: Levinas and Variations on God with Us*, is only a book. At best it points to a responsible ethical life lived in flesh and blood. At worst, it is hagiographical hypocrisy. The book certainly is not a goal that has been reached in itself and for itself. If a book serves its best purpose, it will point beyond itself as a testimony to what inspired its composition. And inspiration is ultimately a phenomenon not of abstract impersonal ideas, but of concrete personal lives. No matter what this book says about Emmanuel Levinas and his work, it will remain sorely incomplete. According to Levinas's son, Michael, who is a prolific pianist and composer: "My father is the one who said to me, in the course of composing, when I was at an impasse or felt it impossible to write, that it was ultimately necessary to accept incompleteness . . . 'Sometimes, the thing suffices in its incompleteness.'"[23] The figure we must keep in mind here is the ellipse, both as a shape and as a grammatical technique.

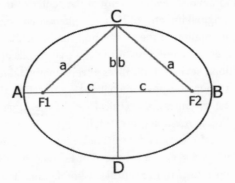

An ellipse, unlike a perfect circle, is an oval shape, or an elongated circle. It has not only one focal point, but two foci that make the original circle shape stretch and dilate to even more generous contours. Levinas's philosophy has this effect. Because the self is decentered and reoriented around an-other-than-the-self that is the very source of the awakening of the self, more room is made for thought and for the possibilities of ethical living.[24]

22. Malka, *Emmanuel Levinas*, 268.

23. Malka, *Emmanuel Levinas*, 264.

24. For more on the philosophical figure of the ellipse, in relation to the method of phenomenology, see the section entitled "Trilectic of Testimony" in Wallenfang, *Dialectical Anatomy of the Eucharist*, 42–48.

For the remainder of chapter 1, I would like to present a summative outline of the philosophy of Emmanuel Levinas according to four main headings: (1) Thinking in Hebrew, (2) Selfhood and Enjoyment, (3) From Enjoyment to Responsibility for the Other, and (4) From Responsibility to Obsessive Substitution. I think it most helpful to understand Levinas's work according to these four primary terms. We also may notice a progression from the first to the fourth sections—a kind of musical crescendo that culminates in the self-abandonment of the martyr as an unexpected inversion of the narrative of the fourth movement of Hector Berlioz's 1830 Symphonie fantastique, "Marche au supplice." Instead of the self-inflicted tragic fate of the solitary lover whose love is scorned by the beloved, Levinas presents the universal human vocation as a sober inversion of the suicidal excesses of self-centered erotic desire in the paradoxical form of self-forgetful martyrdom. Just like music that uses the same sounds, basic notes, rhythms, harmonies and motifs to express a broad range of feelings and thoughts, the writing of this book uses the same letters and words to attempt to say something new and original, even if it is primarily a retrieval of a past hoped for and a future remembered. We will gather up the memories of the future while always anticipating the fresh unfolding of the past. I will present to you Levinas in the remainder of chapter 1, not so much with direct reference to his work through the use of many quotations and footnotes. What you will find is a revoicing of Levinas in my own words, though painted from a predetermined palette of Levinasian grammar. Now let us turn to the first section, "Thinking in Hebrew," in order to become better familiarized with the Talmudic trademark of Levinas's thought.

II. Thinking in Hebrew

Levinas said that "philosophy, I believe, is derived from religion. It is summoned by religion that is adrift, and religion is probably always adrift."[25] Religion (re-ligare, "to bind together again") proceeds from the deepest questions we human beings ask. It is our spiritual marrow and tends toward what is most sublime and meaningful in life. Yet often religion gets carried away with mythology, mystical ecstatic rituals, and theologoumena. It quickly can divorce things spirit from things matter and neglect responsibility lived through the material fibers of life. In response to these excessive and irrational tendencies, Levinas insists that Judaism involves "a rejection of effusiveness, of religious enthusiasm, of ecstasy. Judaism is a religion for

25. Quoted in Malka, *Emmanuel Levinas*, 136.

adults, sober adults. The approach to God is never a mystical adhesion. It
is an obedience to the Most High. It is not a communion."[26] Judaism recognizes and is on guard against the perennial violence of the sacred. Divine
adoration quickly can become forgetfulness, exclusion and even extermina-
tion of the human other. And this is to think in Hebrew: to think along with
Torah, to think in the tradition of Rabbinic Judaism that puts one in the
thicket of the midrashic (interpretive) procedure inscribed in the Talmud.
To think in Hebrew is to study the mitzvot (laws) that have been handed on
from our ancestors. It means for these mitzvot to circulate in our minds as
the primary content of thought. It results in an ethical life—a life oriented
around that of the other person who faces you.

Judaism is a religion of adults because it does not concede to an arrested development that is naïvely unaware of the mature summons to responsibility for the other. What predominates in the heritage of the Jewish
people is ethical signification written on the face of the other. It calls for an
atheism of idolatry—that worship of everything on the side of the wretch-
edness, poverty, estrangement, misery, destitution, nakedness, vulnerability
(susception), and useless suffering of my neighbor and the stranger—the
one for whom I must be responsible before all else. Judaism—Jewish philosophy—thinks all the way by letting the other be thought in me, or better,
to let the other think in me and speak in me (prophecy). Jewish philosophy
operates always within a covenant relationship sealed from time immemorial between the self and the other. It is an obligation not so much elected as
imposed on the self. It is an imposition that appears to violate my autonomous freedom, but rather opens a collective freedom of a solidarity of persons in which my neighbor (and even the stranger) are always my brother,
sister, and dependent. An inherent fraternity obtains among human beings
when faithful paternity (fatherhood) and maternity (motherhood) signify
the heights of humanity. Judaism is the highest humanism to the degree
that it is a pedagogy of hospitality and welcome, as expressed in the gentleness of the feminine face: "As a mother comforts her child, so I will comfort
you; in Jerusalem you shall find your comfort."[27]

Judaism introduces us to a chaste eroticism that never intends to
separate the truth and meaning of sexuality from the universal vocation of
becoming father and mother in relation to the child. The Hebrew Scriptures
remind us of the divine intentionality of our sexual configuration: fertility,

26. Quoted in Malka, *Emmanuel Levinas*, 121. And further, see Malka, *Emmanuel
Levinas*, 123, where Malka paraphrases Levinas's charge that Judaism "derides chatter,
this speaking to everyone without taking responsibility. The redundancy of the word,
the free word, or the excessive word—that is the beginning of prostitution."

27. Isa 66:13 (NABRE). Cf. Isa 40:1; 49:13; Ps 131.

fecundity, procreation; marital fidelity and allegiance that lasts a lifetime and beyond inasmuch as these habits of fidelity are imbibed by the next generation of witnesses; a nuptial bond that serves to memorialize YHWH's unfailing fidelity to his chosen covenantal people. And they are a chosen people because they are a responsible people. They are chosen insofar as they respond affirmatively to the call of and ongoing dialogue with the God of Abraham, Isaac, and Jacob. The pattern of this attentiveness to YHWH— the Lord and Creator of the heavens and the earth—was established from the beginning (Adam), continued through successive generations (Noah, Abraham, Isaac, Jacob, Moses, David), and is renewed in the significations of an ethical monotheistic culture that refuses to forget (anamnesis) the saving history of a chosen people. This alliance with YHWH is sustained through a liturgical ethics that reenacts the oath in the dailiness of justice and the economics of the common life. It is proclaimed through both work and sabbath, both the secular and the sanctified saeculum, both enjoyment and sacrifice, both mountain (Mount Zion) and valley (Canaan), both call and response, both homestead and exodus, both spirit and matter, both what is said and what goes unsaid, both joy and sorrow, both telling (Haggadah) and retelling, both yes and no, both speaking and listening, both fasting and feasting, both losing and finding, both past and future. Judaism and her history encompass both the tragic and the comical wherein there is no shortage of visitation of the surprising guest. In Judaism, normativity is paradoxical because paradox is normative.

The Jewish people are a people who are accustomed to "loving the Torah more than God."[28] What can we suppose Levinas means by this provocative statement? He certainly is not saying that he does not love God, but rather that to love the Torah is to love God and to love God better than claiming to love God aside from the Torah. It is a paradoxical saying that trusts the Torah more than any philosophical or theological concept of "God" per se. For Jewish belief, the Torah is the ethical plentitude of divine revelation, and, therefore, God need not be sought on the side of the Torah. To do so would risk falling prey to some idolatrous adoration of an unethical deity. The living God comes to mind precisely in his commandments and in the lived ethical prescriptions they bear. Levinas indicates, even at a more preliminary level of reflection, that the world is borne by propositions. The world is said, and Judaism presents the world to its addressee through a kerygmatic verbal expression in which ethical metaphysics (being-for-the-other) exceeds the reach of ontological metaphysics (being as being, being-for-oneself). This is a stern and patient invocation

28. Malka, *Emmanuel Levinas*, 248 (Malka quoting Levinas).

that proceeds from the elsewhere of the other's vocal visage. A Jew is a man or woman who understands him or herself not as being, but as being addressed by the imperative signification of a past anticipated and a future remembered—both a modern past and an ancient future. This imperative signification is at once refuge and risk. It is a prophetic and proleptic eschatology. It demands its perennial incarnation in the materiality of dailiness. "Sublime materialism!" as Levinas would say.[29] Not a Marxist ideological material reductionism, but a just economic materiality of daily enjoyment and labor. It is a lifestyle in which glory is proclaimed in humility, transcendence is announced in lowliness, and freedom is expressed in obedient wandering in the direction of a call that precedes my steps. It is the evolution from orientation to disorientation to reorientation. It is where home is exile and yet where exile is not home. Upright materialism in which goodness is held to be the very meaning of creation.

Peace is the recognition of the "Thou shall not kill" that is inscribed on the visage of the other and proclaimed in the "Here I am" from the voice of the self. And holiness is the responsible offering of the self to the other in the tangible form of flesh, blood, and material goods. A broken world is repaired to the degree that responsibilities outstrip the claim to rights, entitlements, and social privileges, and I begin to act for the world to come instead of only for the sake of my own miserable lifespan. To quote the great Levinasian principle: "The Other has nothing but rights and I have nothing but obligations."[30] Repentance, mortification, and self-denial are necessary in the wake of every irresponsible inaction and in expectation of my sociopathic egocentrism that threatens the renewed exodus of the self, taking leave of itself. Judaism recalls us to a tenacious sincerity and frankness that prefers prose to poetry, thereby overcoming the empty rhetoric of preaching, promises, and progress. Technology is embraced and utilized to the degree that it promotes the urbane sociality of the face-to-face.[31] A candidness of the everyday liberates the self from suffocating hubris and neurosis alike. It is the history of the Jewish people that teaches the gift of adversity and the nobility of martyrdom in witness to the transcendent elevation of the Good.

29. Levinas, *Nine Talmudic Readings*, 97.

30. Malka, *Emmanuel Levinas*, 249.

31. Levinas, *Difficult Freedom*, 232–33: "Technology wrenches us out of the Heideggerian world and the superstitions surrounding Place. From this point on, an opportunity appears to us: to perceive men outside the situation in which they are placed, and to let the human face shine in all its nudity. Socrates preferred the town, in which one meets people, to the countryside and trees. Judaism is the brother to the Socratic message."

III. Selfhood and Enjoyment

Dwelling on Mount Zion, or at least climbing somewhere on its steep slope, Levinas presents an itinerary of the universal human vocation: an exodus of the self out of itself in radical responsibility for the other—to live as one-for-the-other. There is a threefold progression within this humanizing itinerary: (1) self-forgetfulness through enjoyment of any other (*l'autre*), (2) redoubled self-forgetfulness through sacrificial responsibility for the personal other (*l'autrui*), and (3) sustained self-forgetfulness and self-abandonment in responsibility for the personal other become obsessive substitution, one-for-the-other. The present section will discuss the first of these three steps and the following two sections of this chapter will treat steps two and three.

To describe the experience of enjoyment, we must begin with the craving self. What does the self crave if not to evacuate itself irrevocably? Levinas gives a haunting depiction of the stale, smothering, and paralyzing experience of "the white noise" of being. Being as being is the essence of boredom and even frenzied panic. I am, and I cannot escape the sheer facticity and weight of my being, my inevasible existence. Being presses in on me on all sides and I cannot slip out of my own skin. I have been consigned to being without my permission, which itself would require being. Levinas calls this dead weight of being the *il y a*, the "there is." Even as early as *Existence and Existents*, a work he began to write while detained as a prisoner of war, Levinas describes this claustrophobia of being. He suggests that it always haunts us, even if subconsciously. It plagues us when we are alone and in silence. It presses in on us when we lie awake in the dark of night, terrified by an insomnia that we cannot tell to go away. It hems us in while awake or asleep, while in good health or infirm. It menaces while nauseous and affected by a feeling that we did not invite as a beguiling guest. We are chained to being with nowhere to flee since any somewhere is still in the land of being. Yet these molesting reflections on the *il y a* serve only to set the stage for the raison d'être of the self: not simply to be, but to be in the direction of . . .

The stagnation of being is overcome by the call to encounter the other (*l'autre*) that is inspired by desire for not more of the same, but desire for something other-than-the-self. Enjoyment (*jouissance*) is the name of the experience in which the self forgets itself and its riveted-ness to being and instead undergoes an ecstatic evasion of the same and nothing but the same. In making contact with an-other-than-the-self (whether food, drink, delightful activity, pleasure, etc.), desire leads the self away from its self-preoccupation and hypnosis of being, and propels the ego-ipsum outside of itself through a disruptive and anarchic orgasm of the elemental. This is not a religious mystical ecstasy, but simply an unrevealed enigmatic and heteronomous experience that is comprised by the alimentation of enjoyment wherein the world nourishes me and bathes me. The world comes to be as an ensemble of nourishments in which a secular exteriority overtakes the sacred insufficiency of the I (sub-jectum). Sexuality, too, signifies the otherwise-than-the-self that never ceases to face the self as a contrariety of the self's specified psychosomatic configuration. The ego is inverted by the exceedance of sensation's orientation toward an-other-than-the-self—the contrariety of woman facing man and man facing woman. Life is experienced as an innocent childhood opposed to theoretical speculation and calculation, though be it merely a preliminary stage of psychological development. Ego-life pulsates according to the voluptuosity of this erotic sense of enjoyment, the ego, though always wanting to recollect itself in its habitation, its dwelling, its vestibule, only goes out again in search of a pleasure that might finally keep its promises of permanent evacuation from the stalemate of being.

In Levinas's description, however, no pleasure ever keeps its promises. When I experience any pleasure, let us say the pleasure of eating a piece of fruit, I am taken on a ride of ecstasy for a fleeting moment, only to recoil on myself afterwards with a sense of shame, embarrassment, and regret (at least subconsciously) that I could not escape the self-sameness of my own being through this new pleasure after all. Within the experience of enjoyment, my desire for this or that is satiated temporarily, only to well up at the next involuntary opportunity. In enjoyment my will is only half-engaged since so many of these innate desires stem from the involuntary neediness of the body and soul. In order for the will to be fully engaged, a greater distance is required to traverse between the self and the other. Enjoyment involves the assimilation of the impersonal other (*l'autre*) in the form of use, reducing the other to just another part of the self's sameness. Reestablished in itself, the self goes only as far as reinstating itself and its malaise of being. However, Levinas proposes a determinate exit of the self in which the will is fully engaged and stretched to its furthest destination: to live in resolute responsibility for the personal other (*l'autrui*) who faces me. While enjoyment served as an initial departure of the self from itself, enjoyment alone cannot deliver the definitive escape and ultimate signification of the self in relation to the other. We must turn now to the stern vocation of responsibility to go the distance in the direction of the other who has a face and a name.

IV. From Enjoyment to Responsibility for the Other

In the assignation of responsibility for the personal other (*l'autrui*), a movement is made from plain consciousness to wakeful conscience. With reference to Levinas, Malka writes that "there is no rest for the righteous, insists the master, the righteous may not slumber. To be righteous is to be awake."[32] The absolute otherness of the other prevents a reductionism of the other to more of the same. Through a critique of egological interiority that tends to dominate the life of the self, the sovereignty of the ego is put into question. A profitable guilty conscience ensues so that the masturbatory self might be overcome by a non-erotic love without lust. Herein a yearnful desire desires the other without temporal satiation and without lack. Outside of the world of being, and even the world of enjoyment, an ethical world of dis-inter-est-edness and non-indifference toward the other opens.

Wakefulness of the ego rises according to the sensation of the nudity of the face and the decisive religious intersubjectivity of the face-to-face. Hyperboles, superlatives, excess, saturation, and exorbitance signify the time of the other wherein the Cartesian idea of the infinite attests to its completely external difference through the trace of its passing as ethical exigence. Responsibility for the other, as an immortal vocation ordained by an elsewhere beyond being, introduces the possibility of impossibility (the non-phenomenon) into the arena of phenomenology. A paradoxical unity between the proximity and the transcendence of the other obtains.

As assigned and ordained, my vocation finds its expression in the accusatory indictment and judgment delivered by the mastery of the other. I discover myself to be in an asymmetrical and asynchronous relationship with the other, exposed to the paroxysm—a sudden violent interruption—of the proximity of the neighbor. An unresolvable equivocation persists between me and the other—a beatific fissure of the self, sustained by the refraction, deflection, separation, divergency, disturbance, and pluralism between me and him that does not merge into an egocentric manageable and manipulatable unity.

Responsibility for the other happens to the measure of a personal fiat that enacts a passivity of subjectivity in response to the surplus of sociality, the uniqueness, and the extra-ordinariness of the other as an appresentation of a hypostasis and non-presence (absence) proclaimed as an-anonymous caress.[33] Solicited by the other to live in responsibility for her, elected and

32. Malka, *Emmanuel Levinas*, 112.

33. Hypostasis as person/relation rather than as substance/being—a personal signification beyond a phenomenology of manifestation and the hypostasis of the present. Levinasian ethical phenomenology refuses the domination of manifestation as an

homeless, I struggle against the return of the *conatus essendi* ("struggle to be") and instead hearken to the hither side of a social collectivity that resists its collapse into hyper-unified communion. Spirit speaks through the interstices of responsibility where the ego takes the place of the same and the other (*l'autrui*) takes the place of the other (*l'autre*).

Again, here I am attempting to repurpose Levinas's language with the goal of condensing some of his core ideas so as to introduce them to non-expert yet critically minded seekers of truth. So far, we have followed Levinas's progression of thought from the first instance of self-forgetfulness, namely, enjoyment, to the terminal velocity of the self, stretching outside of itself through responsibility for the other. Yet, in his later work, Levinas seems to dare one step farther in his analysis: responsibility for the other to the point of a daily martyrdom. To this daunting vocation we now turn.

V. From Responsibility to Obsessive Substitution

I am responsible for the other insofar as the other calls me and I say yes. However, there remains the possibility that this yes might become the very definition of my life, to the degree of self-abandonment. Levinas describes this covenantal reach of responsibility as living as hostage to the other by substituting oneself completely for the other. Herein subjectivity of spirit proves its sincere intentionality through matter—a glorious materialism in which matter serves as the locus of the one-for-the-other. A perpetual vigilance, insomnolence and solicitude overtakes the self, wherein the self lives in obsessive denudation, bareness, dispossession, and divestment (*dépouillement*) before the other who faces me. My skin turns inside out as I assent in discalced self-donation to the gift that costs.

Through a glorious abasement that is bare yet not barren, my body, in its nakedness and indigence, yields as a servant to the turgescence of responsibility that renders my passivity of passivity an astonishing traumatism of the regime of tenderness. A surplus of spontaneity and sociality prevails in which pathos becomes a test of the will and suffering becomes redemptive. Diaconal suffering the other takes the character of respiration. Breathing signifies the denucleation of self-presence—a coring out of the self by virtue of the afflicting circulation of the other that dephases and displaces the self as an ultimate. With irremissible guilt, here I am vis-à-vis the other in nonerotic proximity as hemophiliac, mature infant, and atheistic adorer of the

---

absolute. This is a phenomenological concept radically opposed to that of Heidegger, where both the self and a world of manifestation predominate. See Wallenfang, *Dialectical Anatomy of the Eucharist.*

ethical Name. As transubstantiated flesh, faithful fatherhood and mother-hood express the universal human vocation lived to the end.

On the steep crags of responsibility, met with a reverse conatus, en-nui finds itself overcome by a persecuting unconditional trial that sustains the scandal of sincerity, the prevenient election of the self, and the non-absolution of the absolute. The ubiquity of substituting responsibility forms a utopia of weakness—a virility without cowardice as the soul of the other takes its place within me. I discover myself, not for the last time, as someone uniquely summoned, expiring on the mouth of God in response to a kiss that I cannot turn away. Holiness respires in the martyr who yields to the chase of the other, refusing to die. A perennial ambiguity and skepticism clouds around the self as I never can say for sure whether or not I have accomplished this missionary vocation to responsibility, as it remains un-finished by definition. Only the other can decide.

VI. Recapitulation

Why must I pay tribute to the life and work of Emmanuel Levinas? Because his is a thinking that goes all the way, and his was a life that bore witness to the very things he wrote. As you can tell from the insufficient summary above, these ideas are serious, complex, and humanizing. He is not asking, "How can I make more money?," or "How can I use the other as a means to an end?," or even "How can I procure many goods in this world for myself and my family?" His is a much deeper question: "Who is the other and what does he need of me?" If these kinds of questions rule our lives, how can we go wrong? Is this not the very meaning of being human after all? I have found it to be so. I cannot help but refer to Emmanuel Levinas and his work. It proceeds from both traumatic and zestful lived experiences in the flesh, and I believe that he serves as a model of humanity for all of us. Though of course limited in his social context and cultural milieux, constrained by language and certain conventional modes of expression, Levinas nevertheless has left us a testament of perseverance and determined determination (Teresa of Ávila) that speaks to the human situation that we share.

Stemming from the ethical monotheism of Judaism, Levinas under-scores the ethical implications of his name, Emmanuel—"God with us." For Levinas, God is with us inasmuch as the call of the other person who faces me is a fresh proclamation of a personal divinity who summons me to responsibility for my neighbor, through my neighbor, in this wander-ing wilderness of life. God comes to mind precisely in the fray of the self against itself within the sober arena of daily ethical exigency. As categorical, unqualified, and unconditioned imperative, the silent siren call of the other assigns my steepest and most transcendent meaning of being: being given up, one-for-the-other, to the point of unregretable abandonment. Martyrdom sets the seal on the life lived to the end in endless obedient and faithful responsibility for the other who has a face and a name. May the chapters to follow in this book provoke us all to tread the highest heights and excessive exterior recesses of our common humanity.

—————— CHAPTER 2 ——————

AVATARS OF ALTERITY

I. Introduction

ACCORDING TO WILLIAM JAMES, the formidable task of interreligious dialogue today is to take place in a life which feels like a fight. If this is indeed
the case, says James, "why not be the Happy Warrior willing to listen to all,
struggle with and for all, help all to hear the other voices than the self?"[1] It
is precisely this disposition of the Happy Warrior which Emmanuel Levinas
promotes through the method of phenomenology over and against all
methods which would pretend to reduce the other to more of the same.
However, the method of phenomenology has evolved along two primary
currents, which can be identified by the terms "manifestation," on the one
hand, and "proclamation" on the other hand. Jean-Luc Marion, a propo-
nent of manifestation phenomenology, suggests that all phenomenality be
rendered according to the common denominator of givenness. Levinas, a
champion of proclamation, insists that the other cannot be reduced to any
mode of manifestation without violently destroying the exorbitant integrity
of the other.[2] Marion's approach results in a *theo*logy of childhood while that
of Levinas results in a theo*logy* of adulthood. Is it possible that a dialectical
method which harnesses the fruitfulness of the polarity between manifestation and proclamation—between childhood and adulthood, between contemplation and ethics—will be most productive for the task of interreligious
dialogue in the twenty-first century? Let us find out.

1. As quoted in Tracy, *Dialogue with the Other*, 29.
2. See Levinas, *Totality and Infinity*, 200 (italics original): "To speak to me is at each
moment to surmount what is necessarily plastic in manifestation. To manifest oneself
as a face is to *impose oneself* above and beyond the manifested and purely phenomenal
form, to present oneself in a mode irreducible to manifestation."

II. A Goodness beyond Being

Emmanuel Levinas's project in phenomenology has been described as a phenomenology of the other which poses a brash challenge to the egocentric proposals that preceded him, especially those of Edmund Husserl and Martin Heidegger.[3] While Husserl's project was anchored in a stable conception of consciousness, and Heidegger's oeuvre hinged on the disclosive analytic *Dasein*, Levinas recognizes the call of the other as that which predates any and all appearing to consciousness. This recognition leads Levinas to posit ethics as first philosophy, yet he is entirely aware of the suspicion that inevitably will attend such a claim. Nevertheless, he presses on to argue that the very idea of infinity proceeds from the exteriority of the other and the discourse between oneself and another which shatters all pretenses toward totality.

In spite of Levinas's bold claim, even after sixty years of its first proclamation in *Totality and Infinity*, do his revolutionary words not continue to fall on deaf ears? Has Levinas's proposal provoked a decisive sea-change in philosophy and theology that is equivalent to the radicality of his texts? It seems to me that the answer for today is a cowardly no. The egocentric notion of a resolute solipsistic being-towards-death persists in its eclipse of the vocation to substitute oneself for another. Since Levinas's project positions the other as its preface, locus, and postscript, it ever will remain an uncanny prophetic utterance to be shirked by the self-contented self. In other words, the message of Levinas will remain unheeded as long as people refuse to expose themselves in extreme passivity to the other who beckons the self to responsibility. Levinas's message must first be lived if it is to be understood and thereby open the host of self-centered philosophies to what they have neglected perennially, namely, the voice and demands of the other.

In the following reflection I will attempt to explicate the way in which Levinas challenges what could be called a "phenomenology of manifestation." Since its inception in the work of Husserl, phenomenology has been understood as a method which deals with appearances—with the way things show themselves, or more precisely, with the way things give themselves to consciousness. Most often phenomenology is shrouded in a discourse about visibility, privileging the sense of sight over those of touch, taste, hearing, and smell. Even Plato's allegory of the cave evinces philosophy's proclivity for understanding knowledge and mental conversion in terms of light and sight. All such emphases on appearance and visibility can be summed up under the rubric "manifestation," which itself suggests

---

3. Cf. John Wild's introduction in Levinas, *Totality and Infinity*, 13.

an event of revelation. Moreover, Heidegger's understanding of truth as unconcealedness (*alétheia*) privileges the disclosive operation of Being's self-unveiling in and through beings.[4] From its Greek heritage, Western philosophy has tended to understand truth in terms of vision, reason, being, and consciousness. The homogeneous human subject has consistently been located at the helm of the ship *Sophia's* route to the port of truth. Within this scheme, otherness is an obstacle to certainty; alterity is an unwanted detour within the pursuit of self-reassurance.

Not so for Levinas. Instead of giving lip service to mere avatars of alterity, whereby the other is conveniently transposed into the key of the same, Levinas regards the other in her irreducibility. Levinas undertakes the most radical shift ever performed in Western philosophy: a displacement of attention from the self-same self to the perpetually othering other. For Levinas, the relationship between the other and oneself is characterized by asymmetry in which the other activates the self's consciousness long before the self can recognize the other as such. The self is summoned to responsibility for the other with an anteriority proportionate to the exteriority, and yet the proximity, of the other. This is to say that my responsibility for the other precedes my cognitive acts of intentionality and receptivity which consist of a gathering up of manifestation. The call of the other which indicts me and summons me to responsibility does not come through a modality of manifestation, but, more correctly, through proclamation. The face of the other appears to the extent that it speaks. The epiphany of the other's face is precisely the expression of the other's voice which is first audible in my response: "Here I am!" Therefore, for Levinas, ethics is the prevailing structure of phenomenality rather than the traditional categories of manifest truth, knowledge, and being. Ontology is turned on its head in the name of Goodness which eludes all attempts of ontological reduction. Rather than beginning with a conceptual vision which would in turn inform practice, it is the very ethical practice which consummates an attunement toward the other. The exigencies of justice beckon at the beginning of the other's recognition before any theory can be posited. The other announces to me my responsibility for her prior to my recognition of her manifest being given to my sight, cognition, and representation to consciousness.

---

4. Cf. Heidegger, *Being and Time*, 263 (italics original): "Hence only with Dasein's *disclosedness* is the *most primordial* phenomenon of truth attained. . . . In so far as Dasein *is* its disclosedness essentially, and discloses and uncovers as something disclosed to this extent it is essentially 'true'. *Dasein is 'in the truth'*."

III. Face-off

Such is a preliminary sketch of Levinas's project of which the reader is most likely all too familiar. However, my intent here is to bring these bold claims of Levinas into direct confrontation with a contemporary thinker whose work, on the surface, seems to be quite similar to that of Levinas. This thinker is French phenomenologist Jean-Luc Marion. While much of Marion's phenomenological innovations build directly on those of Levinas, I wish to argue that Marion does so at the expense of Levinas's claims to radical alterity. Marion, in the end, concedes to the Western philosophical tradition's privileging of vision, appearance, and manifestation. Marion's project can be summed up adequately as a "phenomenology of manifestation," or more precisely, a "phenomenology of givenness." For Marion, drawing from the work of Husserl and Heidegger, givenness (*Gegebenheit/donation*) is asserted as the universal category for phenomenality: so much reduction, so much givenness.[5] If something is a phenomenon, it must appear; if something appears, it must be due to its inherent degree of givenness. Thus, in Marion's phenomenological framework, givenness serves as the ultimate criterion of veracity and the placeholder for any and all appearing.

A key text which positions Marion at a distance from Levinas is found toward the end of Marion's 1997 book *Being Given: Toward a Phenomenology of Givenness*. Marion writes that "the pertinent question is not deciding if the gifted is first responsible toward the Other (Levinas) or rather in debt to itself (Heidegger), but understanding that these two modes of responsibility flow from its originary function of having to respond in the face of the phenomenon as such, that is to say, such as it gives itself."[6] Marion adds a footnote at the end of this sentence which reads: "In this sense, I will not speak of a 'responsibility for the Other, older than any commitment . . .'—precisely because no 'commitment' (not even for the Other) would be thinkable without responsibility, taken in its phenomenological radicality."[7] Now I will proceed to elucidate these texts of Marion which cut to the chase and explicitly contrast his view with that of Levinas. This text occurs in the course of Marion's reflection on the notion of the call. Both Heidegger and Levinas speak of the call, but in completely different ways. For Heidegger, the call refers to the appeal of conscience to *Dasein* in order to realize its ownmost potential for authenticity. *Dasein* is summoned to its ownmost Being-guilty in which it ultimately incurs a debt to itself. For Levinas, the

5. See Marion, *Being Given*, 14. Also, see chapter 1, entitled "Phenomenology of Givenness and First Philosophy," of Marion, *In Excess*, 1–29.

6. Marion, *Being Given*, 294.

7. Marion, *Being Given*, 374.

call is precisely an anterior call to responsibility for the other. It is this call which functions as the primordial phenomenon and serves as precursor and initiator of all ensuing phenomena.

Marion departs from both Heidegger and Levinas by identifying the call with givenness itself. Marion argues here that there can be no talk of responsibility without first recognizing the givenness of the phenomenon of responsibility as such. It is necessary to recall Marion's phenomenological adage: so much reduction, so much givenness. In carrying out the most radical *epoché* possible, Marion inevitably brackets any ethical configurations in favor of sheer givenness. For Marion, responsibility is not a question of an ethical response to the epiphany of the face of the other, or an authentic response to one's own conscience, but a response of the gifted (*l'adonné*) to the pure manifestation of the phenomenon as such. The identity of the call is not only a question of what happens first in a sequence of phenomena, but a question of phenomenological precision. What is at stake is the determination of phenomenality at its utmost nakedness. Marion describes this nakedness in terms of givenness and manifestation, while Levinas describes this nakedness in terms of alterity and proclamation. In sum, Marion adopts Levinas's turn toward alterity but in a significantly different tonality than that of Levinas. Instead of attending to the call of responsibility issued by the other to me, Marion displaces this call onto the givenness of phenomena in general. His justification for this displacement includes the prevailing exigencies of the phenomenological method and its central task of applying the reduction in order to describe phenomena in their stark nakedness. In the end, Marion's project borrows from Levinas while neglecting its most striking stroke of genius, namely, the recognition of the personal other and her demands on me as that primordial word which resounds from an immemorial past. A paradigm of givenness clings to modes of manifestation while foregoing the contextual elements of language, hermeneutics, and horizon.[8]

8. Cf. "On the Gift: A Discussion between Jacques Derrida and Jean-Luc Marion, Moderated by Richard Kearney" in Caputo and Scanlon, *God, the Gift, and Postmodernism*, 66: "Derrida: Then would you dissociate what you call phenomenology from the authority of the as such? If you do that, it would be the first heresy in phenomenology. Phenomenology without as such! / Marion: Not my first, no! I said to Levinas some years ago that in fact the last step for a real phenomenology would be to give up the concept of horizon. Levinas answered me immediately: 'Without horizon there is no phenomenology.' And I boldly assume he was wrong."

IV. The Limits of Manifestation

Having drawn the distinction between the respective phenomenological configurations of Marion and Levinas, the next step is to discuss Levinas's critique of manifestation. In honor of the seventieth anniversary of the inaugural publication of *Totality and Infinity*, the following discussion will draw primarily from that groundbreaking text. Levinas, mindful of the ambivalent history of Western philosophy, recognizes those tendencies of thought which underlie profound social ills. Conducting a post-Holocaust philosophy, personally tinged with the experience of having family and friends murdered in the name of progress, Levinas is acutely sensitive to the propensity of philosophy toward totality in its insatiable thirst for truth. Likewise, Levinas recognizes the privileged place ipseity has held throughout the history of Western philosophy and questions the unchecked warrants for such a lofty status of the self. Levinas begins by asking if there are any alternatives to totality and the preponderance of the sovereign self. By employing the rigors of the phenomenological method, as he learned it from his mentors Husserl and Heidegger, Levinas is able to describe a host of alternatives to the status quo of Western philosophy.

Overturning totality, Levinas points to realms of phenomenality such as infinity, eschatology, transcendence, and a consummating ethics. Subverting the sovereign self, Levinas listens attentively to the face that speaks, the indictment of the other, the summons to responsibility and substitution, and the diachronic reverberation of illeity. Levinas ultimately issues a severe critique of manifestation by recognizing the function of expression, language, testimony, and prophecy in all human experience. Levinas seeks to preserve the irreducible and incommunicable otherness of the other by bracketing the various modes of manifestation that would purport to assimilate the other as a plastic and familiar form of manifestation to be digested without qualms by consciousness.

Levinas writes that "to speak to me is at each moment to surmount what is necessarily plastic in manifestation. To manifest oneself as a face is to *impose oneself* above and beyond the manifested and purely phenomenal form, to present oneself in a mode irreducible to manifestation, the very straightforwardness of the face to face, without the intermediary of any image, in one's nudity, that is, in one's destitution and hunger."[9] The plasticity of manifestation is overcome by the straightforwardness of naked, vulnerable, and fragile discourse. By the potency of speech, the otherness of the other is prevented from being usurped by the totalizing force of manifestation. The

---

9. Levinas, *Totality and Infinity*, 200 (italics original).

imposition of the other is not denied when the discourse between the other and me is not stifled. The poverty-stricken other incessantly knocks on the door of my self-domesticated home in which I would pretend to enjoy the fruits of my labor without concern for the destitution and hunger of the other who haunts me at every turn. Levinas insists that the relation between the same and the other, sustained by language, does not form a totality but rather persists in an asymmetrical relationship wherein thematization is turned into conversation. Within such a relationship conversation is not an equitable exchange of ideas that would contribute to the founding of a totality system. Conversation is instead enacted as teaching, where the other, as my master, teaches me more than I already possess. This teaching "signifies the whole infinity of exteriority."[10]

For Levinas, the cleavage that obtains "between the idea of infinity and the infinity of which it is the idea"[11] is attested in the relationship between the same and the other. The idea I have of the other never exactly coincides with the other of whom I have an idea. Rather, to recognize the other as such is to proclaim the unassailable disproportion between myself and the other: the other will never be absorbed into the same. The very idea of the other contests such a defacing absorption, doubly contested by the other about whom I have an idea. The other never ceases to teach me; I am resigned to be a perpetual pupil of the other who is forever my pedagogue. There remain two possibilities for the blameworthy I: obedience or feigned ignorance. For no one can pretend to be agnostic before the screaming voice of the other who holds me hostage in the name of freedom and justice—a silent scream heard most acutely in my response to this call which proceeds from the mouth of the infinite, landing on my ears and echoing in my mouth as a prophetic trace from the lips of the other. The call of the other does not proceed by way of manifestation, but by way of proclamation. It is language and discourse that engender the otherness of the other while manifestation contorts the other into the same.

V. The Sacred and the Other

The clash between the phenomenological proposals of Levinas and Marion may seem akin to the proverbial question, "What came first, the chicken or the egg?" For Levinas argues for the anteriority of the call of the other while Marion argues for the primordiality of the call of givenness. The question of the first comer (le premier venu) is not equivalent to the question of causality.

10. Levinas, Totality and Infinity, 171.
11. Levinas, Totality and Infinity, 171.

Both thinkers duly seek alternatives to the age-old philosophies constructed on ontology and etiology. Yet the question "What came first, ethics or givenness?" is not simply a matter of semantics or a matter of methodological correctness. Above this question hovers implicit moral implications which demand an account according to the criterion of justice. In other words, the way one answers this question bears profound consequences for how one treats the stranger (*l'étranger*) to oneself.

Levinas provides a clear ultimatum in the wake of this question akin to the ultimatum between life and death, the blessing and the curse, as propounded by Moses in the Torah.[12] The ultimatum of Levinas can be detected in the title of his provocative 1961 book, put another way, "What will come last, totality or infinity?" For Levinas the question of origin is more exactly the question of *eschaton*, for the beginning cannot be reached as such, but the eschatology of messianic peace can be realized day by day through ethical responsibility for the other. To inquire about the beginning is therefore to inquire about the end. To return to the chicken/egg analogy: in the end, to argue about the priority of either the chicken or the egg turns out to be a misnomer of the ultimate question. The fact of the matter is that here are chicken and egg, and the crucial question becomes whether or not the chicken will accept responsibility for the egg. Likewise, the human situation is one in which we face one another and bear the most serious possibility of responding affirmatively to the cry of help from the other. It is as if Levinas applies a reverse phenomenological reduction in order to arrive at the most posterior in its naked pronouncement, asking the question of justice from the trajectory of time's consummation rather than its elusive inception. For Levinas, ethics is the mouthpiece and playing field of infinity in which subjectivity is understood to be the welcoming of the other, that is, hospitality. This understanding poses a grave challenge to those phenomenologies of manifestation which posit the human subject as the one who intends a world (Husserl), the one who interprets a world (Heidegger), or the one to whom the world is given (Marion).

Through a prophetic proclamation of the messianic consummation of peace, Levinas determines ethics as that which signifies the nexus between justice and love. One is never finished with living justly; neither does love reach a point of static satisfaction. Ethics is the realm of possibility where

---

12. See Deut 30:19–20: "I call heaven and earth today to witness against you: I have set before you life and death, the blessing and the curse. Choose life, then, that you and your descendants may live, by loving the LORD, your God, obeying his voice, and holding fast to him. For that will mean life for you, a long life for you to live on the land which the LORD swore to your ancestors, to Abraham, Isaac, and Jacob, to give to them."

the transcendent may be enjoyed as transcendent and the delightful difference between the other and me is sustained by discourse. Justice consists
of a lifelong labor at the mercy of the other—a labor which does not end
at death, but which breathes on through the transubstantiated life of the
child. The vocation to justice labors not for one generation alone but for all
generations. Yet how do I know if I labor rightly? By heeding the voice of the
other: my master, my teacher, my sister, my brother. Now that we have set in
sharp relief the distinct phenomenological approaches of Marion and Levinas, let us apply these, respectively, to the topic of interreligious dialogue,
with the hope of transcending mere avatars of alterity.

First, let us recall Levinas's understanding of truth as it is generated
through Talmudic method. The Talmud reveals the play of truth through
dialectical confrontation. Jewish Midrash probes the truth of a text by
keeping the dialectical dance of interpretation alive. Not content with only
simple face-value meanings, Rabbinic hermeneutics unearths allegorical,
parabolic, and even mystical meanings generated by the text through the
interpretive stages of *P'shat*, *Remez*, *Derash*, and *Sod*. Talmudic method
refuses to let the ambiguity of problems and the dialectics of truth resolve
into facile solutions and singular meanings. Instead, as Levinas insists,
the Talmud signifies "an eternal dialogue taking place within human
consciousness."[13] Truth is spoken and heard through the plurality of conversation and unresolved dialectical discourse. Levinas observes that "the
relation between the same and the other—upon which we seem to impose
such extraordinary conditions—is language" and that "truth arises where a
being separated from the other is not engulfed in him, but speaks to him."[14]
Language constitutes the insoluble bridge between the self and the other. It
is the field of truth-telling that maintains the irreducibility of the other to
the same. Even within human consciousness, truth is announced through
the infinite play of discourse between interlocutors, at least one of which is
always other than the self. Levinas applies this hermeneutic of dialectical
truth to the diversity of civilizations emerging throughout history and to
the human vocation to tolerance: "We can tolerate the pluralism of great
civilizations and even understand why they cannot merge. The very nature

13. Levinas, *Difficult Freedom*, 65.

14. Levinas, *Totality and Infinity*, 39, 62, respectively (italics original). For Levinas,
the epiphany of the face appears inasmuch as it speaks, for the essence of language is
the very "bond between expression and responsibility" (Levinas, *Totality and Infinity*,
200). Through language, the other becomes my teacher and master, opening new vistas
of recognition by implicating me in her suffering. Whereas Marion interprets all phenomena according to the totalizing criterion of givenness, a Levinasian hermeneutics
of alterity unlocks the infinite possibilities of discourse between others.

of truth explains how this is impossible: truth manifests itself in a way that appeals to an enormous number of human possibilities and, through them, a whole range of histories, traditions and approaches."[15] Truth cannot be packaged exclusively within a monocultural totality of expressions. Instead, truth is expressed through an unlimited variety of signs, symbolic orders, and modes of communication.

This insight is crucial for the formidable task of interreligious dialogue on a global scale. According to the nature of truth itself, there must be an inherent plurality of distinct civilizations and religious traditions. The saturating host of religious traditions articulates the innate impossibility of manipulating truth as truth in its global epiphany of a united plurality of voices. Instead, we encounter a genealogy of world religions which have evolved over the course of time in various geographical and cultural centers: Judaism and Christianity from the Mediterranean region; Zoroastrianism and Islam from Arabia and the Middle East; Hinduism, Buddhism, Jainism, and Sikhism from India; Taoism and Confucianism from China; and Shintoism from Japan. Several other religious traditions could be mentioned as well, but the point here is to set forth the first principle of interreligious dialogue as inspired by Levinas: "Truth is consequently experienced as a dialogue . . . [which] does not reach a conclusion, but constitutes the very life of truth."[16] The unresolved dialogue of truth prevents the premature closure and falsification of truth. If the dialogue of truth comes to an abrupt end with nothing left to say, what becomes of truth as a living and universal summons to action and responsibility—a perennial personal quest of personal (not relative) ethical meaning?

Levinas affirms that "to respect the Other is, before all else, to refer to the Other's opinions."[17] Interreligious dialogue begins, and is sustained, by first seeking to understand the other and to affirm the seriousness of the other's religious convictions and the particular expression of those beliefs. Without the essential disposition of mutual respect and intellectual hospitality, the open quest for truth is reduced to a bland contest of rhetoric, as well as conquest of opinion, untethered from truth and its radical alterity in relation to the self. One always must remember the Parmenidean distinction between truth (*alétheia*) and opinion (*dóxa*) inasmuch as one could pretend to regard one's own opinion (*dóxa*) always to be truth (*alétheia*) and the position of the other as always and only opinion (*dóxa*). Truth (*alétheia*) as such always transcends interlocutors by definition. It maintains

15. Levinas, *Totality and Infinity*, 52.

16. Levinas, *Totality and Infinity*, 163.

17. Levinas, *Totality and Infinity*, 239.

an alterity over and above the alterity between conversation partners and never can be identified exclusively and absolutely with the opinion (*dóxa*) of any one of the interpreting correspondents. This does not imply thereby that truth cannot be known and communicated. Truth is spoken precisely in and through the play of conversation. It can be said but neither possessed exhaustively nor commodified costively.

In my 2017 book *Dialectical Anatomy of the Eucharist: An Étude in Phenomenology*, and as alluded to above, I argue that two distinct strands have evolved within the general method of phenomenology. The first is rooted in the original Husserlian brand which fixates on the field of intellectual vision for consciousness. Its empirical material is indexed according to degrees of appearance, intuition, and, above all, givenness (*Gegebenheit*). This first type of phenomenology privileges seeing and the intellectual vision of consciousness above all other modes of sense perception. It can be summarized under the term "manifestation" as it organizes every phenomenon according to the optical dimensions of eidetic disclosure. Anything which cannot be determined according to the contours of manifestation, in effect, would not appear in its in-the-flesh self-givenness. A clear trajectory extends from Husserl, through Heidegger, to Jean-Luc Marion for this phenomenology of manifestation and givenness. These three phenomenologists permit givenness to reign supreme, though in different, nuanced ways. When approaching the religious phenomenon, there is naturally a predilection for the sacred and for the event—that which manifests itself by itself in some kind of saturating vision. For his part, Marion is very careful to distinguish between the idol and the icon when considering the numinous power of the sacred. Whereas the idol freezes the intellectual gaze in a narcissistic reflection of the self, the icon opens onto the prosopic difference of the other. Nevertheless, one may wonder whether or not givenness itself ultimately hardens into a phenomenological idol obstructing "the nonphenomenality of the other."[18]

18. Levinas, *God, Death, and Time*, 201: "The nonphenomenality of the other who affects me beyond representation, unbeknownst to me and like a thief, is the Illeity of the third person. I hear an order in my own voice and not from someplace where the gaze could come to look for its authority as it would before an idol." Cf. Levinas, *Otherwise than Being or Beyond Essence*, 120: "The tropes of ethical language are found to be adequate for certain structures of the description: for the sense of the approach in its contrast with knowing, the face in its contrast with a phenomenon"; and, once again, Levinas, *Otherwise than Being or Beyond Essence*, 200 (italics original): "To speak to me is at each moment to surmount what is necessarily plastic in manifestation. To manifest oneself as a face is to *impose oneself* above and beyond the manifested and purely phenomenal form, to present oneself in a mode irreducible to manifestation, the very straightforwardness of the face to face, without the intermediary of any image, in one's nudity, that is, in one's destitution and hunger."

This question leads us to recount the second primary strand in phenomenology which has evolved since the time of Husserl. While it commences with the early Heidegger and his attention to the role of the interpreting human subject, as well as to the play of meaning and signification, it makes a more distinct break with the Husserlian optics of manifestation as observed in the work of Paul Ricoeur and Emmanuel Levinas. Greatly influenced by their personal religious contexts—Reformed Christianity and Rabbinic Judaism, respectively—Ricoeur and Levinas develop what can be called a phenomenology of proclamation in contrast to a phenomenology of manifestation. This strand of phenomenology emphasizes dialogue, interpretation, text, word, testimony, ethics, and the other, while it cautions us about the dangerous notion of the sacred.[19] Levinas, especially, pioneers a new phenomenology of the other by detecting the primary asymmetrical structure of intersubjectivity, which is issued through an inescapable ethical imperative that precedes any gathering up of manifestation and givenness.

For Levinas, the ethical is always primary, and he makes it clear that his notion of expiation for the other "is not a manifestation of the sacred."[20] To give oneself in loving responsibility for the sake of the other is not a modality of manifestation, but an ethical act performed through the frankness and resoluteness of intersubjective dialogue. Further, Levinas contends that

> for religion, and primarily for Christianity, the ethical appears to be only an approach, a beginning: the religious stands over the ethical. For thinking, the sacred appears as something which stands in essence higher and belongs to the metaphysical. I believe, on the other hand, that the ethical is the spiritual itself and

19. See Ricoeur, *Figuring the Sacred*, 72: "I am frightened by this word 'sacred.'" Cf. Levinas, *Totality and Infinity*, 77: "To relate to the absolute as an atheist is to welcome the absolute purified of the violence of the sacred. In the dimension of height in which his sanctity, this is, his separation, is presented, the infinite does not burn the eyes that are lifted unto him. He speaks; he does not have the mythical format that is impossible to confront and would hold the I in its invisible meshes. He is not numinous: the I who approaches him is neither annihilated on contact nor transported outside of itself, but remains separated and keeps its as-for-me." Cf. Levinas, *Difficult Freedom*, 15: "The rigorous affirmation of human independence, of its intelligent presence to an intelligible reality, the destruction of the numinous concept of the Sacred, entail the risk of atheism. That risk must be run. Only through it can man be raised to the spiritual notion of the Transcendent. It is a great glory for the Creator to have set up a being who affirms Him after having contested and denied Him in the glamorous areas of myth and enthusiasm; it is a great glory for God to have created a being capable of seeking Him or hearing Him from afar, having experienced separation and atheism."

20. Robbins, *Is It Righteous To Be?*, 99.

that there is nothing that surpasses the ethical. The surpassing
of the ethical is precisely the beginning of all violence.[21]

In this quote, Levinas lays down his cards. Here, as in several other texts,
he draws a sharp contrast between the notions of immanence and transcendence, between totality and infinity, between contemplation and ethics, between incarnation and illeity. For Levinas, God is "an immanent
transcendence" rather than a transcendent immanence as in Christianity.[22]
Within the realm of human experience, Levinas hears something which
neither Husserl nor Heidegger nor Marion detected because they were too
bedazzled by what manifests itself to vision: Levinas hears the voice of the
other and therein the voice of God. His phenomenology of the other is
bound to a phenomenology of proclamation which prioritizes speech above
sight. Ethical exigency, as enacted through spoken discourse, humanizes
humanity insofar as it empties all dehumanizing idols of their banal nu-
minosity and their false pretenses to surpass the goodness inherent in the
anthropological face-to-face ethical encounter.[23]

On guard against the idolatrous disclosure of truth as *alétheia*, that is,
truth as non-concealment, Levinas's phenomenology is inspired by Torah,
"the book of anti-idolatry, the absolute opposite of idolatry!"[24] Torah, defined as instruction, law, and command, transpires through speech, recita-
tion, rumination, and exegesis of text. Torah defies every idol by resisting
the hypnosis of manifestation and its bedazzling *mysterium fascinans et
tremendum* in relation to the spoken word. Even more, Torah is enacted
in daily ethical performance within interpersonal relationships that hinge
on divine standards of justice. Levinas frequently describes Judaism as "a
religion for adults."[25] Adults are the ones identified as those who recognize
themselves as responsible for the other—responsible for the child, responsible for the poor and marginalized persons of society, responsible for the
disabled person and those who live in radical vulnerability and fragility. Mature adults have entered the stage of post-naïveté through the sophistication
of language and culture. Adults compose and interpret texts, recognizing
human existence as taking place within a density of texts and interpretive

21. Robbins, *Is It Righteous To Be?*, 131. We hear this quote, of course, with implicit
critique of the Kierkegaardian suspension of the ethical in the name of religious faith.

22. Robbins, *Is It Righteous To Be?*, 148. Cf. Levinas, *Otherwise than Being or Beyond
Essence*, 140: "This transcendence is not convertible into immanence."

23. One need only think of Friedrich Nietzsche's idea of *Übermensch*, that is, above
the "human, all too human," and its devastating dehumanizing consequences as manifest in the way it was incarnate in Nazi ideology.

24. Levinas, *In the Time of the Nations*, 58.

25. Levinas, *Difficult Freedom*, 11.

layers of meaning. Centered on the phenomenality of proclamation, a theology of adulthood stands opposite a *theology* of childhood that stems from
the primacy of manifestation.[26]

VI. *Theology* of Childhood versus Theo*logy* of Adulthood

In contrast to Marion's phenomenology of givenness and *theology* of childhood, Levinas develops a phenomenology of the other and theo*logy* of adulthood, scolding the idolatry of the sacred in the name of the One proclaimed
in the face of the other. In order to understand the placement of Levinas's
critique of the sacred, let us first explain what is meant by a *theology* of
childhood as revealed in the work of Marion. Marion's entire oeuvre can be
categorized properly as a *theology* of childhood—with its express emphasis
on the *theos* rather than on the *lógos*—since givenness privileges the wonder
and awe in the gaze of the child. As the one who lacks a highly developed
vocabulary and symbolic order, the child most especially personifies the fitting disposition of the human subject in the face of the free and unmasterable phenomenon. Unlike the adult, the child is the one most uninhibited
by presuppositions and biases. The child, unlike the adult, does not view
that which appears through calloused interpretive lenses. In Marion's phenomenological world, the child would be the quintessential representative of
counter-intentionality and openness of intuition. The child's world is much
more saturated than the adult's world because the child does not place limits
on what may or may not appear. The child's world is a world of grand possibilities. It contains fewer obstacles for love—fewer experiences of betrayal,
of hurt, of crustaceous ideology. Marion writes in *Prolegomena to Charity*
that "love opens the eyes . . . not in the way violence opens the eyes of the disabused, but as a child opens his eyes to the world, or a sleeper opens his eyes
to the morning."[27] A child's experience is charged with openness, mystery,
and surprise. A child does not calculate and predetermine what may or may

26. By "*theology* of childhood" is not meant childish but the *theo*logical genius,
spiritual maturity, and religious potential of the child. Cf. Cavalletti, *Religious Potential
of the Child*, and Matt 18:3–5: "Amen, I say to you, unless you turn and become like
children, you will not enter the kingdom of heaven. Whoever humbles himself like this
child is the greatest in the kingdom of heaven. And whoever receives one child such as
this in my name receives me." In this respect, I would liken the humble, receptive and
contemplative attitude of the child to the phenomenological bracketing of the natural
attitude that is necessary to receive all that gives itself by itself without prejudice or
adjudication. For more on the distinction between a theology of childhood and a theology of adulthood, see Wallenfang and Wallenfang, *Shoeless*, 27–37.

27. Marion, *Prolegomena to Charity*, 69.

not occur in her experience. Rather, the child approaches life with a natural sense of fascination and affinity toward beauty and magnificence. Love is the hermeneutic key to beholding the world like a child, since love melts away the hermeneutic apprehensiveness which drains the phenomenon of its immaculate autonomy of self-revelation. For Marion, love serves as the "insufficient reason" to see and to act.[28] Love is that which inspires the authentic *theo*logian for whom "the referent [of *theology*] is not taught, since it is encountered by mystical union."[29] In Marion's view, authentic *theology* is that which peels away all hermeneutic filters in order to attain the purest mystical encounter with divinity. In the final analysis, divine revelation is not a matter of human investigation and contribution but depends entirely on letting the divine manifest divinity to the human being considered as pure recipient of divine gift, in a word, grace. When applied to theology, the perception of the child serves as the premier *mise-en-scène* upon which the phenomenon may show itself by itself without qualification or limitation. The child exhibits the genius of wonder and the propensity for the beautiful and the sacred. This is what is meant by a *theo*logy of childhood.

In contrast, with his accent on frank discourse and ordinary ethical movements, Levinas chides the notion of the sacred and the naïveté of the child's worldview. If responsibility is the key term for Levinas's lifelong project to establish ethics as first philosophy, it is the adult who is the responsible one. Levinas develops what can be called a theo*logy* of adulthood because the accent is on language, speech, and signification. For Levinas, the divine is proclaimed in the human through ethical action, not through an incarnate manifestation of divine presence. In a 1984 interview with Salomon Malka, Levinas says, "contrary to what my friend Derrida says, philosophy is not a subject matter for children of preschool age or in the first grade."[30] Philosophy and theo*logy* are fields which require the developmental competence to recognize and rise to the place of responsibility for the other. The vocation to responsibility is a mission for the mature—for adults who have been initiated into the election of virtue and responsibility. Adulthood is ushered in by *bar mitzvah* and *bath mitzvah*, through which a child becomes an adult within the human community. Quoting his teacher Shoshani, Levinas quips that "one should not give steak to newborns."[31] Infants and children are incapable of becoming responsible for the other to the degree that an adult

---

28. See Marion, *Erotic Phenomenon*, 79: "When loving is at issue, reason is not sufficient: reason appears from this point forward as a principle of *insufficient reason*" (italics original).

29. Marion, *God without Being*, 155.

30. Robbins, *Is It Righteous To Be?*, 102.

31. Robbins, *Is It Righteous To Be?*, 102.

is: infants and children are instead those for whom adults are responsible. In his 1963 Talmudic reading entitled, "Toward the Other," Levinas writes that "decidedly, with Judaism, we are dealing with a religion of adults."[32] The Jewish law is intended for adults who are able to perceive it, understand it, and respond to it. Through dialectical discussion and debate, the *logos* of reason comes of age when we recognize our responsibility for and serve the other not without risk to the self.

In *Difficult Freedom*, Levinas writes that "for a long time Jews thought that every situation in which humanity recognizes its religious progress finds in ethical relations its spiritual meaning—that is to say, its meaning for an adult."[33] Ethics is a territory of adulthood, and theo*logical* reflection on the spirituality of ethical action is a task suited to adults. In this same text he goes on to say that "the adult's God is revealed precisely through the void of the child's heaven. This is the moment when God retires from the world and hides His face. . . . This condition reveals a God Who renounces all aids to manifestation, and appeals instead to the full maturity of the responsible man."[34] One ascends into the state of adulthood as the fondness of the child's world of manifestation fades away through the experience of the tragic and the iron discipline of self-mastery. The word of God is issued not through the manifestation of a numinous presence, but through righteous and just living for the other. For Levinas, a God revealed in manifestation perpetuates an arrested development of the human spirit, which only lives in the *imago Dei* to the extent that it assumes responsibility for the other. Levinas again draws a serious contrast between the mystical sacred and the sober Torah as he writes,

> Here I believe we see the specific face of Judaism: the link between God and man is not an emotional communion that takes place within the love of a God incarnate, but a spiritual or intellectual [*esprits*] relationship which takes place through an education in the Torah. It is precisely a word, not incarnate, from God that ensures a living God among us . . . [Torah] is a protection against the madness of a direct contact with the Sacred that is unmediated by reason.[35]

What is to fear in contacting the sacred in a way unmediated by reason? Levinas warns us that such enthusiasm quickly leads to dehumanizing activity. When the ethical is suspended, so is the human, so is the divine. A theo*logy*

32. Levinas, *Nine Talmudic Readings*, 15.
33. Levinas, *Difficult Freedom*, 4.
34. Levinas, *Difficult Freedom*, 143.
35. Levinas, *Difficult Freedom*, 144.

which respects the transcendence of God refuses to manipulate the divine as a mode of human affectivity. The radical otherness of God is maintained through the unflinching demands of the divine law, which binds the human person through rational assent to the inherent and transcendent goodness of this law and of righteous living. A theo*logy* of adulthood prevents an irrational Dionysian affair with the sacred which would result in a destruction of self, other, and community. A theo*logy* that is rational ensures that the rectitude of God's eternal law will continue to unfold within the terrain of humanity. This is what is meant by a theo*logy* of adulthood.

VII. Toward a Dialectical *Theology* of Ethical Communal Personhood

Now that we have discussed the phenomenological polarity between Marion and Levinas, let us in turn propose the next step for interreligious dialogue in the twenty-first century.[36] Instead of recommending either Marion's *theo*logy of childhood or Levinas's theo*logy* of adulthood as the winning approach, I would like to suggest a new dialectical *theology* of ethical communal personhood. I do not intend to synthesize the respective positions of Marion and Levinas (à la Hegel) into a third position totality, but rather to bring them into closest proximity in order to harness the fruitfulness of the dialectical tension between them. This procedure, in fact, is precisely what Levinas recommends in his Talmudic understanding of truth. By affirming the veracity of both poles of the dialectic, fertile conversation is advanced without breakdown. I term this proposal "*theology* of ethical communal personhood" since both *theos* and *logos* receive emphasis and since both childhood and adulthood are validated as necessary hermeneutic vectors to the phenomenon. My argument is that there is an intrinsic complementarity between childhood and adulthood, between the experience of the child and the experience of the adult. While children are called to the maturity of adulthood, adults are likewise called to the innocence and perceptive openness of children. Are not children creatures of love par excellence? Both children and adults are persons in the full sense of the term, and, therefore, to speak of a *theology* of ethical communal personhood suggests the primacy of relationality within a matrix of otherness. How would this newly devised method work in interreligious dialogue? Let us briefly apply this

36. For a much more thorough foray into the interstices within the field of interreligious dialogue, see my introduction in Cavadini and Wallenfang, *Evangelization as Interreligious Dialogue*, 2:xv–xl.

hermeneutic to the following religious traditions: Judaism, Christianity, Islam, Hinduism, Buddhism, and Shintoism.

Judaism and Christianity

First, we have detected already the character contrast between Judaism and Christianity. While Judaism professes an aperture of proclamation, Christianity reveals one of manifestation—especially in Catholicism and in Eastern Orthodoxy. As witnessed in Levinas, Judaism constantly defends the transcendent otherness of God who is revealed through the law of the covenant. All forms of idolatry are condemned and lambasted in the name of the LORD—YHWH—who is above all nomenclature and representation. Christianity, on the other hand, began as a sort of reform movement within Judaism, but announced an epiphany which overturned the lordship of legislation. For Christians, the law of God has been manifested in the flesh in Jesus of Nazareth who is regarded as Lord.[37] Yet within Christianity there are trajectories of both manifestation and proclamation, with Protestant Christianity taking up the banner of proclamation. With its fundamentalist basis in the Lutheran notion of *sola scriptura*, Protestantism, in a way, returns to the Jewish prominence of language, text, and ethics, as opposed to liturgy, sacraments, and mysticism.

Islam

With its concentration on the textual vitality of the Qur'an, Islam, like Judaism, can be situated as a religion of proclamation. As Levinas writes, "Monotheism marks a break with a certain conception of the Sacred. It neither unifies nor hierarchizes the numerous and numinous gods; instead, it denies them. As regards the Divine which they incarnate, it is merely atheism."[38] Both Judaism and Islam can be defined as atheistic belief structures in regard to deities expressed in polytheistic avatars and incarnations. The preeminence of prophetism in both traditions signals the word of the other—in particular, the word of God—announced in the self and especially in the self's response to this divine summons. Even though Islam can be situated as a religion of

37. John 1:1, 14: "In the beginning was the Word (*logos*), and the Word was with God, and the Word was God. . . . And the Word became flesh and made his dwelling among us, and we saw his glory, the glory as of the Father's only Son, full of grace and truth" (NAB). Notice the language of sight here in verse 14 as it emphasizes the manifestation of God in the flesh.

38. Levinas, *Difficult Freedom*, 14–15.

proclamation, it also has a mystical trajectory within it: Sufism. Through its developed symbolic structures of meaning, Sufism introduces mysticism in the Islamic tradition for the sake of its goal: communion with God through the pathway (*tariqah*) of ecstatic contemplation (*wajd*). Although this mystical itinerary seems close to the notion of manifestation in Christian mysticism, Sufism insists that it is dealing with an awakening to the unmanifest or unseen world (*kashf al-ghayb*).

Hinduism

Hinduism, in contrast to Judaism and Islam but similar to Christianity, asserts a proliferation and multiplicity of divine manifestations.[39] A countless host of divine avatars, for example, Krishna, Rama, Parvarti, Shakti, Kali, and Lakshmi, are derived from the three primary manifestations of Brahman—Brahma, Vishnu, and Siva. In Hinduism, the divine is worshipped in a plethora of manifestations which are taken to be diverse embodiments of the divine. Through the saturating variety of aspects, descents, and personifications of divinity, believers draw near to the Deity for various needs and causes. The Vedas speak of the "thousand-headed Brahman" and of the oneness of truth called by many different names. Likewise, the Vedas depict God as becoming the creation. For Hinduism, the goal of faith is *moksa*, that is, spiritual ascent (*dharma*) and eventual union with Brahman. The dynamic of manifestation is so prominent in Hinduism that oftentimes there is little demarcation between the divine and the universe, resulting in an essentially pantheistic perception of reality, as seen in the principle of *advaita*, or non-dualism. Ornate and intricate *mandalas* depict a refulgence of divine emanation which constitutes the cosmos. The doctrine of reincarnation reinforces the unity and totality of the cosmos in which all beings comprise an organic whole.

Buddhism

Like Protestantism within Christianity, Buddhism can be interpreted as a reform movement within Hinduism, which moves away from an obsession

---

39. Panikkar, *Rhythm of Being*, 216–17: "*Advaita* overcomes the strictures of positing the *logos* to integrate the *pneuma* (spirit) in our approach to reality . . . spiritual knowledge that does not need rational evidence in order to gain an insight into the nature of things. . . . *Advaita* amounts to the overcoming of dualistic dialectics by means of introducing love at the ultimate level of reality . . . "aduality." . . . Reality is-not one; reality is-not two (*a-dvaita*)."

with the sacred toward a concentration on text and ethical behavior. Buddhism, then, is fundamentally a religion of proclamation. Initiated by Siddhartha Gautama in the sixth century BC, Buddhism turns attention away from the cosmological *samsara* (that is, the swirling cycles of death and rebirth) in order to break free from them through *bodhi* (that is, enlightenment) and to reach the final state of *nirvana* (that is, to extinguish [literally, "to blow out"] the fire of ignorance and desire which causes suffering). However, two divergent movements emerged within Buddhism: Theravada Buddhism (which adheres to the values of proclamation in an almost exclusive way) and Mahayana Buddhism (which demonstrates a preoccupation with the captivating sacred, for example, in the worship of *bodhisattvas*). Chan, Zen, and Tibetan Buddhism all stem from the manifestation paradigm of Mahayana Buddhism. On the whole, however, it is accurate to understand Buddhism as a reform movement within Hinduism, moving away from the religious form of manifestation to that of proclamation. As one Hindu believer, Ramaswamy Sharma of Parma, Ohio, has put it: "Buddhism is Hinduism minus God." Indeed, original Buddhism can be construed as an atheistic belief structure in relation to the panoply of divine manifestations which make up Hinduism.

Shintoism

Finally, Shintoism—a religion indigenous to Japan—certainly can be placed in the school of manifestation with its practices of ancestor veneration and belief in *kami*, which are sacred spirits that exist in everything, and are revered as deities. One such *kami* is the venerated Amaterasu, a sun goddess who gives sacred authority to the emperor. Therefore, the national emperor is revered by the people of the nation as a man who has been commissioned directly by the divine to rule. With its diverse array of *jinja*, or shrines dedicated to *kami*, the structure of Shintoism clearly follows the contours of manifestation rather than proclamation. Shintoism envisions an infinite pantheon of deities which oversee all aspects of nature and human life. A fundamental part of Japanese life is to make offerings to *kami* at shrines and temples or at sacred sites, for example, at streams or mountains. Shintoism claims that human beings become *kami* after they die, joining the ranks of the nature spirits which animate the universe. This idea of deification is similar to that within Hinduism and manifestation Christianity, which hold an eschatological teleology of divinization for the human soul.

VIII. Conclusion

This very brief outline of some of the world's great religious traditions shows the value of the phenomenological relationship between manifestation and proclamation, especially as articulated in the confrontation of the works of Marion and Levinas. And this critical phenomenological basis can serve as a foundation for interreligious dialogue today. It sets the standard for an unresolved dialectic enacted in respectful conversation, while furnishing key categories for understanding the fundamental relationships between diverse religious traditions and the reform movements within them. This insight may very well be a real breakthrough for the task of interreligious dialogue today.

The hypothesis advanced here must continue to be developed and tested through actual interfaith encounters, but for now it leaves us with great hope and promise for conversations of peace and mutual respect to unfold between those Happy Warriors who are accustomed to listening to the other. A *theology* of ethical communal personhood contributes to this critical enterprise for today because it provides a model which promotes both otherness and complementarity so that genuine differences can serve as the building blocks of genuine unity. By harnessing the dialectical tension between manifestation and proclamation in a positive way, new pathways are opened for tolerance, fraternity, and responsibility for the other. Violence and antagonism result upon the collapse of dialectical relationships, but human flourishing, just living, and loving service are the result of the centrifugal hope of irreducible alterity united.

CHAPTER 3

ANALYTIC PHILOSOPHY
AND ITS LIMITS

Numquam ponenda est pluralitas sine necessitate.

—William of Ockham, *Quaestiones et decisiones in quattuor libros Sententiarum Petri Lombardi*

If a sign is *useless*, it is meaningless. That is the point of Occam's maxim.

—Ludwig Wittgenstein, *Tractatus*[1]

Givenness thus determines all the levels of phenomenality.

—Jean-Luc Marion, *Being Given*[2]

DANGER LURKS EVERY TIME one pulls out a razor, especially when motivated by the intention to trim off what is judged to be excessive or unnecessary. What has come to be known as Ockham's razor is no exception, and its phenomenon was in use much earlier than the fourteenth century. Philosophy has been tormented perpetually with the temptation to reductionism. The risk of mistaking the part for the whole is never fully overcome. In seeking to know reality with clarity, one is beset by some form of minimalism perhaps because the whole is too vast for any one mind or group of minds to think. To think anything at all implies thinking one part at a time and at no time thinking all parts simultaneously. For this reason, it is only natural for the whole of thought to be parceled out to a variety of academic disciplines and

---

1. Wittgenstein, *Tractatus Logico-Philosophicus*, 31 (italics original). For a discussion on Wittgenstein's employment of Occam's razor as a precursor to pragmatism, see Hallett, *Wittgenstein's Definition of Meaning as Use*, 18–25.

2. Marion, *Being Given*, 26.

subspecialties. Among these subdivisions of knowledge, antithetical trajectories develop quite naturally as well when different starting points and
methods are chosen for approaching any given issue. Two distinct schools
of philosophy have emerged through the course of the twentieth century
and now face each other as strangers: analytic philosophy and continental
philosophy. Each school refers to a broad range of personas and methods,
and, once again, we succeed in furnishing yet another hasty reductionism as
the price to pay for attempting a metanarrative in brief.

At the turn of the twentieth century, two general schools of philosophy
in Europe began to develop simultaneously, geographically separated by the
English Channel. In England, Alfred North Whitehead (1861–1947) and
Bertrand Russell (1872–1970), influenced by the logicism of Gottlob Frege
(1848–1925), co-authored the three-volume work, *Principia Mathematica*
(1910, 1912, 1913) with the goal of reducing the principles of mathematics
to logic. In Germany, Edmund Husserl (1859–1938), influenced by Franz
Brentano's (1838–1917) notion of intentionality, published his two-volume
work, *Logical Investigations* (1900, 1901), thereby commencing the peculiar
philosophical method that would come to be known as phenomenology—
one of the many movements that would comprise continental philosophy.
In short, continental philosophy refers to all European philosophy other
than analytic philosophy that was developing apart from analytic philosophy. Idealism, existentialism, structuralism, deconstruction, and critical
theory (among other philosophical currents and schools) are considered
as part of what is meant by continental philosophy, in addition to phenomenology and hermeneutics. Developing rather independently of one another, analytic and continental philosophy certainly have their differences,
but they also have much in common in terms of what they were trying to
accomplish. For the purpose of this chapter, we will confine continental
philosophy to its subcategory of phenomenology in order to compare analytic philosophy and phenomenology more directly.

Nevertheless, the main point of this chapter is not so much to compare
analytic philosophy and phenomenology as to apply this distinction to the
divergence between Emmanuel Levinas's and Jean-Luc Marion's respective
claims in phenomenology. It will be argued that even though Marion follows
Levinas on many points in his phenomenology, in the end he betrays the sine
qua non of Levinas's entire project: ethics as first philosophy. Coming after
the phenomenological projects of Husserl and Heidegger, Levinas boldly
claims that phenomenality has an inherently ethical character. Nothing gives
itself to consciousness outside of the anterior ethical relationship. The call of
the other and my ensuing responsibility for him precede the so-called call
of givenness (*Gegebenheit*) and form the very anthropological structure of
the perception and reception of givenness. By leaving behind what Levinas

calls the "trauma of transcendence," Marion reverts back to a pre-Levinasian phenomenology by reducing the other to just another form of givenness.[3] In essence, Marion converts the auditory call of the other into a common instance of manifestation. Alterity is swallowed up under the rubric of givenness, thereby reducing the other to more of the same.

At the risk of appearing anachronistic, this chapter presents a Levinasian critique of Marion's phenomenology of givenness. Even though Marion claims to go further than Levinas by a post-Levinasian return to the concept of givenness, I will argue that Marion in fact backslides from the phenomenological gains made by Levinas. In order to issue this corrective of Marion's phenomenology of givenness, the argument will proceed as follows: (1) a brief summary of the phenomenological innovations of Levinas, (2) a positioning of Marion as an "analytic phenomenologist," and (3) a proposal of a dialectical phenomenology of contemplative ethics. In order to observe how Marion's phenomenology departs from that of Levinas, while sharing much in common, let us make a sketch of Levinas's phenomenology of proclamation.

I. Levinas's Phenomenology of Proclamation

As Levinas constructs his phenomenological anthropology, eventually establishing ethics as first philosophy, he chooses his words very carefully.[4] In a conversation I once had with his daughter, Simone, she said that he was very demanding of himself as he wrote, oftentimes crumpling up pages he had written and throwing them in the waste basket. She said that he chose his words with painstaking care. Upon surveying the oeuvre of Levinas, consistency of intentional vocabulary is noticed.[5] Certain words Levinas favors and feature as refrains throughout his works, such as the other, responsibility, the call, substitution, signification, proximity, the face, justice, law, the infinite, transcendence, testimony, witness, prophecy, kerygma, and proclamation. Other words Levinas holds in contempt, such as the sacred, love (at times), forgiveness, appearance, knowledge, the visible, and manifestation. Anything that would pull my attention away from the other person who faces me is an idol to be razed. No theophany and no apparition are to compete with the ethical demands that incessantly call me to responsibility for the other. If the call for me to be responsible for the other

3. See Levinas, *Otherwise than Being or Beyond Essence*, xlviii.

4. In contrast to Levinas's positioning of ethics as first philosophy, Marion posits the phenomenology givenness as first philosophy. See Marion, "Phenomenology of Givenness and First Philosophy" in his *In Excess*, 1–29.

5. See Ciocan and Hansel, *Levinas Concordance*.

were only one of many important aspects of life, those aspects other than responsibility could take priority over responsibility. If the call of the other is one of many forms of manifestation for phenomenology to categorize and manage alongside all other phenomena, then the call of the other is not ultimate or more primordial than anything else.

Levinas's entire project can be regarded as a concentrated critique of phenomenology's preoccupation with manifestation and its proclivity for the visible. Drawing from Heidegger's admission that the meaning of the term "phenomenon" suggests more possibilities than only those of visual appearance, Levinas similarly expands the Husserlian scope of phenomenology to include phenomena that do not appear as such. Using the example of symptoms of a disease, Heidegger writes that, in such a case, "appearance, as the appearance 'of something', does *not* mean showing-itself; it means rather the announcing-itself by something which does not show itself, but which announces itself through something which does show itself."[6] The phenomenality of announcing is other than that of appearing. Some phenomena cannot be seen but can be heard. For Levinas, ethical exigency is not a matter of seeing but of hearing the call of the other announced through the vital interstices of language and signification. Law codifies the requirements of justice in their formal particularities. Ethical precepts are formulated according to that which does not appear as an object, a being, or even as one of many instantiations of givenness. By its very etymology, the term "manifestation" implies manipulation. The first part of the word derives from the Latin noun, *manus*, meaning "hand." The second part of the word derives from the Latin adjective, *infestus*, meaning "hostile, aggressive, warlike." This is to say that manifestation implies an effect of something striking the hand or the hand grasping something in violent fashion. Reminiscent of Heidegger's notion of "ready-to-hand" (*zuhanden*), manifestation conveys the sense of use and utilization—a controlled and calculated subjective situating of objects within a world of objects—a world of tools at one's voluntary disposal.[7] *Dasein* reigns supreme in the phenomenological world of Heidegger due to the centripetal position of the self and not that of the other person who faces me.

Instead, Levinas speaks of "being affected by a non-phenomenon," one that does not appear as such and therefore prohibits me from asserting

6. Heidegger, *Being and Time*, 52 (italics original).

7. See Heidegger, *Being and Time*, 95–102 (¶15). Also, see Levinas, *Totality and Infinity*, 133: "The structure of the *Zeug* ['tool'] as *Zeug* and the system of references in which it has its place do indeed manifest themselves, in concerned handling, as irreducible to vision, but do not encompass the substantiality of objects, which is always there in addition."

mastery over it.[8] A non-phenomenon is that which does not appear per se but nevertheless exerts a force upon the human subject. Similar to the law of gravitational force, the call of the other is the law of intersubjectivity which imposes itself in and through the proximity of the other. Levinas writes that

> the face of a neighbor signifies for me an unexceptionable responsibility, preceding every free consent, every pact, every contract. It escapes representation; it is the very collapse of phenomenality. Not because it is too brutal to appear, but because in a sense too weak, non-phenomenon because less than a phenomenon. The disclosing of a face is nudity, non-form, abandon of self, ageing, dying, more naked than nudity. It is poverty, skin with wrinkles, which are a trace of itself.[9]

In tracing the phenomenality of the naked, vulnerable, and exposed face of the other, Levinas pushes the tradition of phenomenology to the possibility of the phenomenon of the non-phenomenon. A veritable paradox, the non-phenomenon of the fragile face comes as the transcendent context and milieu of every other perceived phenomenon.[10] As at once exposure and command, the face of the other is the proclamatory *mise-en-scène* encompassing all subsequent perception—"immanent transcendence," "where God *works*, where 'God lives.'"[11] The face of the other is the non-spatial

8. Levinas, *Otherwise than Being or Beyond Essence*, 75. Cf. Levinas, *God, Death, and Time*, 201: "The nonphenomenality of the other who affects me beyond representation, unbeknownst to me and like a thief, is the Illeity of the third person. I hear an order in my own voice and not from someplace where the gaze could come to look for its authority as it would before an idol."

9. Levinas, *Otherwise than Being or Beyond Essence*, 88. Cf. Levinas, *Otherwise than Being or Beyond Essence*, 150 (italics original): "This saying belongs to the very glory of which it bears witness. This way for the order to come from I know not where, this coming that is not a recalling, is not the return of a present modified or aged into a past, this non-phenomenality of the order which, beyond representation affects me unbeknownst to myself, 'slipping into me like a thief,' we have called *illeity*"; and Levinas, *Of God Who Comes to Mind*, 106 (italics original): "The Husserlian 'appresentation,' which does not arrive at satisfaction or at the intuitive fulfillment of the re-presentation, is inverted—as a failed experience—into a *beyond experience*, into a *transcendence* whose rigorous *determination* is described by ethical attitudes and exigencies, and by responsibility, of which language is one modality. The proximity of the neighbor, rather than passing for a limitation of the I by another, or for an aspiration to the unity yet to be effected, becomes desire nourishing itself from its hungers, or, to us a used word, love, more precious to the soul than the full possession of oneself by oneself."

10. See Levinas, *Totality and Infinity*, 92: "The Other is the principle of phenomena." Similarly, see Hansel, "Beyond Phenomenology," 17: "Ethics exceeds—or rather, precedes—phenomenology."

11. Robbins, *Is It Righteous To Be?*, 148 (italics original). Although, elsewhere Levinas writes that "this transcendence is not convertible into immanence" (*Otherwise than Being or Beyond Essence*, 140).

locale and untouchable texture where God comes to mind: "the nonmanifestation, the invisibility which language sets forth."[12] As ethical injunction without egress, the face of the other signifies "the essence of communication [which] is not a modality of the essence of manifestation."[13] Face-to-face relationship signifies the asymmetrical proximity between the other and me in which the other summons me as my vulnerable master—master to the degree of his radical vulnerability. My responsibility for the other swells in proportion to the other's near fragility. Levinas contends that "proximity goes from soul to soul, outside of any manifestation as a phenomenon, outside of any given."[14] Ethical proximity to the other transcends the scope

12. Levinas, "Enigma and Phenomenon," in *Emmanuel Levinas*, 67. Cf. Levinas, *En découvrant l'existence avec Husserl et Heidegger*, 204: "Fixons le point de départ: la nonmanifestation, l'invisibilité que le langage profère." And further in Levinas, *Emmanuel Levinas*, 67: "This refusal to exhibit itself does not necessarily contain a complacency for hidden abodes. The extravagance or hyperbole which language can express by the superlative of the supreme being retains the trace of a beyond-being where day and night do not divide the time that can make them coexist in the dusk of evening, the trace of a beyond borne by a time different from that in which the overflowings of the present flow back to this present across memory and hope. Could faith be described then as a glimpse into a time whose moments are no longer related to the present as their term or their source? This would produce a diachrony which maddens the subject but channels transcendence."

13. Levinas, *Otherwise than Being or Beyond Essence*, 190. Cf. Levinas, *Totality and Infinity*, 200 (italics original): "To speak to me is at each moment to surmount what is necessarily plastic in manifestation. To manifest oneself as a face is to *impose oneself* above and beyond the manifested and purely phenomenal form, to present oneself in a mode irreducible to manifestation, the very straightforwardness of the face to face, without the intermediary of any image, in one's nudity, that is, in one's destitution and hunger"; and Levinas, *Totality and Infinity*, 174: "Transcendence is not a vision of the Other, but a primordial donation. . . . The 'vision' of the face is inseparable from this offering language is. To see the face is to speak of the world. Transcendence is not an optics, but the first ethical gesture."

14. Levinas, *Otherwise than Being or Beyond Essence*, 190. Cf. Levinas, *Otherwise than Being or Beyond Essence*, 193 (italics original): "The exteriority of *illeity*, refractory to disclosure and manifestation, is a having-to-be in the face of another. In it there is announced not a *Sollen*, which is always asymptotic, but glory"; and Levinas, *Collected Philosophical Papers*, 116, 118, 121 (italics original): "Proximity is *by itself* a signification. . . . To approach, to neighbor, is not tantamount to the knowing or consciousness one can have of approaching. In contact the things are near, but are so in a quite different sense from the sense in which they are rough, heavy, black, agreeable, or even existing or nonexisting. The way in which they are 'in flesh and bone' (the usual translation of Husserl's '*leibhaft gegeben*') does not characterize their manifestation, but their proximity. . . . To not be an autochthonous being, to be torn up from culture, law, horizon, context, by reason of an absence which is the very presence of infinity, finding itself in the null site of a trace, is not to take on a certain number of attributes that might figure in a passport; it is *to come facing, to manifest oneself by undoing one's manifestation.* Such is the face, as we have said, the point at which an epiphany becomes a proximity."

of phenomenological immanence within consciousness. In contrast to
Husserl's regard for that which is transcendent to consciousness as suspect,
superfluous, and illusory, Levinas contends that the exteriority and transcendence of the other signifies more significantly than any pure datum of
immanence. As "counterconsciousness," expiation for the other "is not a
manifestation of the sacred," but a signification "which refers to the proclamatory, kerygmatic intention of thought [in which] every phenomenon is
a discourse or a fragment of discourse."[15] Opposed to vision which has to
do with unity, reducibility, and comparability, Levinas describes the structure of phenomenality in terms of hearing which implies diversity, multiple
languages and meanings. Whereas vision is silent and enveloped in solitude,
hearing is musical and rhythmic, adhering to the cadences of ethical life:
"rhythm certainly does have its privileged locus in music, for the musician's
element realizes the pure deconceptualization of reality. Sound is the quality
most detached from an object."[16] For Levinas, phenomena are musical and
have more to do with signification and language than with appearance and

15. Levinas, *Entre Nous*, 58; Robbins, *Is It Righteous To Be?*, 99; Levinas, *Collected
Philosophical Papers*, 112. Cf. Levinas, *Collected Philosophical Papers*, 111–13, 123–24,
126 (italics original): "Everything, is, one might say, imaged in experience, except the
identity of individuals, which holds sway over the instants of the images. This identity
is possible only as *claimed*. . . . The *proclamatory* character of identification destroys
the analogy. And it shows how the kerygma, which is sovereign through the word that
establishes and consecrates beyond the given, will play in historical tongues and their
system of signs. . . . To be taken as . . . , to be understood or claimed or maintained
as this or as that, is for what appears to have signification. But what appears cannot
appear outside of signification. . . . Language is not meaningful because it would come
out of some play of meaningless signs; it is meaningful because it is a kerygmatic proclamation which identifies this as that. . . . Language, contact, is the obsession of an I
'beset' by the others. Obsession is responsibility. . . . The ethical language we resort
to does not proceed from a special moral experience, independent of the description
developed until then. It comes from the very meaning of the approach, which contrasts
with knowledge, of the face which contrasts with phenomena. Phenomenology can
follow the reverting of thematization into ethics in the description of a face. . . . The first
saying is to be sure but a word. But the word is God." See also, Levinas, *Otherwise than
Being or Beyond Essence*, 6, 35, 62, 65, 99, 120 (italics original): "The correlation of the
saying and the said, that is, the subordination of the saying to the said, to the linguistic
system and to ontology, is the price that manifestation demands. . . . Identification is
kerygmatical. The said is not simply a sign or an expression of a meaning; it proclaims
and establishes this as that. . . . The intention that animates the identification of this as
this or as that is a proclamation, a promulgation, and thus a language, a stating of the
said. . . . Philosophy, which is born with appearing, with thematization, tries, in the
course of its phenomenology, to reduce the manifest and the manifestation to their
preoriginal signification, a signification that does not signify manifestation. . . . This
identification is not the *counterpart* of any image; it is a claim of the mind, proclamation, saying, kerygma. . . . The tropes of ethical language are found to be adequate for
certain structures of the description: for the sense of the approach in its contrast with
knowing, the face in its contrast with a phenomenon."

16. Levinas, *Collected Philosophical Papers*, 4.

static knowledge of objects. Just as music signifies the deconceptualization of reality, so does the inherent ethical structure of intersubjective relationships signify the de-phenomenalization of phenomena according to the exorbitance of the primordial phenomenon of the non-phenomenon: the call of the other. Levinas's distinction between the saying and the said attests to the phenomenal non-phenomenon before and behind every perceived phenomenon: "the responsibility for another is precisely a saying prior to anything said. The surprising saying which is a responsibility for another is against 'the winds and tides' of being, is an interruption of essence, a disinterestedness imposed with good violence."[17] Responsibility for the other, as diachronic non-phenomenon, disrupts the manageable influx of immanent essences within consciousness. Levinas describes this incessant vocation to responsibility as a good violence because it protects against the eruption of bad violence at the point at which the self otherwise would be paralyzed by the *il y a*, by boredom, or by seething self-interest which reduces the other to a tool for use at best and an obstacle to be destroyed at worst.

Levinas argues that "the meaningfulness of the face is the command to responsibility . . . the face is not at all what has been seen. . . . The face speaks. The manifestation of the face is already discourse. . . . The eyes break through the mask—the language of the eyes, impossible to dissemble. The eye does not shine; it speaks."[18] When Levinas speaks of the face, it is not for him primarily a phenomenon of manifestation or vision. To envisage the face of the other is to deface the other. Before the face becomes manifest to sight, it has spoken already as ethical injunction: thou shall not kill. Twice exposed, first as saying and then as said, the face of the other proclaims my vocation to responsibility for her. Responsibility, as first phenomenon, deduces ethics as first philosophy according to the method of phenomenology: "a method for philosophy, but phenomenology—the comprehension effected through a bringing to light—does not constitute the ultimate event of being itself."[19] While phenomenology tends to frame phenomena exclusively in terms of conscious vision and manifestation, it runs ashore in the encounter with the face of the other. In the nakedness of the face, "humility

---

17. Levinas, *Otherwise than Being or Beyond Essence*, 43.

18. Robbins, *Is It Righteous To Be?*, 135, 144; Levinas, *Totality and Infinity*, 66. See also Robbins, *Is It Righteous To Be?*, 235–36 (italics original): ". . . why I have been so interested in language. Language is always addressed to the other, as if one could not think without already being concerned for the other. In the profundity of thinking, the *for-the-other* is articulated, or, said otherwise, goodness is articulated, love for the other, which is more spiritual than any science . . . To see or to know the face is already to deface the other. The face in its nudity is the weakness of a unique being exposed to death, but at the same time the enunciation of an imperative which obliges me not to let it alone. This obligation is the first word of God."

19. Levinas, *Totality and Infinity*, 28.

unites with elevation. And announces thereby the ethical dimension of visitation."[20] Phenomenology must be humbled before its prize catch: the paradoxical non-phenomenon of call and responsibility proclaimed in the summons of the naked face. The call of the other, neither manifest nor given nor seen, constitutes the awakened playing field for the light of consciousness rather than vice versa. In attending to the non-manifest *mise-en-scène* for consciousness, phenomenology is scandalized once again by the metaphysics of transcendence that goes before and behind it.[21] The face of the other indicts and absolves "the idolatry that brews in all contemplation."[22] Thanks to Levinas, phenomenology must confess that neither givenness nor manifestation are the first or the last word. The call of the other precedes and predetermines the call of givenness, and the face of the other can be reduced neither to a category of manifestation nor to a subspecies of conscious data. Humiliated by its own provenance, phenomenology is awakened to its most decisive vocation: to testify to the call of the other issued in the poverty and destitution of the naked face, at once unique and universal.

II. Marion's "Analytic" Phenomenology of Givenness and Manifestation

"What has Athens to do with Jerusalem?"[23] For our purposes, Tertullian's timeless question can be applied to the following terms of juxtaposition: What has analytic philosophy to do with continental philosophy? What has a phenomenology of manifestation to do with a phenomenology of proclamation? What has Marion to do with Levinas? At this juncture, we will pair the broad category of analytic philosophy with Marion's phenomenology of givenness and manifestation in order to expose its shortcomings vis-à-vis Levinas's phenomenology of proclamation. First, it must be admitted that Marion's phenomenology is in no way part of the tradition of analytic philosophy. It is to be located, instead, within the tradition of continental philosophy. However, the prerogatives of analytic philosophy may aid to show how Marion's phenomenology of givenness falls prey to the potential reductionism of the phenomenological reduction. Let us begin, then, with a brief assessment of the aims of analytic philosophy in order to compare them with those of Marion's phenomenology of givenness.

20. Levinas, *Humanism of the Other*, 32.

21. See Levinas, "Metaphysics and Transcendence" in *Totality and Infinity*, 33–52.

22. Levinas, *Totality and Infinity*, 172.

23. Tertullian, *De Praescriptionibus Adversus Haereticos*, 7 (*Patrologia Latina* 2.20): "Quid ergo Athenis et Hierosolymis?"

Upon the 1910 publication of Alfred North Whitehead's and Bertrand Russell's first volume of *Principia Mathematica*, analytic philosophy was conceived. As a peculiar school of philosophy on the world stage, its trademarks were announced in the opening pages of Whitehead's and Russell's seminal work: "It is framed with a view to the perfectly precise expression, in its symbols, of mathematical propositions: to secure such expression, and to secure it in the simplest and most convenient notation possible, is the chief motive in the choice of topics. . . . In fact the very abstract simplicity of the ideas of this work defeats language."[24] Its mission is clear, hearkening back to Ockham's razor: reduce all plurality and ambiguity to the most simplified formulas; do not go beyond what is necessary. Perfection is regarded as precision of symbolic expression which claims to underwrite all mathematical formulas. To this end, textual notation is reduced to a symbolic nomenclature of meaning. A universal language is proposed that would disqualify the need for multiple languages and expressions of meaning. Language is reduced to symbolic computations and logical deductions. Whatever falls outside the scope of the predetermined symbols of the logical system's totality is deemed meaningless and irrelevant. In the spirit of fourteenth-century English Franciscan, William of Ockham, analytic philosophy subscribes to the law of parsimony concerning the deliberations of reason. Binding itself to the economy of logical deduction, analytic philosophy reduces all reality and meaning to the lowest common denominators of expression. For example, take the following basic formula of inference from *Principia Mathematica*:[25]

$$\vdash p \supset \vdash q$$

24. Whitehead and Russell, *Principia Mathematica*, 1:1–2. "The adaptation of the rules of the symbolism to the processes of deduction aids the intuition in regions too abstract for the imagination readily to present to the mind the true relation between the ideas employed" (Whitehead and Russell, *Principia Mathematica*, 1:2). For a helpful description of the common prescriptions of analytic philosophy, see Rea, "Introduction," 5–6. Rea lists the following as the central prescriptions of the analytic style of doing philosophy: "P1. Write as if philosophical positions and conclusions can be adequately formulated in sentences that can be formalized and logically manipulated. P2. Prioritize precision, clarity, and logical coherence. P3. Avoid substantive (non-decorative) use of metaphor and other tropes whose semantic content outstrips their propositional content. P4. Work as much as possible with well-understood primitive concepts, and concepts that can be analyzed in terms of those. P5. Treat conceptual analysis (insofar as possible) as a source of evidence." In addition to such intellectual commitments, A. P. Martinich and David Sosa suggest that what analytic philosophers have in common is "a stronger and more practical commitment to the spirit of naturalism, if not to naturalism or physicalism themselves" (Martinich and Sosa, *Analytic Philosophy*, 4). On this score, see "The Ultimate Constituents of Matter" in Russell, *Mysticism and Logic and Other Essays*, 125–44.

25. Whitehead and Russell, *Principia Mathematica*, 1:9.

This symbolic formula signifies the linguistic statement: proposition p is asserted; the proposition that p implies q is asserted; and proposition q is asserted. The symbolic statement also may be read as "p, therefore q."[26] In effect, the reduction of any and all statements of meaning and truth to symbolic formulas such as this one, claims to accomplish the philosophical quest for absolute certainty, indubitability, and exactitude. Analytic philosophy claims to cut to the chase of meaning and truth by reducing all words to the basic abstract building blocks of concepts and propositions expressed in symbolic code. Making recourse to Ockham's razor, what is unnecessary is cut out.[27]

Functioning in a similar way to Ockham's razor, the phenomenological reduction (*epoché*) works to bracket and set aside everything which obscures and hinders the pure givenness of the phenomenon. At the same time, the intentionality of the *epoché* is to reduce all reductionisms that infiltrate interpretation. Givenness and its possibilities are freed up to the degree that the reduction is exercised with rigor. Marion claims: "so much reduction, so much givenness."[28] This is to say that the more a particular phenomenon is reduced, its unwarranted subjective and hermeneutical accoutrements shaved off, the more the phenomenon appears as itself by itself. Similar to analytic philosophy, Marion's phenomenology of givenness works to defeat language by unleashing the overwhelming force of givenness. Just as analytic philosophy is welded to its so-called primitive principles or propositions, the phenomenology of givenness is beholden to the primitive principle of givenness.[29] Marion contends that "givenness thus determines equally, if not indifferently, the phenomenality of the self, the Other, and the truth. This is not, evidently, a matter of chance nor of a homonym."[30] For Marion, givenness alone is absolute and is the determin-

---

26. Whitehead and Russell, *Principia Mathematica*, 1:9.

27. Like many currents in continental philosophy, analytic philosophy regards metaphysics as meaningless and attempts to break away from all forms of onto-theology by setting aside the question of being and the question of God. By the definition it claims for itself, analytic philosophy is rigorously atheistic since the concept of God is positioned at best as a limit-concept for thought. While inheriting Kant's placement of the divine as a postulate of pure reason (a concept virtually inaccessible for thought), analytic philosophy unfortunately left behind Kant's preeminent notion of the categorical imperative.

28. Marion, *Reduction and Givenness*, 203.

29. See Whitehead and Russell, *Principia Mathematica*, 1:13–22.

30. Marion, *Being Given*, 331 (endnote 23). Marion's reduction to givenness is so radical that it takes little account of the hermeneutic filters which channel givenness to consciousness. For his glaring oversight of hermeneutics, Marion has been roundly critiqued. See Kearney, "Jean-Luc Marion: The Hermeneutics of Revelation" in his *Debates*

ing factor of all phenomenality. In effect, Marion reduces all phenomenality to givenness, including the other person who faces me. While adopting many of Levinas's phenomenological insights, such as the notion of counterconsciousness or counterintentionality, Marion breaks company with Levinas at the most crucial point. Levinas argues that responsibility for the other transcends all attempts to bracket it and categorize it as just another manifestation of givenness. Marion, on the other hand, writes that:

> Responsibility cannot be restricted to just one of the paradoxes—the icon, however privileged it might be—nor confined to just one horizon, be this the ethical. Responsibility belongs officially to all phenomenality that is deployed according to givenness: what is given (the call) succeeds in showing itself as a phenomenon only on the screen and according to the prism that the gifted (the responsal) alone offers it. . . . The pertinent question is not deciding if the gifted is first responsible toward the Other (Levinas) or rather in debt to itself (Heidegger), but understanding that these two modes of responsibility flow from its originary function of having to respond in the face of the phenomenon as such, that is to say, such as it gives itself. . . . Levinas collapsed difference into the relation to the Other. . . . Only givenness, unfolded in all its instances, differs/defers.[31]

---

in Continental Philosophy, 15–32; Shane Mackinlay's "Phenomenality in the Middle: Marion, Romano, and the Hermeneutics of the Event" and Richard Kearney's "Hermeneutics of the Possible God" in Leask and Cassidy, Givenness and God: Questions of Jean-Luc Marion, 167–81 and 220–42, respectively; Westphal, "Vision and Voice"; David Tracy's "Jean-Luc Marion: Phenomenology, Hermeneutics, Theology" in Hart, Counter-Experiences, 57–65; Mackinlay, Interpreting Excess; Gschwandtner, Degrees of Givenness; and Wallenfang, Dialectical Anatomy of the Eucharist.

31. Marion, Being Given, 293–94, 296. Likewise, see Marion, Being Given, 267, 268, 269, 287 (italics original): "Isn't the call Levinas recognizes in the Other just as much exhausted therein as the call Heidegger assigns to Being is confined to it? For that matter, didn't Husserl himself already describe counter-intentionalities, therefore sketches of the call apropos of neither ethical nor ontological phenomena? Wouldn't it therefore be appropriate to disconnect once and for all the figure of the call (therefore of the receiver and the gifted) from its successive uses? . . . The call institutes the gifted phenomenologically in terms of the four characteristics of its own manifestation. . . . It is no longer a case of understanding oneself in the nominative case (intending the object—Husserl), nor in the genitive (of Being—Heidegger), nor even in the accusative (accused by the Other—Levinas), but in terms of the dative: I receive my self from the call that gives me to myself before giving me anything whatsoever. . . . [The call] is nevertheless transcribed in visibility by way of the response. . . . The gifted holds the place of a horizon of visibility for the paradox that gives itself. It makes the call visible by accepting it in its own visibility; it manifests the a priori in the prism of its a posteriori. What gives itself [the call] becomes a phenomenon—shows itself—in and through what responds to it and thus puts it on stage (the gifted)."

Marion displaces the priority of the call from the face of the other to the face of givenness.[32] Whereas for Levinas the call is heard in its response, for Marion the call is seen in its visible manifestation.[33] According to Marion, responsibility for the other is not a privileged venue of phenomenality. It is just like the rest, even if saturating in character. The self is no more responsible for the other than for any manifestation of givenness whatsoever. To respond in the face of the phenomenon as such is the cardinal responsibility. Difference is transcribed not so much in the self's relation to the other (*l'autrui*) as in the self's relation to the alterity (*l'autre*) of givenness. Marion accuses Levinas of reducing difference to the relation to the other alone rather than to the allegedly more anterior difference of givenness, the other being merely one of its many manifestations. Marion goes so far as to claim that the priority of givenness is necessary for responsibility to go as far as love since love insists on "atomic particularity."[34] In other words, the reduction of the phenomenon to givenness is necessary to access its individuality and its atomic particularity. Reenter analytic philosophy.

32. See Marion, *Reduction and Givenness*, 204: "the pure form of the call"; and Marion, *Being Given*, 266–80.

33. See Marion, *Being Given*, 287. For further discussion on the difference of the place of ethics in Levinas and Marion, see Gerald McKenny's "(Re)placing Ethics: Jean-Luc Marion and the Horizon of Modern Morality" in Hart, *Counter-Experiences*, 339–55.

34. Marion, *Prolegomena to Charity*, 95 (italics original): "The injunction itself now remains to be determined, so that it will not settle into any figure of the Neuter. If we want to secure responsibility all the way to the point of love, then the injunction must designate not only the other as such, but *just such* an other as the invisible gaze that crosses my own. That *just such* an other enjoins me implies that he sets himself up as unsubstitutable and strictly irreplaceable. . . . Love passes beyond responsibility only if the injunction reaches atomic particularity: love requires nothing less than *haecceitas*, which is also situated beyond essence (unless we must say on the hither side of essence)"; and Marion, *Idol and Distance*, 199: "No third, neuter (Levinas), and colorless pole could offer itself to express distance equitably." Perhaps analytic philosopher G. E. Moore likewise would accuse Levinas of what he calls the naturalistic fallacy in how Levinas converts the simple idea of the good into responsibility for the other. See Moore, *Principia Ethica*, 9–17; and Burggraeve, "Violence and the Vulnerable Face of the Other," 34: "This responsibility, which establishes the nonkilling of the other and which begins as from the summons of the face—and, finally, which is therefore radically heteronomous—Levinas characterizes time and again throughout his writings as 'goodness.'" See what would amount to a Levinasian response to the above charge of Marion in Levinas, *Otherwise than Being or Beyond Essence*, 194 (italics original): "The singularity of the subject is not the uniqueness of an *hapax*. For it is not due to some distinctive quality, like fingerprints, that would make of it an incomparable *unicum*, and, as a principle of individuation, make this unity deserve a proper noun, and hence a place in discourse. The identity of the oneself is not the inertia of a quiddity individuated by an ultimate specific difference inherent in the body or in character, or by the uniqueness of a natural or historical conjecture. It is in the uniqueness of someone summoned."

In 1918, Bertrand Russell delivered a course of eight lectures in Gordon Square, London, under the heading, "The Philosophy of Logical Atomism."[35] These lectures articulate Russell's theory which holds that all reality is made up of atoms, i.e., those individual elements that result from logical analysis. In contrast to the monistic logic of Hegel, Russell argues that there is no single indivisible reality that encompasses the whole of atomic multiplicity. He writes that "the process of philosophizing, to my mind, consists mainly in passing from those obvious, vague, ambiguous things, that we feel quite sure of, to something precise, clear, definite, which by reflection and analysis we find is involved in the vague thing that we start from, and is, so to speak, the real truth of which that vague thing is a sort of shadow."[36] Reminiscent of the allegorical cave of Plato's *Republic*, Russell's philosophy of logical atomism seems to occur in the same genus as Marion's phenomenology of givenness. Methodological intent is the same for both: reduction to the irreducible. For Marion, givenness is the irreducible fruit of the phenomenological reduction. Yet how does Levinas respond to the reductionism apparent in analytic philosophy and in Marion's phenomenology of givenness?

Such sparring partners were not far from the mind of Levinas, even if he did not engage them as directly and explicitly as one would like. In considering the reduction of language to a system of signs, Levinas writes that the proximity of the other is "a sign given from one to the other before the constitution of any system of signs, any common place formed by culture and sites, a sign given from null site to null site. The fact that a sign, exterior to the system of evidences, comes into proximity while remaining transcendent, is the very essence of language prior to every particular language."[37] The dimension which analytic philosophy lacks is verticality. There is no transcendent height or elevation within analytic philosophy, only horizontal

35. Russell, *Logic and Knowledge*, 177–281.

36. Russell, *Logic and Knowledge*, 179–80.

37. Levinas, *Collected Philosophical Papers*, 121–22, and further on 121: "Is to not place oneself in the universe of common language, in culture, still a saying? . . . This saying no doubt precedes the language that communicates propositions and messages: it is a sign given from one to another by proximity about proximity. This sign is not already a discourse that would be still stammering." See also Levinas, *Totality and Infinity*, 92, 96 (italics original): "The world is offered in the language of the Other; it is borne by propositions . . . the interlocutor cannot be deduced, for the relationship between him and me is presupposed by every proof. . . . [Objectivity] is *posited* in a discourse, in a *con-versation* [*entre-tien*] which *proposes* the world. This *proposition* is held between [se tient entre] two points which do not constitute a system, a cosmos, a totality"; and Levinas, *Of God Who Comes to Mind*, 165: "The Same destined irrevocably to the Other: this is an ethical thought, a sociality that is proximity or fraternity, and not synthesis."

anthropology at best. Analytic formulas only run left to right, only run side-
ways. If they do move vertically on occasion, it is only in the direction of
descent. For all that logical deduction can assume at its outset, it cannot assume everything. If it attempts to do so, it amounts to assuming nothing
of real and lasting value. Nihilism commences with its ambition of omniscience. Yes, at every point in time we know some things, but we never know
all. The other, instead, is proclaimed as perpetuity of mystery and witness
to the infinite. Levinas insists that "from the outset, we think more than we
can think. . . . The things that we have without our horizon always overflow
their content."[38] Whereas analytic philosophy is a reduction of meaningful
sentences, assertions, propositions, arguments, metaphors (and the inherent
diversity of discourse) to trite symbols which inevitably reduce the excess of
meaning contained in the play of language, Levinas demands "the elevation
of meaning by the metaphor."[39] Rather than capitulate to the violent banality
of minimalism on display in analytic philosophy and in a phenomenology of
givenness, Levinas's phenomenology of proclamation maintains the indis-
solubility of ethics and the proximity of the other: "Ethics is not a simple region of being. The encounter with the other offers us the first meaning, and in
the extension of this encounter, we discover all the others. Ethics is a decisive
experience."[40] Ethics precedes givenness inasmuch as the face of the other is
irreducible to some other subcategory of the same, even that of givenness.
Any category which claims to include the face of the other within its domain
fails to recognize and comprehend the deflecting non-phenomenon of call
and unsubstitutable ethical responsibility which encompasses phenomenality as such. Levinas chastises all attempts at manipulating the alterity of the
face of the other in saying that "nothing, in effect, is absolutely other in the
being served by knowledge wherein variety turns into monotony. . . . Everything is absorbed, sucked down and walled up in the Same . . . *the fiasco of the
rationality of the Same*."[41] Are not analytic philosophy and the phenomenology of givenness guilty of reducing the whole of reality to the same? For the
former, a reduction to logical atoms of meaning; for the latter, a reduction to

38. Robbins, *Is It Righteous To Be?*, 159. Also, see Robbins, *Is It Righteous To Be?*,
199: "The study of the Torah is this infinity that is never finished, where the light gained
illumines above all the insufficiencies of the light acquired."

39. Levinas, *Of God Who Comes to Mind*, 106.

40. Robbins, *Is It Righteous To Be?*, 160. See Robbins, *Is It Righteous To Be?*, 131: "To
recognize the unsurpassable quality of the ethical is, rather, the fundamental lesson and
the first truth. It seems to me extremely important in this connection that the relation
of myself to the other not involve a collapsing together of the two, but that the two-ness,
the non-unity, is actual in the ethical. Proximity is a value in and for itself."

41. Levinas, *Of God Who Comes to Mind*, 12, 49.

givenness in all its avatars of manifestation. To the contrary, Levinas reminds us that sometimes less is not necessarily more.

III. Toward a Dialectical Phenomenology of Contemplative Ethics

If less is not always more, must we not turn the question to Levinas's phenomenology of proclamation and his priority of responsibility for the other? Can the whole of phenomenology be reduced to a phenomenology of proclamation? Is the solution, after all, to eradicate a phenomenology of givenness in favor of a phenomenology of proclamation? This would seem to contradict the alterity which Levinas champions all along. Instead, what about the possibility of a dialectical phenomenology of givenness and proclamation? Is this possible? We are of the affirmative opinion.

The phenomenological reduction poses as a double-edged sword. On one side it has a tendency to function as an effective razor of Ockham. And at times this can be helpful and necessary to get to the things themselves. However, its other side can pare away so much of a phenomenon that virtually nothing is left to consider. Even in the case of Levinas's face of the other as non-phenomenon there prowls the temptation to neutrality, indecision, banality, and even nihilism. In the final analysis, appearance and manifestation, too, are important and vital components of phenomenality. The face speaks and appears. If reduced to its speech alone or appearance alone, the face goes unheeded or disappears from view. One of the glaring weaknesses of Levinas's ethics as first philosophy is the lack of detail about specific ethical questions. Sure, all can agree that it is good to feed the hungry and so forth in general terms. But what about issues such as euthanasia, capital punishment, abortion, embryonic stem cell research, marriage, immigration, just warfare, global warming, human trafficking, commercial surrogacy, etc. At a certain point a verdict must be submitted regarding concrete ethical situations. If Levinas indeed capitalizes on the power of phenomenology to determine the intersubjective ethical locus of phenomenality, why does he not go one step further and apply the general commitment to responsibility for the other to its specific regional contours? The reason is that a phenomenology of proclamation can go only so far in its determinations. It is determined to act but it lacks the vision to know how to act. In other words, it knows it must act—this is certain—but it is deprived of contemplation because it has cursed its enterprise from the start in fear that it would lead to the idolatry of more of the same. A legitimate fear indeed, but must contemplation always proceed to idolatry? Is there not still a meaningful place of the sacred that is at once the other and other than the other who faces me? While the naked and destitute face of the other commands me to be responsible for him, does it always tell me how to go about this? Does the other not lack the clarity of vision to know the right course of action in each and every ethical predicament? My contention is that a phenomenology of proclamation is deficient on its own, and so is a phenomenology of givenness and manifestation on its own. I propose a dialectical phenomenology opening onto a dialectical theology which harnesses the genius of both manifestation and proclamation, of both contemplation and ethics, of both Marion and Levinas, of both Catholic Christianity and Judaism, of both sacrament and word.

Even though the term "dialectic" often implies conflict, tension, and contradiction in its common usage, I suggest that it bears the fertile possibility of paradox.[42] In the case of dialectical phenomenology, a fertile paradox is met between manifestation and proclamation. Dialectical phenomenology becomes theological when it deals with questions of divinity and everything meant by the term "God." Conflict does not necessarily lead to violence and destruction. Tension is not always bad. In fact, tension often implies the positive polarity and complementarity of genuine difference that prevents the premature and impatient reductionism to destructive violence. Contradiction sometimes appears as the face of paradox. Paradox does not imply outright contradiction even though it includes the phenomenon of contradiction within its term. In a similar way, metaphor and symbol function to hold together two distinct worlds of meaning in order to give rise to a thought which thinks more than it is able to think.[43] This is the meaning of both Levinas's non-phenomenon of responsibility and Marion's saturated phenomenon, whether in the figure of the idol, the icon, the event, or the flesh. Dialectical phenomenology urges the tensive rapprochement between the disparate schools of manifestation and proclamation.

This proposal does not imply that every ethical dilemma furnishes a cut-and-dry solution. However, it does intimate the fact that whenever there is ambiguity in the ethical domain—whenever there is the experience of the grey haziness of uncertainty as to what to do in the situation—there is, at the same time, the black-and-white clarity of truth and goodness

42. See Wallenfang, *Dialectical Anatomy of the Eucharist*, xxv–xxix, 42–48; and Wallenfang, "Paradox" in *Phenomenology*, 73–100.

43. See Ricoeur, *Rule of Metaphor*, 315, 358: "My own thesis regarding the plurality of spheres of discourse and the fecundity of the intersection of their semantic aims. . . . Metaphor is living by virtue of the fact that it introduces the spark of imagination into a 'thinking more' at the conceptual level. This struggle to 'think more,' guided by the 'vivifying principle,' is the 'soul' of interpretation."

that guide us along the right, just, responsible, and loving course of action in every situation. Dialectical method implies dialogical discourse, but it does not insinuate ambiguity and only ambiguity. This, too, would be a reductionism to the same: the banality of ambiguity. Levinas speaks of "the dialectic of rabbinic thinking . . . to make an always restless dialectic rebound sovereignly . . . a certain intellectual discipline which takes precedence over immediacy."[44] Rabbinic thinking is showcased in the dialogical reverberation of the Talmud.[45] It is a disciplined way of thinking which does not regard truth to be a shifting target subject to the arbitrary whims of interpretive manipulation. However, it does recognize the dialectical nature of truth which comes to mind precisely through the course of candid conversation. It is where "truth is consequently experienced as a dialogue . . . [which] does not reach a conclusion, but constitutes the very life of truth."[46] It is the divinely human site where "to respect the Other is, before all else, to refer to the Other's opinions."[47] Truth is played out through the course of conversation, not only to hide itself therein but to disclose itself therefrom. Making a truth claim is the risk to be run for judgment and decision. But Talmudic wisdom reminds us that clear judgment derives from critical and open conversation—a conflict of interpretations.

Levinas's intuition of Talmudic wisdom is corroborated by the following self-description of Paul Ricoeur: "My inclination is to see the universe of discourse as a universe kept in motion by an interplay of attractions and repulsions that ceaselessly promote the interaction and intersection of domains whose organizing nuclei are off-centered in relation to one another; and still this interplay never comes to rest in an absolute knowledge that

44. Robbins, *Is It Righteous To Be?*, 24, 75, 93.

45. See Levinas, *Difficult Freedom*, 65: "The Talmud is content to emphasize the ambiguity of the problem . . . an eternal dialogue taking place within human consciousness." For an application of Levinas's ethical anthropology to the task of interreligious dialogue, see Burggraeve, "Dialogue of Transcendence."

46. Levinas, *Difficult Freedom*, 163. Likewise, see Levinas, *Difficult Freedom*, 52: "We can tolerate the pluralism of great civilizations and even understand why they cannot merge. The very nature of truth explains how this is impossible: truth manifests itself in a way that appeals to an enormous number of human possibilities and, through them, a whole range of histories, traditions and approaches"; and Levinas, *Discovering Existence with Husserl*, 30–31: "It is the essence of objective truth to be truth for everyone; this intersubjective world is thus ideally presupposed in the very essence of truth. . . . But all the investigations of egological phenomenology must be subordinated to the 'intersubjective phenomenology' which alone will be able to exhaust the meaning of truth and reality. . . . All the 'constitutional' problems must be formulated for the absolute sphere of intersubjective consciousness which precedes all worlds and all nature, and in which all worlds and all nature are constituted."

47. Levinas, *Difficult Freedom*, 239.

would subsume the tensions."[48] Ricoeur identifies the intrinsic polarity
within the cosmos—whether of discourse, atoms, or interpersonal relationships—that serves as the very condition for the possibility of motion. Polarity involves attraction and repulsion because not everything is identical, yet
everything holds together as a unified whole. Individual existents, though
centered as individuals in themselves, orbit according to the alternative individual centers of gravity that surround them. This interplay of individuals
and forces never comes to rest as long as polarity subsists. Absolute knowledge remains illusory as long as there is more than one. Tension, therefore,
is not to be subsumed by force against force but promoted to the measure
that it is good, true, and fruitful.

Taking its warrant from Talmudic wisdom and cosmological polarity,
dialectical phenomenology is poised to approach adequately a specific ethical issue and submit a verdict. Granted that volumes have been written and
left to be written on each and every ethical issue under (and beyond) the
sun, the following is an abbreviated exercise in dialectical phenomenology
as applied to the issue of abortion. First, dialectical phenomenology does
not fear offending anyone because its concern is not to keep everyone su-
perficially happy. Its concern is to call a thing what it is even with all the risk
its methodological procedure entails. Second, dialectical phenomenology
liberates the issue from its ideological strongholds by categorizing the issue
as neither liberal nor conservative. The phenomenon under investigation is
politically neutral as such and must be interpreted apart from the natural
attitude in which it is typically ensconced.[49] Third, dialectical phenomenology—in good dialectical fashion—borrows a crucial insight from analytic
philosophy, namely, Wittgenstein's notion of language-games.[50] Dialectical
phenomenology attends to hermeneutical phenomena at every turn and realizes that language and reality-as-it-is-perceived go hand in hand. Fourth,
dialectical phenomenology always will begin and end with responsibility
for the other as articulated by Levinas. This is the sine qua non milieu of
all phenomenality and is philosophy come of age. It articulates the truth of
being human more accurately and decisively than any other philosophical
assertion recorded throughout human history. Nothing trumps responsibility for the other, not even all the tropes of love. For if love attests to the

48. Ricoeur, *Rule of Metaphor*, 357.

49. For more on the term "natural attitude" according to Husserl's original meaning, see Levinas, *Discovering Existence with Husserl*, 11–12.

50. See, for example, Wittgenstein, *Philosophical Investigations*, 236: "Am I less
certain that this man is in pain than that $2 \times 2 = 4$?—Is the first case therefore one of
mathematical certainty?—'Mathematical certainty' is not a psychological concept. The
kind of certainty is the kind of language-game."

infinite, it is responsible love. This is the only kind of love worthy of respect. Therefore the universal human vocation of responsibility for the other is absolute and irreducible. Conscience disrupted by the plight of the other without ceasing makes all the difference in approaching any ethical issue. For dialectical phenomenology, bad conscience is normative and regulative.[51] Finally, dialectical phenomenology resolves to contemplate before prescribing action. The first ethical act is to contemplate for the sake of the other, both in and through the course of conversation and in solitude with the divine, which is still conversation—a communion of persons—but often one in which no words are spoken and heard.

Bearing these non-negotiable characteristics of dialectical phenomenology in mind, we return to the specific issue of abortion.[52] Step one: unmask language-games surrounding the issue. Every ethical question is enmeshed in a density of language-games. Contemplation is necessary before appropriate ethical action can be determined. And so we commence a dialectical phenomenology of contemplative ethics. Given the issue of abortion, it is necessary to articulate what and who is at stake. What is being aborted? Pregnancy, cells, embryo, fetus, the abortion—in a word, it? Or is that which is being aborted properly called human life, human being, human person, infant, child, the other—in a word, him or her—illeity! Does this other issue a call to the mother, to the father, to anyone who would listen? Do not kill me! Does this other have a face? Does this other have a name? What gives? How does the phenomenon give itself? How does the phenomenon relate to the context of ethical exigency which goes before and behind every passing phenomenon? What is the ontological constitution of the other in light of the relational matrix of persons asking such questions about the person-status of the phenomenon? Because we ask the question, does that mean the answer precedes its asking? If so, what is the answer? Who do you say that I am?[53]

---

51. See the positive meaning of "bad conscience" in Levinas, *Entre Nous*, 123–32, and Levinas, *Of God Who Comes to Mind*, 172–77.

52. For an insightful reflection on the phenomenology of pregnancy and the issue of responsibility in pregnancy, see Hanoch Ben Pazi's essay, "Teaching as an Internalization of Feminine Aspects," in Hansel, *Levinas in Jerusalem*, 171–200. Similarly, see Claire Katz's illuminating discussion of Levinasian hospitality of the feminine in Katz, *Levinas, Judaism, and the Feminine*, 55–65; and, for a Levinasian-influenced ethical anthropology, see Wallenfang, *Dialectical Anatomy of the Eucharist*, 183–214; Wallenfang, *Human and Divine Being*, 1–20, 174–95; and Wallenfang, *Phenomenology*, 73–127.

53. See Gen 4:9–10; 22:1–18; 34:1–4; Exod 20:13; 21:22–25; Pss 127; 128; 139; Jer 1:5; Matt 16:15; Mark 8:29; Luke 9:20.

——————— CHAPTER 4 ———————

LAW AND FREEDOM

I. Introduction[1]

THERE IS A PERENNIAL ambiguity within the relationship between law and human freedom. Does law inherently promote freedom or restrict it? Emmanuel Levinas proposes that law—precisely Torah—is the gateway of freedom to the degree that law attests to the obligatory summons to responsibility for the other. In his 1964 Talmudic lecture entitled, "The Temptation of Temptation," Levinas presents the paradoxical beginning of freedom in "a non-freedom which, far from being slavery or childhood, is a beyond-freedom . . . overcoming the temptation of evil by avoiding the temptation of temptation."[2] In other words, law demands a restraint of freedom understood as arbitrary license in order to open onto a collective and coexistent freedom of responsibility. Levinas's thesis bears significantly on crucial ethical dilemmas of today, for example, ecological degradation, severe poverty, and eugenic movements on a global scale. In demonstrating the direct correlation between freedom and responsibility, Levinas supplies the philosophical framework needed to undergird the practical remedies for our most dire social and ecological ills.

However, Levinas's turn to Torah is not enough. His ethical phenomenology of proclamation must be paired with a contemplative phenomenology of manifestation so not to engender action without considering what exactly gives itself to act upon. Enter, once again, Jean-Luc Marion. While Levinas's attention to the call of the other opens the ears to ethical exigency, Marion's attention to givenness opens the eyes to contemplative recognition of phenomena as they give themselves by themselves. An adequate

1. I would like to thank two anonymous readers for helping to enhance this essay beyond its original form. All remaining shortcomings are, of course, my own.

2. See "Temptation of Temptation" in Levinas, *Nine Talmudic Readings*, 40–41.

assessment of the relationship between law and freedom requires a holistic phenomenology rooted in the polarity between ethics and givenness. Moreover, a comprehensive understanding of law and freedom exacts a return to metaphysics in dialectical proximity to phenomenology. The paradoxical relationship between law and freedom can be comprehended clearly only through a combined methodology which harnesses the fruitful tension between metaphysics and phenomenology.

In this chapter, I will trace this threefold series of dialectical relationships in method in order to account for the paradoxical relationship between law and freedom. First, I will provide a brief account of the "beyond-freedom through law" of which Levinas speaks in "The Temptation of Temptation." The phenomenality of the Internet will be employed as a kind of case study for Levinas's claims as evinced in the twenty-first-century world. Second, I will outline Marion's conception of freedom informed by an Augustinian theology of grace. And third, I will advance the need to partner the contributions of Levinas and Marion in order to render a coherent understanding of the perplexing relationship between law and freedom. Altogether, a move toward a new dialectical theology will be made that metes out justice to God, to humanity, and to the entire cosmos.

II. Tempted by Temptation

In order to approach Levinas's understanding of law and freedom with clarity, it is necessary to begin with his critique of what he calls "the temptation of temptation" as introduced in his 1964 Talmudic lecture.[3] In her 2002 book, *Emmanuel Levinas: The Problem of Ethical Metaphysics*, Edith Wyschogrod articulates well what Levinas means by "the temptation of temptation" and its relevance for people today:

> According to Levinas, the difficulty of Western man is rooted in his need to experience everything that can be experienced, to taste all the possibilities that life affords. This is the temptation of temptations. The paradigms of Western man are Ulysses, whose life is filled with novel and perilous adventure, and Don Juan, for whom a multiplicity of seductions provides a heightened sense of existence. It is of great moment to engage one's passions

3. For an analysis of Levinas's translation of the Jewish Hebrew idiom into the tradition of French (Greek) philosophy, especially within this Talmudic lecture, see Herzog, "Levinas and Derrida on Translation and Conversion." Similarly, for an assessment of Levinas's appropriation of Talmudic discourse into mainstream Western thought, especially in "The Temptation of Temptation," see Kavka, "Is There a Warrant for Levinas's Talmudic Readings?"

in life and to live dangerously. Innocence seems infantile and
merely provisional, awaiting transformation by life itself.[4]

"Leave no stone unturned"—this is the essence of twenty-first-century
wisdom, especially within a materialist paradigm that interprets the whole
of reality as matter in motion, and nothing more. Wyschogrod's summary
of Levinas's original concept called "the temptation of temptation" is made
with precision. The heightened sense of existence is the prize won for ceding
all constraints of law, conscience, religion, authority (other than the self),
and any predetermined conception of the Good whatsoever. Life is lived
to the fullest inasmuch as it is filled with new and unpredictable experiences, endless prospects of enjoyment, and sensational excursions ever on
the brink of peril and misfortune. Ulysses and Don Juan are paragons of the
good life because of their promiscuous pursuit of the varied flavors of life.
Innocence and childlike naïveté are to be awakened and vacated for the sake
of becoming a seasoned adult who assumes the privilege of connoisseur in
relation to the plethora of stimulating experiences life has to offer. There is an
acronym in circulation among young people today, "YOLO," which stands
for, "You Only Live Once." Many young people (at least subconsciously)
swear allegiance to this life philosophy before any other tradition of faith or
standard of rationality. In other words, Epicureanism and Hedonism have
resurfaced today, even if in effigy, supplanting traditional religions as an
absolute source of personal values and moral decision-making. However,
instead of pleasure itself as the guiding goal of action, experience for its own
sake reigns supreme, whether resulting in pleasure or pain for the actor. It
is more desirable for experience to be untethered to any guiding principle
in order to preserve its purity and anarchical formless form. Rationality as
such is dropped for the Dionysian predilection for experience absent justification: "just for the hell of it." If there be any justification at all, actions

4. Wyschogrod, *Emmanuel Levinas*, 208. Commenting on the work of Luiz Cláudio
Figueiredo, a Brazilian scholar of the epistemology of psychology, Emanuel Meireles
Vieira writes that "ideas of freedom and of the individual are essential to reason for
it to legitimize itself as a suitable form of knowing the world . . . [resulting in] the
self-centered individual postulated by Modernity" in Vieira, "Ethics and the Person-
centered Approach," 799. Similarly, commenting on the work of Immanuel Kant, Richard Cohen writes that "the moral agent is free, and hence subject to moral judgment
(unlike objects which are caused) only insofar, Kant argues, that the agent is rationally
self-legislating" in Cohen, "Judaism and Philosophy," 71. Both of these references un-
derscore the deep influence of the Western Enlightenment, including the Scientific
Revolution, of the seventeenth and eighteenth centuries on modern-day notions of human freedom as uninhibited self-determination. For a Levinasian-inspired alternative
to autonomous self-determining freedom, termed "heteronomous freedom," see Zhao,
"Freedom Reconsidered."

are justified merely in the name of pillaging virgin experience. Many would rather regret what they have done rather than regret what they have not done. Enter the temptation of temptation.

For Levinas, the temptation of temptation refers precisely to the temptation of knowledge in which "what tempts the one tempted by temptation is not pleasure but the ambiguity of a situation in which pleasure is still possible but in respect to which the Ego keeps its liberty, has not yet given up its security, has kept its distance. . . . What is tempting is to be simultaneously outside everything and participating in everything."[5] In other words, the temptation of temptation occurs in the dark interstices of ambiguity between the object of temptation and the tempted, between marginal culpability and accusation, between anonymity and personal identity. In the experience of being tempted by temptation, the ego is disengaged just enough to render itself incognito before the light of conscience.[6] Being tempted by temptation escorts the ego to the threshold of the threshold of sin, all the while suspending an explicitly sinful act, though advancing as far as possible before the buffer of actual temptation. Living in the temptation of temptation is to enjoy the anonymous autonomy before all that is possible, all that is knowable, and all that is pleasurable. The temptation of temptation exalts free will as divine since the very notion of free will indicates self-determination rather than being determined from without. The temptation of temptation brackets and sets aside all that would impinge upon the sovereignty of the will. This becomes the essence of freedom: unrestraint. Anything that would impinge upon the will is regarded as a hindrance to absolute freedom. To help us clarify the distinction between the temptation of temptation and a Levinasian freedom beyond freedom, let us turn our attention to the Dutch Dominican moral theologian, Servais Pinckaers.

Strikingly similar to Levinas's idea of the temptation of temptation is Servais Pinckaers's concept of the freedom of indifference. In his groundbreaking 1985 work in moral theology, *The Sources of Christian Ethics*, Pinckaers contrasts the two primary ways of understanding human freedom today: (1) freedom of indifference and (2) freedom for excellence.[7] Stemming from the arguments of fourteenth-century English Franciscan theologian William of Ockham, and his critique of the moral teleology of Thomas Aquinas, freedom of indifference intuits the essence of freedom

5. Levinas, *Nine Talmudic Readings*, 33–34.

6. See Fleming, "Primordial Moral Awareness," for a brief systematic analysis of conscience in light of the Catholic tradition of moral theology and the place of conscience in the work of Levinas.

7. See Pinckaers, *Sources of Christian Ethics*, 327–78, and Pinckaers, *Morality*, 65–81.

as the operation of free will in its autonomous and uninhibited choice between contraries. This nominalist approach views ultimate freedom as the will unrestrained by anything greater than itself, whether divine will, right reason, natural law, predetermined ends of action, or any particular impression of beatitude. This type of freedom is linked to the genitive "of indifference" to refer to its indifferent attitude toward what the will chooses. One is most free the more one exercises an attitude of indifference in relation to competing objects parading before the will. In a freedom of indifference, each free act is independent of all others and law is external to freedom, which would otherwise limit it by some sense of obligation to obey the law. Each individual act is measured neither in relation to past acts nor to future acts. Law neither proceeds from nor promotes this freedom of indifference but curtails the naturally unalloyed power of free will. In a freedom of indifference everything is fair game for the will, just as in the temptation of temptation all temptations are neutralized by the distance between the self and each instance of actual temptation. In both the freedom of indifference and in the temptation of temptation, free will is identical to freedom; free will is absolute.

Tracking with Pinckaers's description of the freedom of indifference helps us to comprehend Levinas's articulation of the temptation of temptation. Likewise, by following Pinckaers's outline of the freedom for excellence we will be able to follow Levinas's solution to overcome the temptation of temptation more exactly. The freedom for excellence is traceable back to the scholastic theology of Thomas Aquinas wherein freedom is always defined in relation to the Good.[8] To draw closer in proximity to the Good through personal acts expands not only personal freedom but the freedom of all and enhances the common good. The freedom for excellence is constantly ordered to the Good and the universal summons to communal beatitude. It proceeds from reason and the will, but free will is not absolute. Free will must submit perpetually to the teleology of the mature virtuous life and the principal end of happiness oriented toward the Good. Within a freedom for excellence all of one's actions are united in an ordered

8. While I am suggesting a significant similarity between Thomistic virtue ethics and Levinasian phenomenological ethics, it is important to note that they are not univocal. For example, in comparison see Levinas, *Of God Who Comes to Mind*, 69: "The goodness of the Good—of the Good that neither sleeps nor slumbers—inclines the movement it calls forth to turn it away from the Good and orient it toward the other, and only thus toward the Good." The basis of Levinas's phenomenological ethics is not an abstract notion of the Good but a concrete proximity of the other. The Good is proclaimed in the goodness of the other. The Good is good inasmuch as the other is good. Special thanks to Georges Hansel, Levinas's son-in-law, for illuminating for me this important distinction for me.

whole and law plays a pedagogical role in shaping the will to choose freely and habitually what is good. Freedom grows to the degree that the Good is pursued and evil is avoided. The perfection of freedom mirrors the perfection of the Good. In biblical language, one must enter into a covenant relationship with the Good to be truly free. However, it is important to note that, whereas for Thomas, the Good is something distinct from the personal other, for Levinas, the Good is identical to the glorious face of the other, signified by her incessant call for me to become responsible for her. Goodness is active responsibility itself, as desperate call and affirmative response. The Good, the divine, comes to mind within the context of the interpersonal ethical relationship and nowhere else.[9]

Levinas's strategy for surmounting the temptation of temptation is quite similar to Pinckaers's portrayal of the freedom for excellence over and against the freedom of indifference. Levinas argues that "Westerners, opposed to a limited and overly well defined existence, want to taste everything themselves, want to travel the universe. But there is no universe without the circles of Hell!"[10] Levinas insists on the sober reality that not everything is good and therefore we should conduct our search for knowledge with careful discretion. Who desires to roam about the circles of Hell? Yet it is the temptation of temptation which wants to keep the circles of Hell within its ambiguous range of possibilities. Levinas says that "the temptation of temptation is philosophy, in contrast to a wisdom which knows everything without experiencing it."[11] The philosopher feeds on the ongoing temptation of temptation, arrested in the pretense to omniscience without admitting limit or restriction. The covenantal sage, in contrast, is the one who binds himself or herself to divine wisdom through filial trust.[12] Unlike the primordial human couple who ate from the symbolic tree of the knowledge of good and evil, the wise one is the person who trusts YHWH's command and renounces the possibility of transgressing this life-giving

9. See Levinas, *Of God Who Comes to Mind*, for example, 69: "We have designated this manner for the Infinite, or for God, to refer, from the heart of its very desirability, to the undesirable proximity of the others, by the term 'illeity'; this is an extra-ordinary turning around of the desirability of the Desirable, of the supreme desirability calling to itself the rectilinear rectitude of Desire. . . . [God] is Good in this very precise, eminent sense: He does not fill me with goods, but compels me to goodness, which is better than to receive goods."

10. Levinas, *Nine Talmudic Readings*, 33.

11. Levinas, *Nine Talmudic Readings*, 34.

12. See Levinas, *Nine Talmudic Readings*, 49: "We think, like our text, that consciousness and seeking, taken as their own preconditions, are, like naïveté, the temptation of temptation, a tortuous path leading to ruin. The *bogdim* are the unfaithful, breaking a fundamental covenant. To them are opposed the *yesharim*, the upright."

command.[13] The truly wise one knows what is good and evil by trusting in divine testimony rather than demanding to determine this knowledge on his or her own apart from God. Levinas writes that "overcoming the temptation of temptation would then mean going within oneself further than one's self."[14] Toward whom does one go further than oneself if not the other?[15] To overcome the temptation of temptation requires going further than complacent and solipsistic self-sufficiency by committing oneself at all times to responsibility for the other.

Levinas defines the freedom which transcends the self in its movement toward the other as "a freedom of responsibilities."[16] Freedom is revealed as a paradox, for it is not realized by shedding responsibility for the other but by embracing it. Levinas develops his freedom of responsibilities by reflecting on the Talmudic excerpt of the Tractate *Shabbath*. Within this text, Israel is depicted as the people who commit themselves to doing before hearing in the context of the giving of the Law on Mount Sinai.[17] Before

13. See John Paul II, *Veritatis splendor*, 35 (italics original), in speaking of the divine prohibition to eat from the tree of the knowledge of good and evil: "With this imagery, Revelation teaches that *the power to decide what is good and what is evil does not belong to man, but to God alone.* The man is certainly free, inasmuch as he can understand and accept God's commands. And he possesses an extremely far-reaching freedom, since he can eat 'of every tree of the garden'. But his freedom is not unlimited: it must halt before the 'tree of the knowledge of good and evil', for it is called to accept the moral law given by God. In fact, human freedom finds its authentic and complete fulfillment precisely in the acceptance of that law. God, who alone is good, knows perfectly what is good for man, and by virtue of his very love proposes this good to man in the commandments."

14. Levinas, *Nine Talmudic Readings*, 34.

15. See Levinas, *Nine Talmudic Readings*, 48: "An innocence without naïveté, an uprightness without stupidity, an absolute uprightness which is also absolute self-criticism, read in the eyes of the one who is the goal of my uprightness and whose look calls me into question. It is a movement toward the other which does not come back to its point of origin the way diversion comes back, incapable as it is of transcendence—a movement beyond anxiety and stronger than death." Cf. Pascal Bruckner's idea of innocence (used in a different yet similar sense in comparison with Levinas's use of the term) as "the disease of individualism" in Bruckner, *Temptation of Innocence*, for example, 8–9 (italics original): "I call *innocence* the disease of individualism; it consists in trying to escape the consequences of our own acts, attempting to enjoy the advantages of liberty without suffering any of the disadvantages."

16. Levinas, *Nine Talmudic Readings*, 37.

17. See Levinas, *Nine Talmudic Readings*, 42–43 (italics original): "One accepts the Torah before one knows it. . . . It is a perfectly adult effort . . . acting before understanding. . . . The excellent choice that makes doing go before hearing does not prevent a fall. It arms not against temptation but against the temptation of temptation. . . . This undoubtedly indicates that the doing which is at stake here is not simply *praxis* as opposed to theory but a way of *actualizing without beginning with the possible*, of knowing without examining, of placing oneself beyond violence without this being the privilege of a

hearing the words of the Torah, the Israelites bind themselves to it by virtue of its divine origin. Their unwavering trust in divine Goodness is the beginning of the Law's fulfillment in their daily lives. Because they completely trust the Lawgiver, they obey the divine command even before hearing it. In other words, they do not insist first on hearing the prescriptions and then considering for themselves whether or not they are amenable to them. That, after all, was the essence of the original sin. Instead of pretending to pass judgment on the divine Judge, the Israelites willfully submit to divine legislation before its articulation. This amounts to an inversion of the original sin and a refusal of the temptation of temptation. Disobedience begins with the temptation of temptation. It begins with the audacity of the finite to pass judgment on the Infinite. It begins with the demand to measure and scrutinize the law of God according to arbitrary standards of human calibration. Disobedience stems from a pretentious subjectivity that considers itself as ultimate authority. Obedience to Torah, in contrast, expresses "the structure of a subjectivity clinging to the absolute."[18] Obedience recognizes the anteriority of Torah before logic, the anteriority of freedom before free will, the anteriority of God before humanity.[19]

Levinas speaks of this obedience to Torah as uprightness that, as "an original fidelity to an indissoluble alliance, a belonging with, consists in

---

free choice. A pact with good would exist, preceding the alternative of good and evil." This passage marks the striking metaphysical character of Levinas's thought within his overarching method of phenomenology.

18. Levinas, *Nine Talmudic Readings*, 48. Cf. Levinas, *Nine Talmudic Readings*, 38: "That the mind needs training suggests the very mystery of violence's anteriority to freedom, suggests the possibility of an adherence prior to free examination and prior to temptation." For further elucidation on the philosophical notion of "the absolute," see Paul Ricoeur's essay, "The Hermeneutics of Testimony," in Ricoeur, *Essays on Biblical Interpretation*, 119–54.

19. See Levinas, *Nine Talmudic Readings*, 37, 40: "The teaching, which the Torah is, cannot come to the human being as a result of a choice. That which must be received in order to make freedom of choice possible cannot have been chosen, unless after the fact. . . . Wouldn't Revelation be precisely a reminder of this consent prior to freedom and non-freedom? . . . To receive the gift of Torah—a Law—is to fulfil it before consciously accepting it. . . . Without being less pure than the freedom that would arise from freedom (in the non-engagement of the one who is tempted and who tries his luck), the freedom taught by the Jewish text starts in a non-freedom which, far from being slavery or childhood, is a beyond-freedom." Cf. Emmanuel Levinas, *Otherwise than Being or Beyond Essence*, 10: "The freedom of another could never begin in my freedom, that is, abide in the same present, be contemporary, be representable to me. The responsibility for the other can not have begun in my commitment, in my decision. The unlimited responsibility in which I find myself comes from the hither side of my freedom, from a 'prior to every memory,' an 'ulterior to every accomplishment,' from the non-present par excellence, the non-original, the anarchical, prior to or beyond essence."

confirming this alliance and not in engaging oneself headfirst for the sake of engaging oneself."[20] The alliance is between Torah and the human subject. A covenant relationship obtains between God and humanity through the mediation and signification of Torah and its ethical imperatives. Fidelity to Torah takes precedence over self-discovery because Torah contains "a lucidity without tentativeness," "a history whose conclusion precedes its development," "a 'practice' prior to voluntary adherence," an ethical order prior to the world.[21] Does any knowledge rival that proclaimed in the Torah? What could compare to the unrelenting ethical summons to responsibility before my neighbor? What other knowledge contains its future history in its past declaration? What other knowledge prescribes a way to live anchored in the infinite because it proceeds from "a past more ancient than any present?"[22] The alliance between Torah and the human subject is the very alliance between the self and the other. This alliance is attestation to goodness itself.[23] Torah is materialized within the fabric of human relationships where it takes on flesh through uprightness and responsibility. No additional knowledge informs Torah or adds to its primordial message.

20. Levinas, *Nine Talmudic Readings*, 49.

21. Levinas, *Nine Talmudic Readings*, 40, 45, 48. Cf. Levinas, *Nine Talmudic Readings*, 36, 41: "It may be, however, that the notion of action, instead of indicating *praxis* as opposed to contemplation, a move in the dark, leads us to an order in which the opposition of engagement and disengagement is no longer decisive and which precedes, even conditions, these notions. . . . The meaning of being, the meaning of creation, is to realize the Torah. The world is here so that the ethical order has the possibility of being fulfilled."

22. Levinas, *Otherwise than Being or Beyond Essence*, 24. Unlike Levinas's admonition to consider Torah as primal and ultimate knowledge, we often regard knowledge as neutral, prior to and apart from lived ethical experience. See Levinas, *Nine Talmudic Readings*, 34: "To join evil to good, to venture into the ambiguous corners of being without sinking into evil and to remain beyond good and evil in order to accomplish this, is to know. One must experience everything through one's own self but experience it without having experienced it yet, before engaging oneself in the world. For experiencing itself is already committing oneself, choosing, living, limiting oneself. To know is to experience without experiencing, before living. We want to know before we do. But we want only a knowledge completely tested through our own evidence. We do not want to undertake anything without knowing everything, and nothing can become known to us unless we have gone and seen for ourselves, regardless of the misadventures of the exploration. We want to live dangerously, but in security, in the world of truths."

23. See Burggraeve, "Violence and the Vulnerable Face of the Other," 35: "The true meaning and real value of goodness, understood as the unconditional of the other despite its 'otherness,' consists precisely in overcoming the evil threatening the other with reduction and destruction, instead establishing another relation with him or her, one resting on attention and devotion to the other."

Especially in a digital age, "the European is certain at least of his retreat as subject into his extraterritorial subjectivity, certain of his separation with respect to any other, and thus assured of a kind of irresponsibility toward the All."[24] The notion of a private life, removed and withdrawn from a public network of transparent relationships, is symptomatic of the postmodern era. To pretend to exercise an imagination entirely absent of consequences and effect on others is the grand illusion of our times. Given the ephemeral phenomenality of the anonymous virtual world, it seems possible to live in windows of time absent of all responsibility toward the other and toward everyone. The frequent experience of solitude relieved of all solicitude has become the premier way of life. News feeds do not so much provoke concern for the other as serve as a form of entertainment at which to gawk, balk, and mindlessly forget in the casual movement to yet another miserable private enjoyment. It is a sinister privilege to sit on the hind side of a screen and watch the world suffer, all the while neglecting the charge to come to its assistance. The temptation of temptation insulates the choice of the self to act or not to act—or at least not to act yet. Action and the sense of responsibility for the other are suspended by the primacy of free will and its self-interested ranking of more urgent matters. However, Levinas avers that the freedom afforded by Torah is rooted in the ultimatum of *eyn berera*, or "no choice": "the Torah or death"—a dilemma pressed on the human subject from without.[25] It is not Torah that is determined by humanity, but humanity which is determined by Torah. Will we humanize or destroy one another? This is the question which confronts everyone at all times, and me before all others. Responsibility does not begin, first of all, with free will. Rather, the call to responsibility precedes free will, is the raison d'être of free will, and compels free will to actualize its latent potential to become truly free.

Within the Levinasian paradigm, being itself is relegated to an ancillary position in relation to Torah: "Being receives a challenge from the Torah, which jeopardizes its pretention of keeping itself above or beyond good and evil. In challenging the absurd 'that's the way it is' claimed by the Power of the powerful, the man of the Torah transforms being into human

---

24. Levinas, *Nine Talmudic Readings*, 36.

25. Levinas, *Nine Talmudic Readings*, 37. Cf. Levinas, *Nine Talmudic Readings*, 49: "The Torah is an order to which the ego adheres, without having had to enter it, an order beyond being and choice. The ego's exit from being occurs before the ego-which-decides. . . . It happens through the weight exerted on one point of being by the rest of its substance. This weight is called responsibility. Responsibility for a creature—a being of which the ego was not the author—which establishes the ego. To be a self is to be responsible beyond what one has oneself done. *Temimut* [i.e., "uprightness"] consists in substituting oneself for others."

history. Meaningful movement jolts the Real."[26] This is to say that Torah serves as guide for the humanization of being. In giving lasting meaning to being through their ethical activity, human persons attest to the ancient primacy of the Good over Being.[27] In other words, being is because it is good to be. Through ethical relationships we likewise testify against all nihilistic worldviews which leave no room for holiness or redemption. Being is stale or even suffocating without its transformation into meaningful acts of love and service by us rational creatures. Torah subverts the propensity toward a self-insulating power which only ever ends in self-consumption and instead relocates power as the prophetic inspiration of responsibility. I am ordered by the other through the interiority of my guilty conscience which holds me responsible for how the other fares. Attunement to the call of the other is neither naïve nor unsophisticated but represents the heights of the human intellect.

Moral sagacity is measured by the standard of recognition and affirmative response to the call of the other. Intelligibility is dialogical and commences with a word from the other through the pedagogical process of mimesis and the development of a symbolic order within consciousness. According to Levinas,

> Intelligibility does not begin in self-certainty, in the coincidence with oneself from which one can give oneself time and a provisional morality, try everything, and let oneself be tempted by everything. Intelligibility is a fidelity to the true; it is incorruptible and prior to any human enterprise; it protects this enterprise like the cloud which, according to the Talmud, covered the Israelites in the desert. Consciousness is the urgency of a destination leading to the other person and not an eternal return to self.[28]

26. Levinas, *Nine Talmudic Readings*, 39.

27. See Levinas, *Totality and Infinity*, 103: "The Place of the Good above every essence is the most profound teaching, the definitive teaching, not of theology, but of philosophy." Cf. "The Divine Names," in Pseudo-Dionysius, *Pseudo-Dionysius*, 71–96; Plato, *Republic*, VI, VII; *Philebus*; *Timaeus*.

28. Levinas, "The Temptation of Temptation," 48. For more on Levinas's treatment of intelligibility, see Levinas, *Totality and Infinity*, 82–83, 123–24, 127. For instance, see Levinas, *Totality and Infinity*, 82–83: "And yet the concern for intelligibility is fundamentally different from an attitude that engenders an action without regard for obstacles. It signifies on the contrary a certain respect for objects. . . . The famous suspension of action that is said to make theory possible depends on a reserve of freedom, which does not abandon itself to its drives, to its impulsive movements, and keeps its distances. Theory, in which truth arises, is the attitude of a being that distrusts itself. Knowing becomes knowing of a fact only if it is at the same time critical, if it puts itself into question, goes back beyond its origin—in an unnatural movement to seek higher than one's own origin, a movement which evinces or describes a created freedom."

Intelligibility first involves a conversation between the self and the other. Further, it requires an object of intelligibility about which the conversation takes place that is identical to neither the self nor the other. This double otherness of intelligibility recognizes truth as a non-manufacturable species which transcends the individuality of self and other. Approaching truth means to take leave of the self and the truth can be approached only vis-à-vis the other. The truth must be communicated between the self and the other.[29] Without personal alterity the truth does not come alive in the course of conversation. A genuine morality is not relative to individual preference but is tethered to truth as such. The phenomenon of consciousness arises from the proclamation of truth outside the self and consciousness remains vigilant to the degree that it stays attuned to the call of the other and to the sober exigencies of truth.[30] Intelligibility grows inasmuch as it takes leave of the self, never to return. Freedom reveals its paradoxical character through the experience of suffering the other in which the self becomes hostage to the other in a relational context of radical passivity.[31] In recognizing oneself as hostage to the other, the self escapes itself and burns its ships upon arriving upon the shores of responsibility. Leisure is exchanged irrevocably in return for the chance to care for the other. Freedom of responsibility engenders authentic love and the solidarity of a communion of persons. Freedom is communal by definition and cannot be achieved alone. The temptation of temptation works only to arrest the natural expansion of freedom through the risk of responsibility. By refusing the risk of responsibility, the temptation of temptation imprisons freedom within the frozen confines of the self. In real responsibility for the other, all must be wagered to the point of abandonment.

---

29. To substantiate this claim, see Ricoeur, *History and Truth*, 50–51; Ricoeur, *Oneself as Another*, 16–23, 317–56; and "Language and Proximity," in Levinas, *Collected Philosophical Papers*, 109–26.

30. For more on Levinas's understanding of consciousness and the notion of human subjectivity as hypostasis, see Levinas, *Existence and Existents*, 64–86, and Levinas, *Time and the Other*, 51–57.

31. See Levinas, *Nine Talmudic Readings*, 50: "It will at least be admitted that this freedom does not have any leisure time in which to assume this burden that, as a result, it is from the start as if compressed or un-done by suffering. This condition (or uncondition) of hostage is an essential modality of freedom—its primary modality—and not an empirical accident of a freedom always remaining above it all. In this impossibility of running away from the imperious cry of the creature, the assumption (of responsibility) in no way goes beyond passivity." Cf. Kaplan, "Israel under the Mountain," 41: "Precisely because the Torah is opposed to violence, both the Torah and those who accept it are always exposed to threats of violence and death. . . . To truly accept the Torah, then, means to accept this exposure to danger, violence, and death."

Morality does not originate with the self or the nebulous dictates of culture. Morality begins with the recognition of the universality of the Good and the intrinsic laws of rationality and nature. Just as sure as we understand the phenomenon of gravity or the universality of mathematics, so does morality emerge from the universal phenomenon of the call of the other. Throughout Levinas's works, he attests to this intersubjective phenomenon which precedes all other perceptions of consciousness. For Levinas, the human being is the responsible being—responsible for every other person and the entire world. Subjectivity commences with a departure from the self toward some other—whether in the form of an intellectual object, an enjoyment, or any perception whatsoever. But subjectivity comes fully alive with the irrevocable departure from the self toward the personal other (l'autrui), that is, in becoming infinitely responsible for the other person who faces me. The suffocation of being, the inescapable experience of being riveted to oneself in existence (il y a), and the banality of pleasure are all overcome through the affirmative response to the call of the other to the point of abandonment. To become human is to become responsible for the other without remainder. Giving up all, including the totality of one's very self, results in the freedom of the other, and, paradoxically, the freedom of the self—the self as oneself-for-the-other. By foregoing the temptation of temptation through responsibility for the other, freedom is born for all.

III. Google and the Limen of Temptation: A Case Study

Given the vocation to radical responsibility for the other, it is necessary to forfeit the temptation of temptation. However, in the twenty-first century, there is one phenomenon that promotes the temptation of temptation like no other, and like never before in human history: the Internet. Presenting the illusion of infinite knowledge and boundless virtual possibilities, the Internet wraps its onlooker in a web of perceptual fantasy. The hiatus between good and evil is suspended inasmuch as the search engine pronounces no judgment on its user. Knowledge is the alibi for every word search under the sun. Even more, it seems that everything needs to be searched and to be made available to encounter in the name of omniscience. Even if I admit that I am not omniscient, I must yield to the pretense that the Internet is. By its very phenomenality, the Internet is an invitation to knowledge almighty and, therefore, an invitation to the temptation of temptation.

I hover over the distinction between good and evil as long as I remain within the temptation of temptation. I pretend to be above the difference between good and evil as long as I suspend the question. Returning to the symbolic tree of the knowledge of good and evil, before partaking of the forbidden fruit, I hearken to the voice of the tempter and consider the possibility of the possibility of possibility, etc. Levinas says as much when he writes that "the temptation of temptation is thus the temptation of knowledge. The repetition once begun no longer comes to a stop. It is infinite. The temptation of temptation is also the temptation of temptation of temptation, etc. The temptation of temptation is philosophy, in contrast to a wisdom which knows everything without experiencing it."[32] Knowledge, as a concept, is identical to neither good nor evil. Knowledge is good insofar as what is known is good. Knowledge could be bad if its object is deficient of goodness in some way or if it distracts in some way from doing what is good. The term "knowledge" bears a rather neutral connotation, or, if anything other than neutral, a positive meaning. It may be readily agreeable that to know is good. So, how can the temptation of knowledge constitute this menacing temptation of temptation? The reason is that the temptation of knowledge mimics the infinite while not being identical to it. Knowledge is an imposture of the infinite since it displays an infinite character that only recoils back into itself upon every additional thing known. By knowing more and more, I am neither closer nor further away from the infinite. Even worse, is Qoheleth correct when he says, "For in much wisdom there is much sorrow; whoever increases knowledge increases grief?"[33] How can Levinas assure us of "a wisdom which knows everything without experiencing it?"

Paul of Tarsus alludes to such a state of affairs when he writes, "'Everything is lawful for me,' but not everything is beneficial. 'Everything is lawful for me,' but I will not let myself be dominated by anything."[34] Again, in the same Epistle to the Corinthians, he writes, "'Everything is lawful,' but not everything is beneficial. 'Everything is lawful,' but not everything builds up. No one should seek his own advantage, but that of his neighbor."[35] In his exhortation to the Corinthians, Paul advocates a similar freedom of responsibility as that of Levinas. Liberty and license are not to be equated. Liberty without limits is no liberty at all since liberty without limits amounts to a finite free will claiming to be infinite. Free will is not infinite because each choice implies one thing rather than another. Moreover, a free will which pretends to exercise a limitless capacity becomes enslaved both to illusion and to some other finite good in a disordered way. To elevate a finite good or set of finite goods to the status of

32. Levinas, *Nine Talmudic Readings*, 34.

33. Eccl 1:18 (NABRE).

34. 1 Cor 6:12 (NAB).

35. 1 Cor 10:23–24 (NAB).

the infinite is dishonest and illusory. Through phenomenological analysis it is clear that liberty turned into licentiousness leads to enslavement to one thing or the other and eventual destruction of the self and the other. Not only temperance but self-mastery is the virtue par excellence which anamnestically remembers the other at all times. It is the unlimited summons to responsibility for the other that pronounces the true character of the infinite. Another word for this limitless responsibility and vocation to serve the other is love. In his same epistle to the church in Corinth, Paul writes, "Love never fails . . . if knowledge, it will be brought to nothing. For we know partially and we prophesy partially, but when the perfect comes, the partial will pass away. . . . At present I know partially; then I shall know fully, as I am fully known."[36] Love is infinite, knowledge is not. How so? There are three ways to demonstrate this assertion.

First, knowledge is contingent on love rather than vice versa. Each act and fact of knowledge does not produce the infinite but merely confirms the finitude and futility of knowledge. If knowledge does not serve the greater vocation to love, it is vain.[37] If I have knowledge of everything under the sun but have not love, it is all to no avail. Knowledge confirms various data series but does not put the data at the service of a higher good than the data themselves. The banality of knowledge confirms the priority of love and the anteriority of the other.[38] Love is what steers knowledge in a meaningful and beneficial direction. Love finds meaning in knowledge because of its desire to share knowledge and rejoice in knowledge with another person.[39] Apart from a communal context of knowledge-sharing, knowledge gained by oneself alone is lonely and short-circuits without being passed on to another. Besides, gaining knowledge always involves another person from whom that particular knowledge comes in the first place. Even if new knowledge is discovered, the discovery was made possible by a sharing of knowledge by a plurality of persons leading up to the discovery.

Second, there is a stoppage of knowledge at points of fatigue, disinterest, and incomprehension. Knowledge is not an infinite process because inquiry

36. 1 Cor 13:8–9, 12 (NAB). Similar to Paul, in his later work, Levinas identifies philosophy come of age as "the measure brought to the infinity of the being-for-the-other of proximity, and is like the wisdom of love . . . the wisdom of love at the service of love" (*Otherwise than Being or Beyond Essence*, 161–62).

37. See Marion, *Erotic Phenomenon*, 11–40.

38. See Levinas, *Of God Who Comes to Mind*, 12: "Nothing, in effect, is absolutely other in the being served by knowledge wherein variety turns into monotony."

39. See Levinas, *Of God Who Comes to Mind*, 106: "The proximity of the neighbor, rather than passing for a limitation of the I by another, or for an aspiration to the unity yet to be effected, becomes desire nourishing itself from its hungers, or, to use a used word, love, more precious to the soul than the full possession of oneself by oneself."

naturally terminates at various levels where love for learning more about a particular topic is lacking. In addition, there are points at which the mind realizes that it has gone as far as it can go and can go no farther. René Descartes taught us as much when he argued that the idea of the infinite comes to us from an elsewhere since our minds are finite. One idea we cannot produce, know fully, or circumscribe by the powers of our minds is the infinite. It is an idea which saturates our limited modalities of comprehension. Concerning the idea of the infinite, we know that we know it in that we do not know it. Knowledge bumps up against many epistemological paradoxes such as that of the idea of the absolute, the idea of God, and many metaphysical ideas such as actuality, substance, form, and the soul. Simply because we cannot fully comprehend these ideas like we can comprehend other phenomena poor in intuition, this fact alone does not rule them out of the real de facto or de jure.[40] It is not that logical evidence is lacking or absolutely no intuition gives itself in these instances. Instead, both metaphysics and phenomenology allow us to detect realities which must be the case in light of realities we know with greater degrees of relative adequacy. We logically posit necessary conditions of possibility in terms of being and causality in metaphysics, and we perceive phenomena that give themselves in saturating ways and that attest to themselves through the indefinability of alterity through the course of intersubjective relationships in phenomenology.

David Tracy has demonstrated sufficiently the relative adequacy of both certainty and knowledge.[41] He writes that

> to lose any belief in pure self-presence as well as any claims to certainty or apodictic knowledge is not to deny the possibility of knowledge itself. What we know, we know with relative adequacy, and we know it is bounded by the realities of language, society, and history. On any particular issue, we can know when we have no further relevant questions. It is possible, therefore, to know when we know enough.[42]

40. See Marion, *Being Given*, 221–47.

41. For example, see Tracy, *Plurality and Ambiguity*, 22–25: "For relative adequacy is just that: relative, not absolute, adequacy. If one demands certainty, one is assured of failure. We can never possess absolute certainty. But we can achieve a good—that is, a relatively adequate—interpretation. . . . Somehow conversation and relatively adequate interpretations suffice. As Hilary Putnam reminds us: in some situations, 'Enough is enough, enough is not everything.' Sometimes less is more. . . . When there are no further relevant questions either from the text of from myself or from the interaction that is questioning, then I find relative adequacy."

42. Tracy, *Plurality and Ambiguity*, 61.

Tracy points out the layers of interpretation which mediate between the objects of knowledge and the knower in every case of knowledge. There is no fact which is self-identical to the knower just as there is no knower self-identical to the infinite. Knowledge is infinite neither in quantity nor in any degree of quality. It is always conditioned upon the limit situation of contingent and interpretively bound realities which surround every act of knowledge. Knowledge reaches its natural limit when questioning on a particular topic ceases. If there are no further questions of interest, there is nothing further to know. We know when we know enough but knowing enough simply attests to the finite process of knowing. Our experience of knowledge is constantly conditioned by our desire—or lack thereof—to know. Again, love is what prompts us to know for the sake of acting in meaningful ways in light of knowledge gained. Paul of Tarsus sums it up well: "'Knowledge' puffs up, but love builds up."[43]

The third way to distinguish the infinity of love and the finitude of knowledge is to describe the respective processes of each. It has been said by highly educated people, "The more I learn, the more I realize I do not know." This is how knowledge works: the more knowledge gained, the more one is aware of the knowledge one lacks. In other words, the more knowledge gained, the greater lack of knowledge is realized.[44] The more knowledge is obtained, the less knowledge one has according to the recognition of the immense deficiency of knowledge by the one who knows. Ironically, knowledge decreases the more one knows. With love, on the other hand, the more one gives away, the more one has. Love is revealed as a gift received to the measure that it is given away. This is the great paradox of love: to receive it, you must give it away all the more. The process of loving is the very opposite of the process of knowing. Knowledge is something to be grasped and consumed by the mind, whereas love is something to be received as gift to be given away in turn. Knowledge operates according to pride and self-assertion, whereas love operates according to humility and self-emptying. Love is the true face of the infinite and knowledge merely mimics the infinite exchange of love through an inverse pattern of self-sufficiency and self-concern. Love is concerned with the good of the other and never ceases to be responsible for the other.[45] It may very well be that

43. 1 Cor 8:1 (RSV).

44. See Eccl 12:11–12: "The sayings of the wise are like goads; like fixed spikes are the collected sayings given by one shepherd. As to more than these, my son, beware. Of the making of many books there is no end, and in much study there is weariness for the flesh" (NABRE).

45. See Levinas, *Of God Who Comes to Mind*, 67: "Love is only possible through the idea of the Infinite, through the Infinite placed in me, by the 'more' that ravages

teaching which adheres to the pedagogy of love subordinates knowledge to the service of love. Charitable teaching puts knowledge always at the service of the other, for the good of the other. If not wedded to ethical considerations and the eschatology of love, knowledge is in vain.

The priority of love fosters a freedom for excellence and the priority of knowledge engenders a freedom of indifference. Love's aim is to act always in accord with the good. Knowledge's aim is to keep a distance from the good so as not to be swayed by anything other than the pure act of knowing and the subsequent purity of free will. For knowledge, the distinction between good and evil is arbitrary inasmuch as the neutrality of knowledge is indifferent to moral distinctions due to its exclusive interest in "raw data and facts." The phenomenality of Google pretends to signify neutrality and, by virtue of its originally blank contents, strikes consciousness with an aura of digital indifference. Just as a computer is indifferent to good and evil, so is the phenomenon of a web search engine. In extending our noetic consciousness through the neutral composition of digital technology, we take on virtual avatars of robotic and androgynous personas that soar above the distinction between good and evil in the name of knowledge. Even more nefarious, when knowledge is blended with curiosity, there is no end to post-innocent virtual exploration. The temptation of temptation commences and sustains this virtual world which hovers above good and evil. The temptation of temptation opens onto a happy place where all is permissible and nothing is taboo.[46] It is reinforced all the more by ideological strongholds—whether liberal or conservative—which, too, claim to be beyond good and evil. For liberal ideology, Google symbolizes emancipation from censorship and a beacon of the freedom of choice. For conservative ideology, Google is a hub of consumerism and the endless foray into the free marketplace of knowledge, enjoyment, and novelty. Extremes meet in the temptation of temptation.

Altogether, the Internet poses as the panacea for every desire, yet provoking insatiable desire all the more. Because it wields the power of access to innumerable virtual worlds and experiences, the Internet provokes the temptation of temptation: Why leave any stone unturned? If the essence of Torah is to know God and to un-know all false gods (idols), the Internet

---

and wakes up the 'less,' turning away from teleology, and destroying the time and the happiness [*l'heure et le bonheur*] of the end."

46. See Jennifer Geddes's essay, "Attending to Suffering in/at the Wake of Postmodernism," in Brooks and Toth, *Mourning After*, 77–78, where she writes, "Because 'temptation makes nothing irreparable,' it also makes nothing forbidden and everything safely permissible. Mistakes can be erased, risks taken safely, and, hence, nothing is really at stake."

surely offers a plethora of distractions from knowledge of the divine insofar as it spurs on the will to explore a legion of alternatives to the narrative
of the people of Israel and their allegiance to the one, true God. Since the
Internet serves as the gateway to so many roads other than that leading to
the promised land, it detracts the sojourner to truth from its singular destination. Even if I search "YHWH," I will find myself searching and searching to no avail because this God, by definition, never will be encountered
in the potency of pixels or in the windows of wandering. Rather, the true
and living God is to be encountered in the departure from the temptation
of temptation and a movement out into the wilderness:

> What is significant is this, that monotheism was not able to de-
> velop in the great cities and fertile countryside of Mesopotamia.
> No, it was in the wilderness, where heaven and earth face each
> other in stark solitude, that monotheism was able to grow—in the
> homelessness of the wanderer, who does not deify places but has
> constantly to put his trust in the God who wanders with him.[47]

The glowing screen must be vacated in order to encounter the living God
in the stark solitude of the natural wilderness. Where celestial luminaries
meet grains of desert sand is that privileged place of theophany. Likewise,
where I encounter the human other face to face is the locale in which God
comes to mind. Because the Internet features a capital experience of the
temptation of temptation, it must be renounced at first in order to be re-
instated as an instrument of virtue and self-forgetful altruism. Whereby
the temptation of temptation aims at preserving a self-insulating notion of
freedom as license, Torah reintroduces a freedom that came before license:
freedom as responsibility for the other. Inasmuch as the Internet serves this
higher purpose, its use is justified.

IV. Overcoming the Temptation of Temptation

Now that the temptation of temptation has been described briefly in its concept and in its application to Internet ethics, let us examine next how the
temptation of temptation can be overcome. Lurking behind the temptation
of temptation is the temptation to evil.[48] A fine line runs between these two
notions of temptation. Once one passes into the field of the temptation of

47. Ratzinger, *Spirit of the Liturgy*, 98–99.
48. See Gen 4:6–7: "The LORD said to Cain, 'Why are you angry, and why has your
countenance fallen? If you do well, will you not be accepted? And if you do not do well,
sin is lurking at the door; its desire is for you, but you must master it'" (RSV).

temptation, one is found at the door of the temptation to evil. Yet Levinas claims a way out: "overcoming the temptation of evil by avoiding the temptation of temptation."[49] So, how is the temptation of temptation to be avoided both in a general sense and as applied to online ethics? In a word: Torah. Binding myself to the eternal law of God is the only way to circumvent the temptation of temptation. We are dealing with a covenant relationship which risks everything for the one thing. All alternatives are renounced for the sake of the singular path of living according to the divine will. Forming a personal covenant with Torah forces one to forsake choice for the sake of responsibility. Free will admits a vocation that precedes it and realizes that responding affirmatively to this vocation is the only way to freedom. Indeed, this is the vocation to the freedom for excellence by renunciation of the freedom of indifference. It is the freedom of responsibility for the other to which Torah is an indicator. As evinced in C. S. Lewis's book, *The Great Divorce*, to live as children in the kingdom of God requires the complete renunciation of the possibility of temptation in any form whatsoever. The temptation of temptation proves to be inimical to the kingdom of God.

Binding oneself to Torah paradoxically limits the self to many perceivable finite goods, pleasures, and enjoyments but at the same time opens the self to the infinite. The finitude of knowledge gives way to the infinity of love. A veritable death to self-assertion and vanity is required to pass over into the terrain of love and responsibility. When Torah rules my life, every thought, word, and action is scrutinized by the exigencies of responsibility. It is not that knowledge is resisted at every turn. Rather, knowledge is viewed as beneficial if it serves the greater good of being responsible for the other. Entering into a covenant with Torah does not only forfeit every temptation to evil, even more importantly, it forfeits the temptation of temptation. The very venue in which one hearkens to the possibility of being tempted is obliterated, never to return. One may respond to such a proposal with the concern that free will likewise is desolated in the face of Torah. If the temptation of temptation is included in the concept of free will, then that is correct: free will is undone before the demands of Torah, and that is the point.[50] For Levinas, Torah is not revealed primarily in a text and in the self's fidelity to a text. Torah speaks through the face of the other and in the heart

49. Levinas, *Nine Talmudic Readings*, 41.

50. See, for example, the moving *Suscipe* prayer of Ignatius of Loyola in his *Spiritual Exercises*: "Take, Lord, and receive all my liberty, my memory, my understanding, and all my will—all that I have and possess. You, O Lord, have given all that to me. I now give it back to you, O Lord. All of it is yours. Dispose of it according to your will. Give me your love and your grace, for that is enough for me" (Ignatius of Loyola, *Ignatius of Loyola*, 177).

of the self. Just as I never can take leave of the call of the other in the name of some autonomous free will, neither can I dodge the prescriptions of Torah as proclaimed through the relational proximity between the other and me. The phenomenological shape of the human being is the asymmetrical relation between the self and the other. The face of the other speaks to me in its radical vulnerability and nakedness: "Do not kill me." My affirmative response to the call of the other takes form in the prophetic words that well up within me: "Here I am!" In a freedom of responsibility which forsakes the temptation of temptation, the self lays down its rights to autonomy and non-disturbance. The self is liberated from itself through forgetfulness of self and awakening to the needs of the other. Freedom of the self from itself is wrought by the incessant disruption of the self by the other.[51]

The point at which the Internet is viewed exclusively as a powerful tool through which to serve the other through love is when the temptation of temptation is eradicated. The point at which the accumulation of the miserable pleasures of the flesh gives way to the sober vocation of responsibility for the other is when the temptation of temptation is despoiled. The point at which the profligacy of "free time" is invested instead in the mission to come to the assistance of the other through prayer and sacrifice is when the temptation of temptation is forgotten. The Gordian knot of original sin is untied by the ethical eloquence of Torah and its transmutation into flesh.[52] Flesh does not take place within a virtual world. It is not composed of a panoply of pixels. True human flesh is that which extends itself in space and time, through a proximity of vulnerable presence, for the sake of the other. Flesh comes alive and achieves its raison d'être when it goes outside of itself because the other has invaded its innermost recesses. This phenomenon

51. See Levinas, *Otherwise than Being or Beyond Essence*, 180: "Freedom is animation itself, breath, the breathing of outside air, where inwardness frees itself from itself, and is exposed to all the winds."

52. See Levinas, *Otherwise than Being or Beyond Essence*, 105, 109, and 195n12 (italics original): "In the exposure to wounds and outrages, in the feeling proper to responsibility, the oneself is provoked as irreplaceable, as devoted to others, without being able to resign, and thus as incarnated in order to offer itself, to suffer and to give. . . . The body which makes giving possible makes one *other* without alienating. For this other is the heart, and the goodness, of the same, the inspiration or the very psyche in the soul. . . . The body is neither an obstacle opposed to the soul, nor a tomb that imprisons it, but that by which the self is susceptibly itself. Incarnation is extreme passivity; to be exposed to sickness, suffering, death, is to be exposed to compassion, and, as a self, to the gift that costs. The oneself is on this side of the zero of inertia and nothingness, in deficit of being, in itself and not in being, without a place to lay its head, in the no-grounds, and thus without conditions. As such it will be shown to be the bearer of the world, bearing it, suffering it, blocking rest and lacking a fatherland. It is the correlate of a persecution, a substitution for the other."

is what Levinas calls inspiration and it is a prerequisite for following the prescriptions of Torah.[53] By adhering to Torah with perfect fidelity, I reject the temptation of temptation manifest in the phenomenality of the Internet, refusing to be frozen to stone as one who gazes transfixed on the face of Medusa. Serpents of paralyzing possibility do not promote the flourishing of humanity after all. The just one who lives according to Torah acts as the hero Perseus by beheading Medusa, only to use her head as a weapon for good. In other words, the one who resolves to live in responsibility for the other anathematizes the temptation of temptation and instead uses its otherwise dissipate energies for serving the needs of the other.

It is a conscious decision to deny the temptation of temptation not only one time but on a daily basis. When I can pray along with the psalmist the following words, I have learned to take leave of the temptation of temptation:

> I have seen the limits of all perfection, but your commandment is without bounds. How I love your law, Lord! I study it all day long. . . . I keep my steps from every evil path, that I may observe your word. From your judgments I do not turn, for you have instructed me. . . . I make a solemn vow to observe your righteous judgments. . . . Your testimonies are my heritage forever; they are the joy of my heart. My heart is set on fulfilling your statutes; they are my reward forever.[54]

The psalmist recognizes that divine law alone is without limit because it attests to the infinite summons to responsibility for the other. The law of the Lord is the singular delight of the faithful one. It is to be studied day and night without ceasing. The temptation to evil is disowned because the temptation of temptation has been abdicated first. Resolute in his life's mission, the psalmist turns not from the judgments of God.[55] He swears

53. See Levinas, *Otherwise than Being or Beyond Essence*, 181–82, 191n3: "In human breathing, in its everyday equality, perhaps we have to already hear the breathlessness of an inspiration that paralyzes essence, that transpierces it with an inspiration by the other, an inspiration that is already expiration, that 'rends the soul'! It is the longest breath there is, spirit. Is man not the living being capable of the longest breath in inspiration, without a stopping point, and in expiration, without return? To transcend oneself, to leave one's home to the point of leaving oneself, is to substitute oneself for another. . . . The soul is the other in me. The psyche, the-one-for-the-other, can be a possession and a psychosis; the soul is already a seed of folly."

54. Pss 119:96–97, 101–2, 106, 111–12 (NABRE).

55. Cf. Josh 1:7–8: "Only be strong and steadfast, being careful to observe the entire law which Moses my servant enjoined on you. Do not swerve from it either to the right or to the left, that you may succeed wherever you go. Do not let this book of the law depart from your lips. Recite it by day and by night, that you may carefully observe all

a sacred oath to follow the divine law with perpetual constancy—literally, he "sevens himself" (שָׁבַע) and irrevocably binds himself to Torah. This is not a temporary promise that comes and goes but an eternal covenant pact that is enacted between God and the human being. Future security depends entirely on the testimonies of the Lord, which are at the same time the constant joy of the psalmist. There is no other reward to be sought save the fulfillment of divine law, which is at once to be responsible for my neighbor. The temptation of temptation is evaded to the measure that the human conscience is attuned unwaveringly to the ethical injunction issued by the other, or, in a word, Torah.

As applied to Internet usage, the adherent of Torah approaches the Internet exclusively as a tool to serve the vocation of responsibility for the other. There is no other purpose. Entertainment, leisure, selfish enjoyment, and curiosity are all set aside in the name of the other. The self forgets itself under the weight of responsibility it senses in relation to the other. One does not stare aimlessly into the blank gaze of Google (read: Medusa) but performs a web search only when a definite purpose is in mind that will serve to build up the other. To be ever mindful of the other is to dismiss the temptation of temptation in every thought, word, and deed. Encounter with the infinite short-circuits in its quest through the accumulation of knowledge. The Internet, posing as a virtual counterfeit of the infinite, indeed may provide the self with countless stimulating pleasures for self-centered mind and flesh. However, the pleasures provided by the Internet never seem to keep their promises of authentic and lasting liberation of the self from itself, wallowing in the cold static of being.[56] Through the phenomenality of the Internet search engine, the temptation of temptation acts as a virtual quicksand that enslaves free will to its alleged sovereignty, indecision, indifference, and autonomous autonomy.[57] Only the intrusive call of the other can rupture the

---

that is written in it; then you will attain your goal; then you will succeed" (NABRE); and Prov 4:25–27: "Let your eyes look straight ahead and your gaze be focused forward. Survey the path for your feet, and all your ways will be sure. Turn neither to right nor to left, keep your foot far from evil" (NABRE).

56. See Levinas, *On Escape*, 62: "Pleasure is a process; it is the process of departing from being [*processus de sortie de l'être*]. Its affective nature is not only the expression or the sign of this getting-out; it is the getting out itself. Pleasure is affectivity, precisely because it does not take on the forms of being, but rather attempts to break these up. Yet it is a deceptive escape. For it is an escape that fails. If, like a process that is far from closing up on itself, pleasure appears in a constant surpassing of oneself, it breaks just at the moment where it seems to get out absolutely. It develops with an increase in promises, which become richer the closer it comes to its paroxysm, but these promises are never kept."

57. See Ricoeur, *Freedom and Nature*, 445–47, 463 (italics original): "The initial act of freedom for the classical thinker is suspicion: it is a doubt, and that doubt is an

entropic force of self-aggrandizement and the apathetic virus of pleasure for pleasure's sake. By diagnosing the phenomenon of Google as the temptation of temptation, we are able to call it out and overcome its suffocating effect on humanity, turning Medusa's severed head into a weapon of virtue. Now, let us transition to considering the contributions of Marion's graceful concept of freedom that will serve to challenge and even to fill out what is wanting in Levinas's concept of an obedient freedom beyond freedom.

V. Jean-Luc Marion and the Freedom to Be Free

In his 1986 essay entitled "The Freedom to Be Free," Jean-Luc Marion proposes a quite different understanding of human freedom than that of Levinas.[58] Even though significantly influenced by the work of Levinas,

---

act of withdrawal: the 'I think' withdraws from the snare of the body and the world. It is exalted in defying the malevolent demon. In the same way freedom, according to the existential thinker, trembles since it is the crisis of being, it is anguished by the wide spaces it creates through possibility, it is anguished by the negation which it introduces into the fullness of antecedent being. Starting with its own infinity, it is the permanent possibility of disproportion, it experiences itself as its own temptation, the temptation to exalt itself infinitely, just as it experiences the world and its body as temptation, the temptation to sink into and lose oneself in the object. . . . I suffer from being one finite and partial perspective of the world and of values. I am condemned to be the 'exception': this and nothing else, this not that. . . . I suffer from being condemned to a choice which consecrates and intensifies my particularity and destroys all the possibles through which I am in contact with the totality of human experience. . . . Ah! If only I could grasp and embrace everything!—and how cruel it is to choose and exclude. That is how life moves: from amputation to amputation; and on the road from the possible to the actual lie only ruined hopes and atrophied powers. How much latent humanity I must reject in order to be someone! . . . Freedom responds to the *no* of condition with the *no* of refusal . . . In effect *what* we refuse, is always, in the last analysis, the limitation of character, the shadows of the unconscious, and the contingence of life. I cannot tolerate being only that partial consciousness limited by all its obscurity and discovering its brute existence. Thus we know the initial content of the refusal: the most remarkable trait of this triple refusal is that it does not present itself at first as a refusal but conceals itself in an affirmation of sovereignty whose implicit negativity it is important to bring to light. The disguised form of refusal is the haughty affirmation of consciousness as absolute, that is, as creative or as self-producing. It is the very sorrow of negation of all experienced parts which stimulates the passion of freedom to engender itself as sovereign, to posit itself as being of itself. Briefly, exaggeration is the privileged form of refusal."

58. For a similar argument made of more recent date, see Marion, *Erotic Phenomenon*, 50–53 (§11, "Whether I Will It or Not"), 70–97 (§§16–19, "Pure Assurance," "The Principle of Insufficient Reason," "The Advance," and "Freedom as Intuition"). For example, see Marion, *Erotic Phenomenon*, 94: "Whether I am beginning to become amorous, or I already love loving, or I imagine myself loving, in each case I am willing it and, in this acquiescence, am deciding for it." Cf. Marion, *Givenness and Revelation*,

Marion's phenomenology ends up in a distant land in comparison to that of his predecessor because of his fundamentally different point of departure. Instead of swearing allegiance to the other as such, Marion makes a pact with phenomenological givenness.[59] For Marion, the other is merely another instance of givenness, whereas for Levinas, the other transcends all phenomenological categories and reductive interpretations of perception.[60] The

---

45 (italics original): "Love knows and makes itself known, but on *one* condition: that its freedom to set the conditions of *its* knowledge be recognized; that is, that it be free to begin with the will, insofar as it can first be converted and convert the mind." Also, see Marion, *In the Self's Place*, 161–62, 173 (italics original): "Nothing defines the self more than the freedom of its decision; nothing belongs to me more as my own than my will. . . . In other words, I will insofar as I live, and I live insofar as I will. . . . The will assumes and assures the self itself . . . the will can of itself will what it wills, that the will secures for itself its own autonomy—in short, that the will *suffices* for freedom. In Augustinian terms there is no conflict between grace and will because without grace there simply is no will. Pelagianism does not constitute a sin of pride but first of all an intellectual fault; it assumes the excellence and even the reality of a faculty whose phenomenological description shows its insufficiency and inconsistency." This final point is Marion's greatest challenge to the Levinasian paradigm of the self portrayed as immediately capable of being responsible for the other. Perhaps the polemic between Augustine and Pelagius resurfaces today in that between Marion and Levinas. See Wallenfang, "Dialectical Truth between Augustine and Pelagius," 122–39. For a passing treatment of the necessity of immortality to accomplish the complete authentication of freedom, see Marion, *In Excess*, 123–27 ("Hermeneutics to the Infinite").

59. See Rogers, "Traces of Reduction," 186: "While Marion carries out a sort of eidetic analysis, where the forms of phenomenal experience are disclosed precisely through interpretation of regularities as they unfold, his position is rationalist to the extent that Marion searches for a sort of conceptual Archimedean point upon which to secure independent philosophical 'evidence' for revelation—even if this evidence is, finally, the admittance into philosophy of the absolutely unconditioned. Marion's is a formalized givenness, sanitized of all of its historical particularity and presented into supposedly 'neutral' phenomenological evidence. Marion's phenomenological analysis is illegitimately reductive to the extent to which it assigns theoretical conditions for pre-theoretical experience"; and Rawnsley, "Practice and Givenness," 693 (italics original): "This denial of the subject without any alternative framework being properly worked out means that Marion's project floats free of the *situational*: it has no proper historical or located dimension. The concepts and categories end up as epistemological factors which subsist within a field of disembodied consciousness, neither fully human nor fully divine."

60. For instance, see Marion's essay, "The Voice without Name: Homage to Levinas," in Bloechl, *Face of the Other and the Trace of God*, 240: "Levinas attests that the other person, as appeal, establishes the possibility of a phenomenology of givenness: 'Transcendence is not a vision of the Other, but an original givenness' (*TeI* 149/*TI* 174). It remains to be determined whether this transcendence offers the only givenness, or if other immanence could add to it, thus deploying a phenomenology of givenness in general"; and Marion, *Being Given*, 294, 331 (endnote 23) and 374 (endnote 73): "The pertinent question is not deciding if the gifted is first responsible toward the Other (Levinas) or rather in debt to itself (Heidegger), but understanding that these two

phenomenological paradigms of Levinas and Marion are radically divergent from the start. While Marion reduces all phenomenality to various epiphanies and manifestations of givenness, Levinas contests the maneuver of reducing the other beneath the tyranny of manifestation. In his 1997 book, *Being Given: Toward a Phenomenology of Givenness*, Marion writes that "nothing of what gives itself can show itself except to the gifted and through it—not by constitution, anticipatory resoluteness, or exposure to the Other, but by the will to see, originally derived from givenness itself."[61] Marion positions the intentionality of free will, in its unconditional relation to givenness, as an absolute hermeneutic. With implicit reference to Levinas, Marion denies "exposure to the Other" as primary, and replaces it with givenness and "the will to see," granted by givenness to the human subject. Dissimilarly, Levinas proposes a phenomenology of proclamation which preserves the integrity and alterity of the other because the face of the other is more a matter of speech than it is of appearance.[62] For Levinas, the face appears inasmuch as it speaks. Even more, the face does not appear as such but its phenomenality emerges from the call to responsibility for the other and the ensuing ethical exigency which binds the ego to the other as the primordial and universal human vocation. The totality of manifestation and conceptual manipulation of the other is ruptured by the power of word which cannot be reduced to yet another mode of noematic appearance.

According to his 1986 essay on human freedom, "The Freedom to Be Free," Marion argues that neither freedom nor ethics proceed from the other or an elsewhere, but from the self. It is with this egocentric point of departure that Marion's conception of freedom will end up in opposition to that of Levinas. Marion claims that the post-metaphysical world of modernity "does not destroy ethics, it refuses it."[63] Since ethics is rooted intrinsically in metaphysics, with the departure from metaphysics comes the departure from ethics. Like Levinas, Marion, too, is concerned with the eclipse of ethics in the modern era, as well as the deceptions of ideologies, the ongoing threat of successive totalitarianisms, violent technocracies, and the Dionysian madness

---

modes of responsibility flow from its originary function of having to respond in the face of the phenomenon as such, that is to say, such as it gives itself. . . . Givenness thus determines equally, if not indifferently, the phenomenality of the self, the Other, and the truth. This is not, evidently, a matter of chance nor of a homonym. . . . I will not speak of a 'responsibility for the Other, older than any commitment" . . . —precisely because no 'commitment' (not even for the Other) would be thinkable without responsibility, taken in its phenomenological radicality."

61. Marion, *Being Given*, 307.

62. For more on the concept of "phenomenology of proclamation," see Wallenfang, *Dialectical Anatomy of the Eucharist*, especially 1–50, 102–43.

63. Marion, *Prolegomena to Charity*, 32.

of unbridled desires which loathe any pretension to universal law. However, Marion's solution to these social calamities parts ways with that of Levinas on the issue of human freedom. In contrast to Levinas, who contends that morality proceeds not from the will but from the imposition of the call of the other on the self, Marion insists that post-metaphysical morality stems from the will in overcoming the ambiguity of motivation to act. In other words, Marion claims to go further than Nietzsche by proposing that the self still can will authentically a perceived good, which surmounts the suspicion that the self only acts from the impetus of the will to power or the determination of desire. For Marion, "the act becomes moral when it assumes the risk of deciding in favor of nonpower through the risk that this nonpower is an illusion. The act becomes moral when it accepts to sacrifice totally its author for, perhaps, the illusion of morality—acting morally is certified when one takes the risk of losing all for, perhaps, immorality."[64] This is to say that, for Marion, morality is ultimately a byproduct of human freedom stemming from the will to decide between good and evil.[65]

By accepting the accusation of Nietzsche that metaphysics has run its course to the point of termination, Marion is forced to overcome Nietzsche's dismissal of a genuine ethics with the only legitimate element Nietzsche has left behind: the human will. By foregoing the hope of the immemorial beyond of metaphysics, Marion simultaneously forfeits the possibility of an ethics proceeding from an elsewhere other than the self. Marion proposes to overcome Nietzsche through Nietzsche, but, for that very reason, does not fully overcome Nietzsche. Marion's morality remains trapped in the inescapable ambiguity of the self and its motivation and in the self's claim to overcome itself by itself and through itself.

Subsequently, Marion's understanding of freedom collapses into a freedom of indifference under the weight of the ambiguities of motivation. Marion writes that "I am free, not because I know the determinations of my choice (Spinoza), nor because I dispense with them absolutely (Kant), but because I can hold them all to be perfectly indifferent . . . freedom demands an entitlement to erring."[66] Unlike the Kantian ethical imperative pronounced in the call of the other for Levinas, Marion declares to go beyond Spinoza, Kant, Nietzsche, and Levinas by relocating the source of ethics in the self-determination of the will within the milieu of indifference. In Kierkegaardian fashion, Marion asserts that "I can always render

64. Marion, *Prolegomena to Charity*, 43–44.

65. See Marion, *Prolegomena to Charity*, 44n9.

66. Marion, *Prolegomena to Charity*, 46–47.

myself free to be free."[67] Because of the saturating context of nihilism in the emergence of the postmodern world, Marion reduces ethics almost exclusively to freedom—understood to be synonymous with free will, even if elevated by grace.[68] He writes further: "To act morally signifies first of all to prove (oneself) by the decision, lacking any assurance other than an *as if*, that one can act freely. Today we have perhaps no better motive for acting morally than to experiment with freedom, to contradict the totalitarian hermeneutic in all of its transformations."[69] Here Marion suggests that we are absolutely free inasmuch as we act as if we are indeed absolutely free. One always can raise suspicious questions as to why another's or one's own self acted in this way or that way.

For example, I could question my motivation for showering this morning and styling my hair. Perhaps I did this because I think that I will gain more material benefit in the end by looking clean and sharp (Marx); perhaps I did this because of a subconscious impulse toward sexual pleasure (Freud); perhaps I did this as a means of asserting more power in my professional and personal life (Nietzsche); perhaps I did this as a means to act with even more responsibility toward the other (Levinas). What Marion is arguing is that no matter what my motivation, or even what combination of diverse motivating factors, the fact is that I acted in this way despite the haunting voices which daily accuse me of base, selfish, or noble motivations for all that I do. I risk acting within the menagerie of motivations which constantly stir my activity and inactivity.

Even though Marion claims Levinas as a key source for his construction of human freedom, Marion's vision of freedom is nevertheless

---

67. Marion, *Prolegomena to Charity*, 47.

68. See Marion, *In the Self's Place*, 188–89, 358 (endnote 26): "There cannot be a conflict between freedom and grace, since without grace (that is to say, its transformation into love) the will cannot will well, since, at bottom, it simply cannot will at all. . . . There is no dispute about what freedom could accomplish without grace, since without grace freedom attains absolutely nothing, because it cannot will anything. . . . The certainty of enjoying a free will, even experiencing it as evil, constitutes a first liberation. Whence the absurdity of opposing grace to freedom of choice, since freedom itself comes over me as a gracious gift." Cf. Marion's essay, "The Final Appeal of the Subject," in Critchley and Dews, *Deconstructive Subjectivities*, especially 104 (italics original): "What succeeds the subject is the very movement of irremediable difference which precedes it, insofar as the subject is given to itself as a *myself*, to which any *I* claiming authenticity only offers a mask, doubly belated and radically secondary, or even originally deceptive. More essential to the *I* than itself, the gesture that the interlocuter appears, freely but not without price, in the figure of the claim—as that which gives the *I* as a *myself* rendered to *itself*. Grace gives the *myself* to *itself* before the *I* even notices itself. My grace precedes me."

69. Marion, *Prolegomena to Charity*, 48.

a phenomenon which originates with the self (even if awakened by grace) and ends in the self. And even though Marion's freedom "unceasingly opens the Same to an Other," it does so at the behest of possibility, the other person appearing as only one of many forms of possibility.[70] In the end, Marion's freedom denies the primacy of the call of the personal other in exchange for the primacy of possibility in general, according to the anteriority of givenness and its variety of modes of manifestation. For this reason, every pretension to law is null and void due to the slippery slope of nihilism and the ambiguities of motivation and their codification in law. Even the notion of divine law, or Torah, would be unhelpful to a Marionian freedom of riskful possibility. For Marion, as it was for Nietzsche, is it too presumptuous to claim with certainty a source of divine command? Is there no longer an infallible source for ethics in today's nihilistic world other than the infallibility of possibility and its provocation of the self? Even though Marion argues that givenness grants us access to the call of the unique other, rather than to just another rendition of the Kantian categorical imperative, is such access worth the price of admission, namely, forfeiting the rank of the ethical summons as transcendent and prior to givenness and its belated index of appearances?

VI. Conclusion

In spite of the fact that Marion's conception of freedom takes a different course than that of Levinas, it remains a helpful counterpart nonetheless. To conclude, I would like to introduce briefly the following suggestion. Held together in polar tension, the respective phenomenological matrices of Levinas and Marion in tandem create something new. This something new is what I call "dialectical phenomenology" and, moreover, "dialectical theology."[71] Concerning the relationship between law and freedom, Marion's work maintains the primacy of gift or, in a word, grace. His basis for the primacy and freedom of grace to give itself to the human subject as it will, thereby elevating the will to love in spite of its detractors, is the pure phenomenality of givenness: "The freedom of the gift implies that the decision to give it obeys only the logic of givenness, therefore its gratuity without return."[72] Levinas, for his part, constantly maintains the primacy

70. Marion, *Prolegomena to Charity*, 48.

71. For a more comprehensive treatment of my notions of "dialectical phenomenology" and "dialectical theology," see Wallenfang, *Dialectical Anatomy of the Eucharist*.

72. Marion, *Being Given*, 106–7. Cf. Marion, *Being Given*, 173: "One must expose oneself to the phenomenon to receive its form—as one receives a blow, a shock, or an emotion."

of responsibility for the other as articulated in Torah or, in a word, law. For him, exposure, or sensibility, to the other is the first phenomenon, prior to the avatars of givenness, even if indicated as a "non-phenomenon."[73] A dialectical relationship is observable between law and grace, between exigency and gift, between ethics and contemplation.

If left to itself, a Levinasian phenomenology of freedom can collapse into a sterile nihilism of the self. If left to itself, a Marionian phenomenology of freedom can self-destruct due to the force of desire and the accompanying paralysis of possibility. Yet together in unresolved tension, without anything like the closure of a Hegelian synthesis or sublation, these two phenomenological proposals cultivate a holistic paradigm of human freedom that is neither too self-abnegating nor too self-assuring. My proposal is not so much a blending of Levinas and Marion as it is an ongoing conversation and confrontation between the two. It is akin to the classic dialectic between agape and eros in considering the privileged phenomenon of love. Levinas would represent the agape side of the dialectic and Marion would represent eros. Granted, my proposal trades on generalities, but it contributes, nevertheless, to the revelation of the dialectical nature of truth. Levinas puts it this way: "Truth is consequently experienced as a dialogue . . . [which] does not reach a conclusion, but constitutes the very life of truth."[74] The unresolved dialogue of truth prevents the closure and falsification of truth. If the dialogue of truth comes to an abrupt end with nothing left to say, what becomes of truth as a living and universal summons to action and responsibility?

Yet Marion's concern is that justice and its duties render the gift impossible.[75] An economy of exchange leaves the gift without license and legislature. For him, the will assumes absolute status as it arbitrates within the ambiguous milieu of the actual and the possible, preferring the latter

73. Levinas, *Otherwise than Being or Beyond Essence*, 75: "On the hither side of the zero point which marks the absence of protection and cover, sensibility is being affected by a non-phenomenon, a being put in question by the alterity of the other, before the intervention of a cause, before the appearing of the other. It is a pre-original not resting on oneself, the restlessness of someone persecuted—Where to be? How to be?"

74. Levinas, *Totality and Infinity*, 163.

75. For example, see Marion's essay, "The Reason of the Gift," in Leask and Cassidy, *Givenness and God*, 109–10: "In principle, the duty of justice obliged the giver to distribute that which—in all justice—did not belong to him. In claiming to give, he has done nothing more than fulfill his duty of justice. Justice, which is the motive (internal reason) for the apparent gift, explains it and commands it as a simple duty. Consequently, the giver's claim to gratuity, and even the gift's entitlement to be called such, collapse in the face of a simple duty of justice—the duty to render to each his account, his due. . . . The gift is abolished in that which is due, and gratuity is abolished in solidarity. All that is operative is the symbolic exchange of sociality—the ultimate economy."

in order to preserve the possibility of the gift in all its lucid purity. Rein-
forcing the primacy of the gift even more, Marion attributes the lambent
arbitration of the will to divine grace. He considers the will and its decision always as gift. Levinas, on the other hand, expresses stern reservations
against the careless liberties of love that are presaged by the grammars of
gift—especially the heights of gift as enacted in forgiveness.[76] After all, the
gift may perpetuate a weak will that is exonerated from responsibility due
to the magnitude of the gift before and behind every noble and ignomini-
ous deed. Does not the gift—grace—prove to be too generous in that it
discharges the self from its messianic task in the name of a Messiah that
assumed all culpability and transgression to himself? Is not the integrity
of personal responsibility threatened by a ubiquitous gift that delivers all
that is good in spite of the irresponsible and negligent self? Nevertheless,
might a conciliation of complementarity be possible between grace and
responsibility? Augustine and Pelagius? Marion and Levinas? Gift and justice? Is it possible to imagine a vocation to justice whose energies match
its demands? An affirmative response to these questions is what is meant
by "dialectical theology." Neither a Lutheran either/or, nor a Hegelian synthesis, the dialectic proposed here is one that resists both opposition and
resolution. It is a relationship without rest or finality. It is that relationship
in which beginning is end, and end is beginning. More distant than the past
of historical memory, time immemorial—what Levinas calls diachrony—is
manifest and proclaimed in the *anamnesis* of the future and in the *prolepsis*
of the past. Liturgy and prophecy. Event and testimony.

My claim is not that Levinas ousts Marion, or that Marion defeats
Levinas, in a match of intellectual sparring. Rather, I suggest that each fills
out the deficiencies of the other inasmuch as neither are reducible to the
other. What I suggest is that freedom is reducible neither to grace nor to
self-sufficient responsibility for the other. Instead, authentic and comprehensive freedom is comprised of empowered responsibility that is inspired
by a law from without and a spirit from within. A plural alterity obtains
between exteriority and interiority. A call issues from without (the other
who faces me) and from within (the other inside of me, namely the divine
other—the absolute, conscience). Within the framework of dialectical theology, interiority and exteriority are not opposed to one another, but form
a union of complementarity. Law is not to be regarded as that which would
obstruct freedom, but that which promotes freedom to its highest measure

76. See Levinas, *Difficult Freedom*, 18, 20 (italics original): "*Justice* is the term Judaism prefers to terms more evocative of sentiment. For love itself demands justice.... No
one, not even God, can substitute himself for the victim. The world in which pardon is
all-powerful becomes inhuman."

by serving as its blueprint and script. Law, or Torah, liberates to the degree that it binds. A stunning paradox: the more I am bound to the other in responsibility for him or her, the freer he or she (and I) become. In the end, the wages of responsibility is freedom, and the elixir of responsibility is divine grace. For the term "grace" signifies not what is given without price and without obligation, but what is given with highest sacrifice, thereby obligating its recipient to reenact and to recapitulate the advent of the gift from an elsewhere without Cartesian coordinates or localized address. Justice transpires when the gift remains in circulation and the horizon of the temptation of temptation is folded happily away.

To suggest "a new dialectical theology of justice" means that, like truth, justice obtains to the measure that the dialectic between the self and the other is not dissolved.[77] Between actuality and possibility, between responsibility and freedom, between the community and the individual, one need not have to decide. Dialectical theology is not a matter of "one or the other," but of both actuality and possibility, both responsibility and freedom, both the community and the individual. Justice is a product of the refusal to reduce the other to the same, or to reduce the intersubjective ethical call to the call of givenness. At the same time, justice rests on the shoulders of the self and its determined determination to act justly for the sake of the other. As a figment of the infinite—the infinite in effigy—the temptation of temptation loses its appeal as grace delivers the reassurance of responsibility as the most precious reward. No other reward awaits on the hind side of responsibility since the illusory spoils of the temptation of temptation vanish back into the vanities that they really are. Grace, as the spiritual energy to be responsible for the other to the end—to the point of abandonment—abandons the field of the temptation of temptation in the name of the other who summons me beyond the claustrophobic world of evanescent stimuli and sensations. In the end, Levinas and Marion together offer voice and vision to the vocation of responsibility, empowered by the freedom of the gift.

77. For an account of how Levinas's notion of justice is the opening that makes relational fecundity possible, see Pinardi, "Expresión y Desnudez."

— CHAPTER 5 —

MATERNITY

But because he wished to justify himself, he said to Jesus, "And who is my neighbor?"

—Luke 10:29 (NAB)

Against the denials inflicted by failure, the simplicity of an extreme complexity, and a singularly mature infancy, is needed. That also is the sense of the death of God. Or of his life.

—Emmanuel Levinas, *Otherwise than Being or Beyond Essence*

ACCORDING TO EMMANUEL LEVINAS, the basic anthropological shape consists of a call and a response. This is what makes us human. The fact that the call of the other impresses itself upon me without relief is the very origin of my humanity. I am the responsible one and the measure I assume responsibility for the other who faces me determines the measure of humanity as humanity. The degree to which I am responsible for the other who faces me is at once the degree to which the other is humanized by my affirmative response to her. Responsibility for the other is that privileged movement whereby the stranger becomes the neighbor, whereby the least becomes the greatest, whereby the foreigner becomes the next of kin. For Levinas, there is no discrimination concerning the other who faces me. One of his principal claims is that it is not for me to decide who is other and, therefore, who calls to me. It is the one who calls who decides me, who decides my vocation, who decides my fate. As agent responsible, I am animated by the prevenient whisper of the other that awakens me to action (see 1 Kgs 19:12). Vigilance for the other defines the mission called human.

Within the arena of Levinas scholarship, the nomenclature of "the other" and "otherness" has witnessed wide application, spanning an innumerable array of social justice issues, ecological issues, and diversity issues in general—and rightly so. However, one glaring gap in recognizing the call of the other in Levinasian terms is that which is most essential within the human experience: the call of the infant in the womb. Even Levinas himself seems to be reticent concerning the call of this hidden other, perhaps due to the ambiguity within Rabbinic midrash as to when human life begins. In any case, it seems entirely fitting for Levinas scholarship to extend its reach into the most essential—where ethical exigency attains to its maximum threshold in relation to the magnitude of the other's call that increases in its acuity in proportion to the vulnerability of the visitant. In other words, as the name "infant" suggests (*in-fans*, "incapable of speech"), the one who lacks a voice calls the loudest. Even more, the faceless face speaks with greater ethical eloquence as it demands to be fashioned according to the steady hands of responsibility that tend its growth and development. With all of the twenty-first-century clarity of human embryology in mind, this essay will proceed to examine the call of the infant as the "first comer" (*le premier venu*) par excellence. After all, is it not the infant who comes on the scene first, before all others? Is not the advent of the infant the very personi-fication of the most extreme vulnerability and dependency?

In the text to follow, I will argue affirmatively in response to these and similar questions. First, I will consider in brief the universal form of hu-man vocation as incarnate responsibility for the other. Second, I will make a phenomenological sketch of maternity as material responsibility exercised one-for-the-other in relation to the infant. And third, I will consider the historical persona of Mary of Nazareth as paradigmatic for the maternal incarnation of responsibility as material corporeality, one flesh given up for the other. Altogether inspired by the Levinasian priority of the call, the voca-tion of motherhood will be revealed as the prophetic locus of intersubjective encounter that resists the cowardice of the *Akedah* ("the binding of Isaac") in favor of a return to the ethical, a return to the authentically human.[1]

I. Human Vocation as Incarnate Responsibility

Is there a universal human vocation, that is, a universal human way of being in the world? According to Emmanuel Levinas, the answer is an undeniable "yes." How should this universal human vocation be described? In many

1. See "Kierkegaard: Existence and Ethics" and "A Propos of Kierkegaard Vivant" in Levinas, *Proper Names*, 68–79; Beach and Powell, *Interpreting Abraham*, especially Laurence Bove's contribution, "Unbinding the Other: Levinas, the *Akedah*, and Going Beyond the Subject," 169–86; and Claire Katz's essay, "The Responsibility of Irresponsi-bility: Taking (Yet) Another Look at the Akedah," in Nelson et al., *Addressing Levinas*, 17–33.

ways, but within the grammar of Levinas, the term "responsibility" holds pride of place. In his 1982 interview with R. Fornetand A. Gómez, "Philosophy, Justice, Love," Levinas defined responsibility as "love of one's neighbor; love without Eros, charity, love in which the ethical aspect dominates the passionate aspect, love without concupiscence."[2] Yet he went on to say: "I don't very much like the word love, which is worn-out and debased. Let us speak instead of the taking upon oneself of the fate of the other."[3] Responsibility is first of all attentiveness toward the other, but so much more than attentiveness. It is solicitude for the other—being incessantly disquieted by the plight of the other. Responsibility signifies my personal affirmative response to the call of the other who faces me at every moment. Responsibility is disinterested, that is, lacking the self-interest that tends to dominate within the egocentric way of being in the world. Responsibility has come of age by disengaging the callow illusions of lust in their legion forms that never deliver on their promises.[4] To be human, in a word, is to be responsible. For responsibility, the fate of the other becomes my own, not because I determine this to be the case, but because the other's call to me designates me in my unique vocation as prophet and witness—a counterconsciousness that besieges me to the point of blessed surrender.[5]

In *Otherwise than Being or Beyond Essence*, Levinas articulates the meaning of responsibility with even more precision: "the-one-for-the-other in proximity . . . the form of sensibility or vulnerability, pure passivity or susceptibility, passive to the point of becoming an inspiration, that is, alterity in the same, the trope of the body animated by the soul, psyche in the form of a hand that gives even the bread taken from its own mouth. Here the psyche is the maternal body."[6] First, responsibility is living for the other. It implies a

2. Levinas, *Entre Nous*, 103.

3. Levinas, *Entre Nous*, 103.

4. See Levinas, *On Escape*, 62: "Pleasure is affectivity, precisely because it does not take on the forms of being, but rather attempts to break these up. Yet it is a deceptive escape. For it is an escape that fails. If, like a process that is far from closing up on itself, pleasure appears in a constant surpassing of oneself, it breaks just at the moment where it seems to get out absolutely. It develops with an increase in promises, which become richer the closer it comes to its paroxysm, but these promises are never kept."

5. See Levinas, *Entre Nous*, 58 (italics original): "Proximity is not a consciousness of proximity. It is an obsession which is not overenlarged consciousness, but counterconsciousness, reversing consciousness. It is an event that strips consciousness of its initiative, that undoes me and puts me before an Other in a state of guilt; an event that puts me in accusation—a persecuting indictment, for it is prior to all wrongdoing—and that leads me to the *self*, to the accusative that is not preceded by any nominative."

6. Levinas, *Otherwise than Being or Beyond Essence*, 67. Cf. Levinas, *Otherwise than Being or Beyond Essence*, 68 (italics original): "In renouncing intentionality as a guiding thread toward the eidos of the psyche, which would command the eidos of sensibility,

closeness and nearness in relation to the other—neighborliness. Responsibility does not attempt to insulate the self against the assailment of the other according to his nakedness and frailty, at times obscene and sensorily offensive,
and always protean, temperamental, and exceedingly fragile. Responsibility
is an active passivity that dutifully, yet courageously, makes itself liable to
the predicament of the other, prone to the trauma of the other, exposed to
the urgent needs of the other. Responsibility secures the warrant for the
passage of the other into the self—prophetic inspiration in which the word
(call) of the other is spoken from the lips of the self: "Here I am (for you)!"
Further, a word not only uttered but incarnate through corporeal solidarity
to the point of self-donation, self-divestment, self-forgetfulness—all the way
to self-abandonment to the point of exhaustion. All that I have is yours! At
the climax of this description, Levinas designates the maternal body, in all
its specificity, as the essence of this alterity in the same, this psychological
animation of the other within the same—in a word, pregnancy. Yet a meaning of pregnancy not only in reference to a particular state-of-affairs of a
woman's body, but the very identification with and vocation to motherhood.
Pregnancy signifies a distinct individuated other within the same. Relational
asymmetry in the flesh whereby the mother's body and entire being is put at
the service of the life within, the life of the infant.

   Why does the image of maternity figure so prominently within Levinas's
writings, especially within his later work? It is clear that, for him, maternity
signifies the paradigmatic instance of embodied responsibility for the other.
However, as Claire Katz points out in her essay, "From Eros to Maternity,"
"the initial ethical relation is one we can all understand through the intimacy
evoked by the image of mother and child. And the image of maternity disrupts the virile model given to us in the philosophical tradition. If Levinas's
philosophy has a specific audience in mind, that audience consists of those
who embody virility, those who rationalize, thematize, and totalize."[7] A secondary effect of Levinas's attunement to the phenomenality of maternity is
its unmasking and deconstruction of the blind spots of the Western philosophical tradition that are all too laden with the masculine optic, stigmatized
as overly detached, distanced, and disinterested. The historical evolution of

our analysis will follow sensibility in its prenatal signification to the maternal, where,
in proximity, signification signifies before it gets bent into *perseverance in being* in the
midst of a Nature"; and Levinas, *Otherwise than Being or Beyond Essence,* 64, 67, 72, 74,
77, 105, 109, 138, 195 (endnote 12).

   7. See Katz's "From Eros to Maternity" in Katz and Trout, *Levinas and the History
of Philosophy,* 2:171. Cf. "Damages Due to Fire" in Levinas, *Nine Talmudic Readings,*
183: "This maternal element in divine paternity is very remarkable, as is in Judaism the
notion of a 'virility' to which limits must be set and whose partial renouncement may
be symbolized by circumcision."

rationality, with its virile inclinations, has tended toward totalization according to its consistent thematic tropes: being, causality, principles, logical deduction, discursive reasoning, management and manipulation of data, for example, the Heideggerian *Zuhandenheit*, "readiness-to-hand." As if everything in the world were there for my self-referential placement of it! For Levinas, in contrast, I am not at the center of the universe. The cosmos is not ordered around me after all. Rather, the call of the other is the locus of meaning and flesh. My flesh protrudes into space in its reach for the other, at the service of the other. Human flesh is responsibility's incarnation for the sake of living for the other to the end. Maternity is the premier instance of the power of the body as responsibility inasmuch as it is the first respondent to *le premier venu*. In fact, the maternal flesh experiences itself as ordered, oriented, and enveloped around the other. The maternal body wraps itself around the body of the other as a vessel of responsibility, at once immanently personal and transcendently mysterious.

Even though maternity is paradigmatic of human responsibility, the-one-for-the-other, it is not a vocation exclusive to woman. Even though woman leads the way through her maternal shape of responsibility in attesting to the universal human vocation of responsibility, man, too, is summoned to these heights of humanity, though he must learn from woman the meaning of incarnate responsibility and responsible flesh for the other who beckons within.[8] Levinas reminds us that responsibility is not an abstract concept, not even a task to be carried out at a safe distance from the other who haunts my daily bourgeoisie existence. Rather, responsibility involves not only a proclamation of affirmative response to the other, but also a manifestation of this "yes" in and through the body. Again, maternity is the quintessential icon for embodied responsibility. From the incipient biological conception of the infant onward, the mother is giving over her body as home for her child: steady migration of the infant down the fallopian tube and into the uterine cavity; implantation of the infant into the

8. For example, see John Paul II, *Mulieris dignitatem*, 18 (italics original): "Motherhood involves a special communion with the mystery of life, as it develops in the woman's womb. The mother is filled with wonder at this mystery of life, and 'understands' with unique intuition what is happening inside her. In the light of the 'beginning,' the mother accepts and loves as a person the child she is carrying in her womb. This unique contact with the new human being developing within her gives rise to an attitude toward human beings—not only toward her own child, but every human being—which profoundly marks the woman's personality. It is commonly thought that *women* are more capable than men of paying attention *to another person*, and that motherhood develops this predisposition even more. The man—even with all his sharing in parenthood—always remains 'outside' the process of pregnancy and the baby's birth; in many ways he has to *learn* his own *'fatherhood'* from the mother."

endometrium; enfolding and nidation of the infant's body within the endometrial epithelium as within a nest; formation of the umbilical cord that establishes a symbiotic exchange of life between mother and child; secretion of amniotic fluid that encases the infant in a warm and hospitable sea of mystery; parturition and birthing the child into the light of day; nursing the infant from her breasts filled with the most nutritious milk for months, if not years, following birth; weaning the child, only to feed him by hand and to teach him how to feed himself so that he, too, one day may feed others from his own hand as he grows to the full stature of maturity. In every way, the body of the mother comports and lends itself to promote the life and development of the child. The phenomenological givenness and signification of the mother's body attest to this self-evident fact.[9]

As proximity of proximity, the body of woman-become-mother reveals the basic anthropological shape of being in relation to the other: being-for, being-from, and being-with.[10] In maternity, the raison d'être of the body is unveiled as gift to be shared, flesh to nourish, flesh to feed, flesh to embrace, flesh to house. In a provocative passage in *Time and the Other*, Levinas relates the paradox of materiality—of having a body—as that in which "the existent is occupied with itself [*s'occuper de soi*] . . . an enchainment to itself. . . . I am encumbered by myself . . . the tragedy of solitude . . . shut up within the captivity of its identity, because it is matter."[11] Matter—the materiality of

9. For a discussion on the relationship between feminist theory and maternity, see Katz, "Lisa Guenther's 'The Gift of the Other.'" In defense of my betrayal of the *Saying* by my descriptive *Said* of the maternal body, I do so in order to bring about more clarity concerning the *Said*—to move beyond the illusory language games that reinforce various political ideologies in favor of speaking accurately about phenomena and their primordial givenness and signification. It needs to be admitted that the *Said* always must be unsaid inasmuch as a person cannot be reduced to body parts, but by definition, transcends body parts, even if in and through the body. The call of the infant in the womb is interpreted in light of the meaning of the mother's body in relation to that of the infant. What signifies most prominently is the "for-you" of existence: I exist, body and soul, for you. I thank Rachel Vogel for her insightful comments and questions in response to my presentation of this material at the 2017 North American Levinas Society meeting at Loyola University Chicago.

10. See Ratzinger, *Truth and Tolerance*, 248: "Being completely free, without the competition of any other freedom, without any 'from' and 'for'—behind that stands, not an image of God, but the image of an idol. The primeval error of such a radically developed desire for freedom lies in the idea of a divinity that is conceived as being purely egotistical . . . the true God is of his own nature, being-for (Father), being-from (Son), and being-with (Holy Spirit). Yet man is in the image of God precisely because the being for, from, and with constitute the basic anthropological shape."

11. Levinas, *Time and the Other*, 56–57. Cf. Katz, "'Before the Face of God,'" 59: "We cannot . . . escape the connection we have to our bodies, or rather the adherence the self has to the body." For Levinas's appreciation, yet critique, of some Marxist insights, see

the body—is what delimits the spiritual self and its pretension to ubiquity. Riveted to myself, I am incapable of unchaining myself from my body—a body that is at once me. A primordial solitude of the self alone with itself, preoccupied with the relentless demands of its material being, I am held captive to myself, by myself and there is no escape. Unless . . . unless I am inspired to make a gift of myself, a gift of my body, to the other who faces me. An inspiration that comes from an elsewhere, redirecting the self to an elsewhere that is in no way concurrent with the self, the call of the other introduces new meaning and possibility for the heaviness and cursed turpitude of my self-absorbed flesh. Responsibility incarnate. So, it seems that I have two options when I come of age and face my flesh, perhaps for the first time. I either can recoil into the misery of my solitude, concerning myself with me and my possessions, or I can take leave of this pitiable place, out of pity and piety for the other who faces me as gift, contestation, and liberator. The latter signifies the predestination of my mortal frame according to the prevenient call of the other that surprises the mortality of individual being with the immortality of responsible relational intersubjectivity. Thanks to the feminine genius that lights the pathway to responsible flesh, I can follow her lead, rise, be on my way—on my way toward the other who was my author and destination all along. Because maternity is paradigmatic of corporeal and material responsibility for the other, let us make a closer examination of the specific contours of maternity.

II. Mother and Child: Maternity as Responsible Flesh

From a Levinasian perspective, the peculiarity of maternity begins with the notion of habitation. It has been said that "be it ever so humble, there's no place like home." The common human experience of departing from and returning to one's home is a copious source for philosophical reflection. Midway through *Totality and Infinity*, Levinas shifts into a discussion of the dwelling in relation to femininity, gentleness, and hospitality.[12] Building on

---

Katz, "'Before the Face of God,'" 59: "Marxism reveals the fundamental material nature of humanity. . . . In [Levinas's] view, the materialists' mistake was to equate the body with the self, at the price of 'a pure and simple negation of the spirit.'"

12. For a critique of Simone de Beauvoir's critique of Levinas as positing woman as privileged other, see Claire Katz's "Reinhabiting the House of Ruth: Exceeding the Limits of the Feminine in Levinas," in Chanter, *Feminist Interpretations of Emmanuel Levinas*, 145–70. For a critique of Luce Irigaray's challenge to Levinas's distantiation of the feminine, see Katz, "'For Love Is as Strong as Death.'" Moreover, see Katz, "'For Love Is as Strong as Death'" for Katz's argument that "(1) the feminine plays a significant if not indispensable role in his philosophical work, and (2) [Levinas's] view of the feminine

his treatment of enjoyment (*jouissance*), a concept that demonstrates the most basic form of the self's exodus from itself toward something other than the self, Levinas describes the dwelling—the home—as one of the most fundamental characteristics of the daily human drama. The dwelling signifies a particular feminine gestalt: "essential interiority . . . the inhabitant that inhabits (the home) before every inhabitant, the welcoming one par excellence, welcome in itself—the feminine being . . . every home *in fact* presupposes a woman . . . the very welcome of the dwelling."[13] Femininity, registered always and necessarily vis-à-vis masculinity, intimates its privileged meanings of motherhood: opening, canal, corporeal hollow, receptivity to gift, space for the other, belly, womb, welcome, wineskin, personal vessel, rich soil, Earth, guardian, gate, porter, mistress, protector, mystery.[14] Even the etymological roots of the word "vagina" are telling: "scabbard, sheath, or hull of an ear of grain or of a ship." Mature womanhood signifies at once motherhood as vocation and relation. In her psychosomatic constitution, woman announces empathy, embrace of the other, the very definition of hospitality. The phenomenality of wombness and pregnancy, in relation to the infant who dwells in the womb, indicates the essence of security and citadel.[15] For Levinas, the feminine face occupies a privileged place concerning the origin

---

is informed by the strong influence of the Judaic on his philosophical thought" (147). Cf. Catherine Charlier's essay, "Ethics and the Feminine," in Bernasconi and Critchley, *Re-Reading Levinas*, 119–29, and Charlier, *Figures du féminin*. For more on Levinas's treatment of the feminine, see "Judaism and the Feminine" in *Difficult Freedom*, 30–38; Levinas, *Time and the Other*, 84–90; and "And God Created Woman" in Levinas, *Nine Talmudic Readings*, 161–77.

13. Levinas, *Totality and Infinity*, 157–58 (italics original).

14. See Stein, *Essays on Woman*, 45, 132–33 (italics original): "Only the person blinded by the passion of controversy could deny that woman in soul and body is formed for a particular purpose . . . woman is destined to be wife and mother. . . . Woman naturally seeks to embrace that which is *living, personal, and whole*. To cherish, guard, protect, nourish and advance growth is her natural, maternal yearning . . . her natural line of thought . . . is directed intuitively and emotionally to the concrete. . . . The soul of woman must therefore be *expansive* and open to all human beings; it must be *quiet* so that no small weak flame will be extinguished by stormy winds; *warm* so as not to benumb fragile buds; *clear*, so that no vermin will settle in dark corners and recesses; *self-contained*, so that no invasions from without can imperil the inner life; *empty of itself*, in order that extraneous life may have room in it; finally, *mistress of itself* and also of its body, so that the entire person is readily at the disposal of every call. That is the ideal image of the gestalt of the feminine soul."

15. For an insightful reflection on the phenomenology of pregnancy and the summons to responsibility in pregnancy, see Hanoch Ben Pazi's essay, "Teaching as an Internalization of Feminine Aspects," in Hansel, *Levinas in Jerusalem*, 171–200. Similarly, see Claire Katz's illuminating discussion of Levinasian hospitality of the feminine in *Levinas, Judaism, and the Feminine*, 55–65.

of alterity—the epiphany of the personal other—inasmuch as the feminine face signifies maternity, welcome, gentleness—primordial *faiblesse* and the very event of vulnerability as the advent of the first comer (*le premier venu*) whereupon the first comer comes on the scene for the first time and indefinitely vis-à-vis the mother's smile.[16]

Is this not, at the same time, the anthropological origin of the meaning of "love?" Love as welcome and responsibility for the other? Levinas says as much when he writes that "love aims at the Other; it aims at him in his frailty [*faiblesse*]. . . . To love is to fear for another, to come to the assistance of his frailty. In this frailty as in the dawn rises the Loved, who is the Beloved. An epiphany of the Loved, the feminine . . . is but one with her regime of tenderness."[17] It seems that Levinas is suggesting that the essence of love is to affirm the call of the other, the good of the other—to assist him in his frailty, weakness, and fragility. The higher the degree of frailty, the higher the degree of assistance is needed. Does not the feminine affirmation of the other commence with the biological, spiritual, and personal conception of the other in the intimate recesses of her womb? Indeed. We are unable to identify any other rational genesis of the call of the other apart from the incipience of the infant's conception within her mother's womb. For this biological and spiritual event marks the inauguration and alpha point of the other's silent yet piercing call, introducing the infant as an individuated and distinct other in relation to his mother and father. Levinas insists that feminine alterity, as the spiritual and corporeal seedbed of transcendence that breaks up the menacing weight of being, initiates the silent language of familiarity, prior to the language between interlocutors.[18]

16. See Levinas, *Totality and Infinity*, 150–51 (italics original): "The welcoming of the face is peaceable from the first, for it answers to the unquenchable Desire for Infinity. . . . This peaceable welcome is produced primordially in the gentleness of the feminine face, in which the separated being can recollect itself, because of which it *inhabits*, and in its dwelling accomplishes separation. Inhabitation and the intimacy of the dwelling which make the separation of the human being possible thus imply a first revelation of the Other." For a phenomenological consideration of the mother's smile in relation to Catholic sacramental theology, see Sweeney, *Sacramental Presence after Heidegger*, especially "Conclusion: Sacramental Presence and the Mother's Smile," 225–39.

17. Levinas, *Totality and Infinity*, 256. Regarding the relationship between the (masculine) lover and the (feminine) beloved, see Levinas, *Totality and Infinity*, 257 (italics original): "The simultaneity or the equivocation of this fragility and this weight of non-signifyingness [non-significance], heavier than the weight of the formless real, we shall term *femininity*. The movement of the lover before this frailty of femininity, neither pure compassion nor impassiveness, indulges in compassion, is absorbed in the complacence of the caress."

18. See Levinas, *Totality and Infinity*, 155 (italics original): "The intimacy which familiarity already presupposes is an *intimacy with someone*. The interiority of

Levinas makes it clear that the face signifies before it appears. The face speaks before it is seen. The face summons to me before it is formed and in spite of its deformation. I encounter the face of the other as ethical expression above all, prior to and following its visual manifestation. Because it "breaks through the form that nevertheless delimits it," and because it is "the primordial *expression*, is the first word: 'you shall not commit murder,'" the face of the other, as "the epiphany of infinity is expression and discourse."[19] Yet "expression is not produced as the manifestation of an intelligible form that would connect terms to one another so as to establish, across distance, the assemblage of parts in a totality, in which the terms joined up already derive their meaning from the situation created by their community, which, in its turn, owes its meaning to the terms combined."[20] Rather, "expression precedes these coordinating effects visible to a third party. The event proper to expression consists in bearing witness to oneself, and guaranteeing this witness. This attestation of oneself is possible only as a face, that is, as speech."[21] The face, therefore, signifies speech that pours forth from the exigencies and exorbitance of responsibility. The word of the other is spoken from my lips—a prophetic wonder—but originates with the other's face as expression. For instance, the paradox of the speech of the voiceless other—the infant, voiceless one par excellence—is spoken audibly by the one who speaks as proxy for the other, the one who acts in responsibility for the other, the one who substitutes herself, one-for-the-other: in a word, the mother. Maternity is conceived in prophetic proximity—one in which the other is borne within the same and in which the other envelopes the same. Alterity of the infant establishes the fait accompli of maternity in proportion to which alterity of the mother establishes the fait accompli of infancy.

In her spiritual reflection on the life and works of Teresa of Ávila, Edith Stein writes that "God is love, and love is goodness giving itself

---

recollection is a solitude in a world already human. Recollection refers to a welcome. . . . And the other whose presence is discreetly an absence, with which is accomplished the primary hospitable welcome which describes the field of intimacy, is the Woman. The woman is the condition for recollection, the interiority of the Home, and inhabitation. . . . The Other who welcomes in intimacy is not the *you* [*vous*] of the face that reveals itself in a dimension of height, but precisely the *thou* [*tu*] of familiarity: a language without teaching, a silent language, and understanding without words, an expression in secret. The I-Thou in which Buber sees the category of interhuman relationship is the relation not with the interlocutor but with feminine alterity. . . . And this is a new and irreducible possibility, a delightful lapse in being, and the source of gentleness in itself."

19. Levinas, *Totality and Infinity*, 198–200 (italics original).
20. Levinas, *Totality and Infinity*, 201.
21. Levinas, *Totality and Infinity*, 201.

away."[22] Similarly, Levinas writes that "goodness consists in taking up a position in being such that the Other counts more than myself. Goodness thus involves the possibility for the I that is exposed to the alienation of its powers by death to not be for death."[23] In stark contrast to the Heideggerian being-toward-death, Levinas points to the possibility of being-toward-the-death-of-the-other, or more precisely, being-toward-the-good-of-the-other, or being-toward-the-life-of-the-other. This selfless and self-forgetful attitude characterizes the heights of responsibility.[24] At the same time, the term "goodness" is related directly to that of "fecundity." The process of love, by which goodness gives itself away, is fecundity, fertility, fruitfulness, procreation. In reproductive fecundity, the possibility of personal transubstantiation is opened, wherein "the I transcends the world of light—not to dissolve into the anonymity of the *there is*, but in order to go further than the light, to go *elsewhere*. . . . Fecundity engendering fecundity accomplishes goodness: above and beyond the sacrifice that imposes a gift, the gift of the power of giving, the conception of the child."[25] Both mother

22. Stein, *Hidden Life*, 38. Cf. Levinas, *Otherwise than Being or Beyond Essence*, 122, 187 (endnote 8) (italics original): "This antecedence of responsibility to freedom would signify the Goodness of the Good: the necessity that the Good choose me first before I can be in a position to choose, that is, welcome its choice. That is my pre-originary *susceptiveness*. It is a passivity prior to all receptivity, it is transcendent. It is an antecedence prior to all representable antecedence: immemorial. The Good is before being. . . . The Good invests freedom—it loves me before I love it. Love is love in this antecedence. . . . The Good as the infinite has no other, not because it would be the whole, but because it is Good and nothing escapes its goodness."

23. Levinas, *Totality and Infinity*, 247.

24. See Levinas, *Otherwise than Being or Beyond Essence*, 115, 117: "An abnegation of oneself fully responsible for the other. . . . This self is out of phase with itself, forgetful of itself, forgetful in biting in upon itself, in the reference to itself which is the gnawing away at oneself of remorse. . . . It is a being divesting itself, emptying itself of its being, turning itself inside out, and if it can be put thus, the fact of 'otherwise than being.'" Note that this "otherwise than being" still depends on the originality and antecedence of being in a metaphysical sense. This is precisely the relationship between the a priori kataphatic movement and the a posteriori apophatic movement, in a theological sense. In other words, no apophasis without first kataphasis; no "otherwise than being" without first being.

25. Levinas, *Totality and Infinity*, 268–69 (italics original). Also, see Levinas, *Totality and Infinity*, 268–69: "The relation with the son in fecundity does not maintain us in this closed expanse of light and dream, cognitions and powers. It articulates the time of the absolutely other, an alteration of the very substance of him who can—his transsubstantiation"; and Levinas, *Totality and Infinity*, 266 (italics original): "I love fully only if the Other loves me, not because I need the recognition of the Other, but because my voluptuosity delights in (her) voluptuosity, and because in this unparalleled conjuncture of identification, in this *trans-substantiation*, the same and the other are not united but precisely—beyond every possible project, beyond every meaningful and intelligent power—engender the child."

and father are transubstantiated in the advent of their child, thereby surpassing the solstices of being and the light of phenomenal appearances.
The conception of the infant signifies the in-breaking of an elsewhere—an
otherwise-than-being—that achieves the transcendent itinerary of goodness by commencing the empowerment of the other and the return-gift of
the infant *ex nihilo*. Even biology and physiology, though included in the
overarching hermeneutic, are exceeded according to the insufficiencies of
their limited ontic capacities.[26] In other words, the call of the infant deflects
an interpretive reductionism to body parts alone. The infant cannot be reduced to a less-than-human conglomerate of cells, or any other language
game that would obscure the veracity of the infant's self-signification, without betraying her clarion call that arises upon the dawn of a single cell,
irreducible to the body of the mother or the father, for it is the new body of
the infant. In fact, the call of the infant is issued long before the biological
unfolding of her anatomical face. In this sense, the expression of the infant's face introduces itself at conception. Those that would demand to see
a naked developed face with naked eye in order to validate the call of the
other miss Levinas's claim entirely: that the call of the other is contingent
on neither appearance nor objective manifestation, but solely on personal
alterity and vulnerability, whether seen or unseen, whether present or absent.[27] What gives itself in the advent of the infant is life, relationality, alterity, vocation. And the only properly human response to incarnate personal
alterity is incarnate personal responsibility.

26. Levinas, *Totality and Infinity*, 277: "The son is not only my work, like a poem or
an object, nor is he my property. Neither the categories of power nor those of knowledge describe my relation with the child. The fecundity of the I is neither a cause nor a
domination. I do not have my child; I am my child. . . . The fecundity of the I is its very
transcendence. The biological origin of this concept nowise neutralizes the paradox of
its meaning, and delineates a structure that goes beyond the biologically empirical." Cf.
Katz, "'For Love Is as Strong as Death,'" 128–29: "Love reaches out beyond itself to make
itself permanent. . . . Levinas's point in stressing fecundity is the emphasis on the asymmetrical responsibility that is characteristically unique to the parent/child relation. . . .
Through my child, I am able to be responsible for the other, even after my own death."

27. See Levinas, *Otherwise than Being or Beyond Essence*, 88–89, 120: "The face
of a neighbor signifies for me an unexceptional responsibility, preceding every free
consent, every pact, every contract. It escapes representation; it is the very collapse of
phenomenality. Not because it is too brutal to appear, but because in a sense too weak,
non-phenomenon because less than a phenomenon. The disclosing of a face is nudity,
non-form, abandon of self, ageing, dying, more naked than nudity. It is poverty, skin
with wrinkles, which are a trace of itself. . . . The proximity does not enter into the common time of clocks, which makes meetings possible. It is a disturbance. . . . The tropes
of ethical language are found to be adequate for certain structures of the description:
for the sense of the approach in its contrast with knowing, the face in its contrast with
a phenomenon."

When Levinas writes about the transubstantiation of mother and father into the life of their child, he has in mind an erotic transubstantiation
in which

> *eros* delivers from this encumberment [of the I], arrests the re-
> turn of the I to itself. . . . Fecundity is part of the very drama of
> the I. The intersubjective reached across the notion of fecundity
> opens up a plan where the I is divested of its tragic egoity, which
> turns back to itself, and yet is not purely and simply dissolved into
> the collective. Fecundity evinces a unity that is not opposed to
> multiplicity, but, in the precise sense of the term, engenders it.[28]

What, after all, is the intentionality of *eros*? Is it not aimed at its fertile fulfillment in the creation of the infant?[29] *Eros* functions as a privileged vehicle
for providing a means of escape for the self from itself. Yet this departure
is secondary to what *eros* intended to accomplish all along, whether or not
the self was consciously aware of its comprehensive circuit or meaning. That
at which *eros* aims is its multiplication—its proliferation and expansion—
inasmuch as Plato's intuition about the transcendental teleology of *eros* is
rooted in and oriented toward truth, goodness, and beauty (not always in
that precise order of attraction). Truth, goodness, and beauty, by their very
nature, are destined to be shared and to be enjoyed. Erotic ecstasy, set out in
pursuit of its raison d'être, encounters its unsuspected and insatiable inversion through the phenomenality of fecundity and its attendant demands of
responsibility. Mother and father are not permitted to return to themselves
because there is no time left to do so. It is all spent in service of their little

28. Levinas, *Totality and Infinity*, 271, 273. Also, see Levinas, *Totality and Infinity*,
276–77, here Levinas critiquing Freud's *libido* principle that dominates his psychoanal-
yses, stopping short of the meaning of the phenomenon of fecundity. Instead, Levinas
proposes to let *eros* reach all the way to its prized destination, namely, fecundity: "What
remains unrecognized [by Freud] is that the erotic, analysed as fecundity, breaks up
reality into relations irreducible to the relations of genus and species, part and whole,
action and passion, truth and error; that in sexuality the subject enters into relation
with what is absolutely other, with an alterity of a type unforeseeable in formal logic,
with what remains other in the relation and is never converted into 'mine,' and that
nonetheless this relation has nothing ecstatic about it, for the pathos of voluptuosity
is made of duality. . . . Sexuality is in us neither knowledge nor power, but the very
plurality of our existing." Cf. Levinas, *Otherwise than Being or Beyond Essence*, 192
(endnote 27): "Beneath erotic alterity there is the alterity of the-one-for-the-other,
responsibility before eros." For an analysis of Levinasian ethics as marked by sexual
difference, see Claire Katz's "From Eros to Maternity: Love, Death, and 'the Feminine'
in the Philosophy of Emmanuel Levinas" in Tirosh-Samuelson, *Women and Gender in
Jewish Philosophy*, 153–75.

29. For similar sentiments, see "Concerning the Third Party, and Its Arrival" in
Marion, *Erotic Phenomenon*, 184–222.

vulnerable ones whose needs crave as an echo of the yearnful romance that gave rise to the life of the infant because life was too precious to keep to oneself: "Two are better off than one, in that they have greater benefit from their earnings. For should they fall, one can raise the other; but woe betide him who is alone and falls with no companion to raise him! Further, when two lie together they are warm; but how can he who is alone get warm? Also, if one attacks, two can stand up to him. A threefold cord is not readily broken!"[30] Plurality is the prerequisite for unity, and unity promotes plurality to the degree that it resists the collapse of the same back into the same and only the same. Identity without *eros* is nothing other than the impersonal rustling of the *il y a* and the ruins of a city not set on a hill. Rather, as premier voyage from the self to the other, fecundity opens the sociality of mother, father, and infant, and the adventure of goodness giving itself away.

III. Mama: Maternity as Susceptibility, Passivity, and Name

The human body makes it possible to give to the other in a human way. Human flesh is the medium whereby incarnate responsibility is exercised, the-one-for-the-other. Flesh empowers spirit inasmuch as it is its antithesis. Because of the material body, spirit is granted the vocation to go as far as incarnation, wherein matter becomes materiality and the signifyingness of responsibility.[31] Because of the material body, spirit can reach as far as its humiliation and humanization in its opposite. In other words, there is nothing further from God than matter, and yet there is nothing dearer to God than matter. So much distance, so much room to love. Love and responsibility express themselves no more eloquently than in and through the frailty of the flesh: nakedness,

30. Eccl 4:9–12 (JPS Tanakh translation).

31. See Levinas, *Otherwise than Being or Beyond Essence*, 74, 77–79: "Only a subject that eats can be for-the-other, or can signify. Signification, the-one-for-the-other, has meaning only among beings of flesh and blood. . . . It is the openness, not only of one's pocketbook, but of the doors of one's home. . . . The immediacy of the sensibility is the for-the-other of one's own materiality; it is the immediacy or the proximity of the other. The proximity of the other is the immediate opening up for the other of the immediacy of enjoyment, the immediacy of taste, materialization of matter, altered by the immediacy of contact. . . . Signification signifies, consequently, in nourishing, clothing, lodging, in maternal relations, in which matter shows itself for the first time in its materiality . . . matter is the very locus of the for-the-other . . . an irrecuperable pre-ontological past, that of maternity. . . . Identity here takes form not by a self-confirmation, but, as a signification of the-one-for-the-other, by a deposing of oneself, a deposing which is the incarnation of the subject, or the very possibility of giving, of dealing signifyingness. . . . The subjectivity of sensibility, taken as incarnation, is an abandon without return, maternity, a body suffering for another, the body as passivity and renouncement, a pure undergoing."

exposure, susceptibility, vulnerability. Passivity signifies the heights of spirit because it is the erotically sober desire of spirit to give itself away. Spirit invites the coring out of the ego, not because that is its highest possibility, but because it recognizes this procedure to be its very identity and hospitable movement—"the trace of this *hither side* of things."[32]

Levinas identifies maternity as the incarnate meaning of responsibility—where responsibility for the other is inscribed upon the feminine flesh: auspicious opening, welcoming womb, delightful dwelling, bountiful breasts, body of embrace. Maternity, Levinas says, is the "gestation of the other in the same."[33] Is this not the meaning of incarnate prophecy, in which the voice of the other calls out from within the self—a fortiori, that in which the flesh of the other is borne within the self? Maternity is the incarnation of universal intersubjectivity, the non-identity of the other emerging within the identity of the self that resists the complacency of indifference:

32. See Levinas, *Otherwise than Being or Beyond Essence*, 197 (endnote 26) (italics original): "This absolute passivity beneath the neutrality of things takes on the form of incarnation, corporeity—susceptibility to pain, outrage and unhappiness. It bears in its susceptibility the trace of this *hither side* of things, as the responsibility for that of which there was no will, in the persecuted one, in ipseity, that is, as responsibility for the very persecution it suffers"; and Levinas, *Otherwise than Being or Beyond Essence*, 64, 109, 180–81 (italics original): "Not in elevated feelings, in 'belles lettres,' but as in a tearing away of bread from the mouth that tastes it, to give it to the other. Such is the coring out (*dénucléation*) of enjoyment, in which the nucleus of the ego is cored out. . . . The expression 'in one's skin' is not a metaphor for the in-itself; it refers to a recurrence in the dead time or the *meanwhile* which separates inspiration and expiration, the diastole and systole of the heart beating dully against the walls of one's skin. The body is not only an image or figure here; it is the distinctive in-oneself of the contraction of ipseity and its breakup. . . . This recurrence is incarnation. In it the body which makes giving possible makes one *other* without alienating. For this other is the heart, and the goodness, of the same, the inspiration or the very psyche in the soul. . . . The approach of the neighbor is a fission of the subject beyond lungs, in the resistant nucleus of the ego, in the undividedness of its individuality. . . . That the breathing by which entities seem to affirm themselves triumphantly in their vital space would be a consummation, a coring out of my substantiality, that in breathing I already open myself to my subjection to the whole of the invisible other, that the beyond or the liberation would be the support of a crushing charge, is to be sure surprising."

33. See Levinas, *Otherwise than Being or Beyond Essence*, 75: "Sensibility is being affected by a non-phenomenon, a being put in question by the alterity of the other, before the intervention of a cause, before the appearing of the other . . . it is maternity, gestation of the other in the same. . . . In maternity what signifies is a responsibility for others, to the point of substitution for others and suffering both from the effect of persecution and from the persecuting itself in which the persecutor sinks. Maternity, which is bearing par excellence, bears even responsibility for the persecuting by the persecutor." Cf. "Damages Due to Fire" in Levinas, *Nine Talmudic Readings*, 183 (italics original): "*Rakhamim* is the relation of the uterus to the *other*, whose gestation takes place within it."

"an animate body or an incarnate identity is the signifyingness of this non-indifference."[34] Maternity serves as the tonic for the tonality of humanity. Non-indifferent to the predicament of the other—the other as recurring crisis for the ego—"the evocation of maternity in this metaphor suggests to us the proper sense of the oneself. The oneself cannot form itself; it is already formed with absolute passivity. . . . In the exposure to wounds and outrages, in the feeling proper to responsibility, the oneself is provoked as irreplaceable, as devoted to the others, without being able to resign, and thus as incarnated in order to offer itself, to suffer and to give."[35] Here Levinas is getting at the phenomenological signification of the self. Before anything else, the self is absolutely passive before the other: the alterity of the elemental, the alterity of every enjoyment, and, above all, the alterity of the personal other who faces me. The rationale of having a material body as a spiritual subject—an incarnate person—is disclosed within the experience of ethical exigency stemming from the more native experience of maternity. This is an experience in which I realize, long after the fact, that my body signifies the potential of offering, the potential of suffering, the potential of making of itself a gift unto the other for the good of the other. Thanks to the anthropological testimony of maternity, I am invited into the fold of gift and responsibility. Due to the responsibility of my anonymous (to me) biological mother and to the responsibility of my adoptive mother, Linda, I live today, summoned, as were they, to make of myself, at once my body and soul, a gift, the-one-for-the-other.

My body circulates, flexes, and moves as gift. Offering is its itinerary inasmuch as "the sensible—maternity, vulnerability, apprehension—binds the node of incarnation into a plot larger than the apperception of the self. In this plot I am bound to others before being tied to my body," all the way to substituting myself for the other because I in no way can peel myself back from the proximity between the other and me.[36] More intimate than my inability to

34. See Levinas, *Otherwise than Being or Beyond Essence*, 69, 71 (italics original): "In the form of responsibility, the psyche in the soul is the other in me, a malady of identity, both accused and *self*, the same for the other, the same by the other. . . . Such a signification is only possible as an incarnation. The animation, the very pneuma of the psyche, alterity in identity, is the identity of a body exposed to the other, becoming 'for the other,' the possibility of giving. . . . An animate body or an incarnate identity is the signifyingness of this non-indifference." For an analysis of Maurice Merleau-Ponty's accounts of intersubjectivity, especially that of the child, see Katz, "Significance of Childhood."

35. Levinas, *Otherwise than Being or Beyond Essence*, 104–5.

36. Levinas, *Otherwise than Being or Beyond Essence*, 76. Cf. Levinas, *Otherwise than Being or Beyond Essence*, 195 (endnote 12): "The body is neither an obstacle opposed to the soul, nor a tomb that imprisons it, but that by which the self is susceptibility

shed my own skin is my bond of responsibility for the other, since it is older
than the unfolding of my nascent skin. In its adolescent course of rebellion,
freedom revolts at its inability to evacuate its corporeal terminus. Freedom
cannot overcome finitude—this menacing fact of being that I am and there's
nothing I can do about it, that I cannot take leave of my body and there's
nothing I can do about it, that I am I and there's nothing I can do about it.
However, Levinas insists that "in the proximity of contact arises every committed freedom, which is termed finite by contrast with the freedom of choice
of which consciousness is the essential modality. . . . This freedom enveloped
in a responsibility which it does not succeed in shouldering is the way of
being a creature, the unlimited passivity of a self, the unconditionality of a
self."[37] As revealed in the Torah and in Talmudic wisdom, authentic human
freedom is a committed freedom. It is a freedom lived out in and through
the finitude of the flesh—a finitude forgotten and surpassed to the degree
of solicitude for the other. For finitude steps foot across the threshold of the
infinite every time a sacramental material offering is enacted from me to the
other and from the other to me. Sacramental because the infinite is signified
(even as a trace) on finite flesh become gift. Even though I am overwhelmed
by the weight of responsibility that presses upon my entire physical frame and
spiritual soul, I admit no conditions to the possibilities of responsibility that
in turn overwhelm the alleged actualities of prejudice.

   Any treatment of maternity that stopped short of reckoning with its
incomparable intimacy and denomination would bypass the very meaning
of the term. Maternity, or motherhood, is a concrete phenomenon before
all else. The mother has a name, and so does the infant, her child. What
is the name of the mother? Who is she that Hebrew Scripture touts as the
lofty mountain (Ps 68:16–17; Isa 2:2), the dwelling of the Most High (Pss
46:5; 65:4; 122), the one who treads upon serpents (Gen 3:15), the bride
bedecked with her jewels (Isa 61:10), the queen bedecked in the gold of
Ophir (Ps 45:10), the royal princess (Ps 45:14), the barren wife who bears
seven sons (1 Sam 2:5)? What mother in history affords us the paradigmatic of maternity whereby "the paradigmatic is the real?"[38] Who is the

---

itself. Incarnation is an extreme passivity; to be exposed to sickness, suffering, death, is
to be exposed to compassion, and, as a self, to the gift that costs. The oneself is on this
side of the zero of inertia and nothingness, in deficit of being, in itself and not in being,
without a place to lay its head, in the no-grounds, and thus without conditions. As such
it will be shown to be the bearer of the world, bearing it, suffering it, blocking rest and
lacking a fatherland. It is the correlate of a persecution, a substitution for the other."

   37. Levinas, *Otherwise than Being or Beyond Essence*, 76, 195 (endnote 13). Cf.
"Temptation of Temptation," in Levinas, *Nine Talmudic Readings*, 30–50.

   38. See Tracy, *Analogical Imagination*, 193, and Wallenfang, *Dialectical Anatomy of
the Eucharist*, 215–44.

faithful mother that mothered for all with the translatable and transposable speech of *fiat*? It is the mother whose womb was blessed, but whose heart was pierced. It is the mother who persuaded water to become wine and men to become warriors through the power of passivity. It is the mother whose state of solicitude was matched only by her passion for the possible. It is the mother who followed her son all the way to his humiliation and execution, all the way to his expiration and grave. It is the mother who radiates the glory of susceptibility in the flesh, radical passivity in the flesh, sensibility in the flesh, exposure in the flesh, signifyingness of non-indifference in the flesh, body given up as the-one-for-the-other in the flesh. Who is she? Mary of Nazareth, the Mother of God, *Madonna della Strada*—"Our Lady of the Wayside": handmaid of alterity, servant of the call, queen of substitution, the-one-for-the-other, all the way to the cross.

CHAPTER 6

MYSTICAL HERMENEUTICS

Be patient toward all that is unsolved in your heart and try to
love the questions themselves, like locked rooms and like books
that are now written in a very foreign tongue. Do not now seek
the answers, which cannot be given you because you would not
be able to live them. And the point is, to live everything. Live the
questions now. Perhaps you will then gradually, without notic-
ing it, live along some distant day into the answer.

—Rainer Maria Rilke, *Letters to a Young Poet*,
  Letter Three, April 23, 1903

LEVINAS LOATHED THE WORDS "sacred" and "mystical" because of their tacit
implications of irrationality and irresponsibility. Yet perhaps it is precisely
such terms and their multiple meanings that would surprise Levinas as the
unsuspected other in relation to the sameness of his own thought.

I. Introduction to a Problem

The problem is called "the natural attitude." A term coined by Husserl as
an imperial obstacle for phenomenology (and for pure perception), the
natural attitude implies unwarranted bias, prejudice, presupposition, and
even dogmatic realism in the one who experiences something. The natural
attitude indicates a judgment made about "the real" before it is experienced as given or signified. According to Husserl, if I am to receive that
which gives or signifies itself within my experience in an unobstructed
way, I must bracket (or set aside) this natural attitude in order to maintain "the most perfect freedom from presuppositions."[1] This bracketing is

---

1. Husserl, *Ideas Pertaining to a Pure Phenomenology*, 148. For a discussion of the
evolution of the phenomenological reduction within the history of phenomenology, see
Wallenfang, *Dialectical Anatomy of the Eucharist*, 12–21.

called the phenomenological reduction, or *epoché* ("cessation, suspension, withholding, bracketing"). By exercising the reduction before, during, and even after an experience, I am able to intuit the fullness of what gives or signifies itself within the experience.[2]

Without performing this intentional reduction within my experience, I inevitably reduce what gives or signifies itself to less than what it gives or signifies. Without recourse to the phenomenological reduction, I experience with less clarity, precision, and fidelity to the phenomenon. To avoid a reductionism within my experience, I must reduce that which threatens to reduce the experience to less than is given or signified. In other words, phenomenology works to reduce the reductionism that often can happen within experience. To prevent a reductive interpretation of experience, I must reduce the impending reductionism. More specifically, I must suspend judgment as to "what is, what is real, what is the case"—in a word, the hasty defining and categorizing tendencies of metaphysics and physics (natural science)—in order to let phenomena give and signify themselves as they may, according to their own terms.

All well and good, but how do I effectively bracket my menacing natural attitude, especially when I have been enculturated into it irrevocably, without withdrawing from a community of interpreters and developing an antisocial and psychopathic personality? This is a difficult task indeed—so difficult that one risks social alienation and ostracism in the very practice of the method, but not because the method is inherently antisocial. Living with a phenomenological perspective puts me at risk of being interpreted by physicians and metaphysicians alike as a fool, a dreamer, a profligate—an intellectual pariah because I have betrayed the socially acceptable system of categories and conventions.[3] If I pause to smell the rose for too long, I am made out to be strange and subversive, laughable and lecherous, pusillanimous (*pusus*: "small child") and prepubescent. The price to be paid by

2. See Merleau-Ponty, *Phenomenology of Perception*, xiii: "The best formulation of the reduction is probably that given by Eugen Fink, Husserl's assistant, when he spoke of 'wonder' in the face of the world. Reflection does not withdraw from the world towards the unity of consciousness as the world's basis; it steps back to watch the forms of transcendence fly up like sparks from a fire; it slackens the intentional threads which attach us to the world and thus brings them to our notice; it alone is consciousness of the world because it reveals that world as strange and paradoxical."

3. For accounts concerning the power of the uncanny and the testimony of the fool, see Tracy, *Analogical Imagination*, 357: "The experience of the uncanny awaits us everywhere in the situation"; and Schrijvers, *Introduction to Jean-Yves Lacoste*, 97: "For Lacoste, the religious fool is able, precisely because of his unsettling otherness, to make others restless. Hence, the phenomenological task of the fool is to make the liturgical transgression of the world visible to all others . . . for it is precisely such a visibility which allows the other to truly see what is hidden through the masks one likes to wear."

every prophet is persecution and potential social failure. So is it worth the risk? If I bracket my natural attitude, and even the collective natural attitude of my socio-cultural milieu, do I not at once hazard a bracketing of my reputation, my honor, my pride? Indeed. But I have heard the uncanny testimony that there are pearls more precious than these, and it is these that I seek.[4] Yet who will guide me in this pursuit?

The natural phenomenologist par excellence: the child. It is the child who questions all: Why? It is the child who perceives with wonder: What? It is the child who is radically dependent and beholden to the other: Who? Because the child childs, and can do no other, she leads the way toward an authentic and unpretentious reduction of the natural attitude (because she has none) and an unadulterated encounter with what gives and says itself in experience. For the child does not analyze experience, but simply experiences. I cannot perform the phenomenological reduction in me by merely willing it. Rather, it depends on an inspiration and instigation from elsewhere—an elsewhere unleashed within the heart of the self. Without the concrete model and guide of a natural phenomenologist, I fail to comprehend lived perception uncircumscribed by the natural attitude. I need someone to show me how it is done—how I, too, can perceive phenomena with near perfect purity and disinhibition.

The remainder of this chapter will aim at expressing the meaning of phenomenology as inspired by the child that leads to theological or religious experience: a theology of childhood. I will argue that the child is the natural phenomenologist and that she is necessary to guide the adult to the threshold of phenomenological perception. First, I will introduce the phenomenological goal of givenness through the work of Jean-Luc Marion. Second, through the work of Maurice Merleau-Ponty, I will make the case that the most valid pathway to access phenomenal givenness is through observation and contemplation of the child. Third, I will suggest a rational theological enclave within phenomenological investigation: the tradition of Carmelite spirituality. An affinity and common genus will be suggested between the phenomenological outlook of the child and Carmelite mysticism. Fourth and finally, I will recapitulate the argument by introducing the concept of a theology of childhood in order to expand the parameters of phenomenology and to intimate the largess of possibility within human experience.

---

4. See Matt 13:45–46 (NAB): "Again, the kingdom of heaven is like a merchant searching for fine pearls. When he finds a pearl of great price, he goes and sells all that he has and buys it.'"

II. Mystical Givenness

In the opening sentence of his 2013 article on the artwork of James Turrell, entitled "Contemplative Recovery," Jeffrey Kosky writes that "one way to understand modernity is as the age in which contemplation is repressed, marginalized, or otherwise forgotten."[5] Surely, this amnesia toward contemplation is symptomatic of our times. Could this condition also be attributed to the inability to see with the phenomenological gaze? It should come as no surprise to those familiar with the writings of Jean-Luc Marion that his phenomenology of givenness would be linked to mysticism. With his innovative recognition of the possibility of the saturated phenomenon, Marion, at the same time, admits the possibility of mystical experience. Once again in the history of Western philosophy, it is rationally permissible to encounter God in a personal way. Proving the limits of possibility as imposed by the overconfidence of the Western Enlightenment to be intellectually illicit, phenomenology has lifted the veil of skepticism and has brought the veracity of saturated phenomena into view.[6] Since his early studies on the Eastern Christian mystics in relation to the Romantic and Nihilist movements of the eighteenth, nineteenth, and twentieth centuries, Marion has given new voice to the question of God, or, rather, has allowed the divine to speak afresh without being interrupted so rudely.[7] Not only has Marion challenged the blanket prohibition of divine revelation and its possibility, he has chided the Christian tradition for thinking the divine in terms of being as the primary analogue. Since making a splash in the English-speaking world with his debut, God without Being, Marion has continued to pursue thinking and encountering the divine in terms of personal and relational love.

5. Kosky, "Contemplative Recovery," 44.

6. See Marion's Introduction in Kessler and Sheppard, Mystics, 5: "Saturated phenomena should not be constituted at all, and what we experience with them is precisely an intuition overwhelming any possible concept. This is not because the saturated phenomenon is irrational but because we are unable to be rational enough to produce concepts matching the intuition that is nevertheless in fact given. . . . Thus in front of the saturated phenomenon, we must admit our lack of concepts, that is, of rationality."

7. For Marion's head-on interface with the work of Nietzsche, Hölderlin, and the Pseudo-Dionysius, see Marion, Idol and Distance. Likewise, see Leask and Cassidy, Givenness and God, for example, 1: "Indeed, the 'postmetaphysical' confrontation with nihilism is probably the defining feature of Marion's intellectual and spiritual project" (from Leask's and Cassidy's introduction); and Marion's "Preface to the English Edition" in Marion, God without Being, xix. For Marion's uptake of the Eastern Christian mystics, especially Dionysius the Areopagite and Gregory of Nyssa, see Jones, Genealogy of Jean-Luc Marion's Philosophy of Religion. For more on the backdrop of Christian mysticism in general, see McGinn, Foundations of Mysticism, and Louth, Origins of the Christian Mystical Tradition.

Most recently, in *The Visible and the Revealed*, he writes of the rationality and logic of love as revealed in Christ, not only in words, but even
more so in deeds, namely, in his passion and resurrection.[8] Likewise, in his
study on Augustine, entitled *In the Self's Place*, he speaks of love in this way:
"Absolute and unconditioned transcendental love operates in such a way
that no condition of possibility can impose any limits on it, nor therefore
any impossibility."[9] This statement sounds remarkably similar to the terms
through which he described givenness, along with Husserl's definition,
nineteen years prior in *Reduction and Givenness*: "Givenness alone is absolute, free and without condition, precisely because it gives."[10] One is left to
wonder, does love lead to givenness or does givenness lead to love or does
it even matter which leads to the other? In any case, there is no question
that a close relationship obtains between love and givenness in the work of
Marion. This chapter will argue that the phenomenological conversion of the
natural attitude and the ensuing access to givenness lead to a recognition of
divine love and contemplative prayer. It will be argued further that Carmelite
spirituality, in particular, lends itself to relating the mystical experiences of
prayer to which a phenomenology of givenness leads. In the end, Marion's
phenomenology of givenness will be characterized as a "theology of childhood" which regards hermeneutic accoutrements to be obstructive for pure
givenness.[11] The child will be portrayed as contemplative par excellence in
the way she demonstrates the intentionality of wonder and awe before the
deluge of intuition emanating from a saturating universe.

III. Givenness: *Manuductio* to Contemplation

The first question concerning the givenness of a particular phenomenon is
how to access this givenness. Once again, according to the tradition of phenomenology, givenness is accessed by performing the phenomenological

8. See "Faith and Reason" in Marion, *Visible and the Revealed*, 152.

9. Marion, *In the Self's Place*, 271.

10. Marion, *Reduction and Givenness*, 33.

11. See Marion, *Givenness and Hermeneutics*, 41–43 (italics original): "Hermeneutics does not give a meaning to the given, by securing and deciding it, but each time,
it gives *its* meaning, that is to say the meaning that shows that given as itself, as a phenomenon which is shown in itself and by itself. The *self* of the phenomenon rules in the
final instance all the givenness of meaning: it is not a givenness by the "*I*" of a meaning
constituted by it into an object to this very object, but to let its own meaning come to
the object, acknowledged more than known. The meaning given by hermeneutics does
not come so much from the decision of the hermeneutic actor, as from that which the
phenomenon itself is (so to speak) waiting for and of which the hermeneutic actor
remains a mere discoverer and therefore the servant."

reduction, or *epoché*.[12] It involves a deliberate suspension and setting aside of the so-called natural attitude in order to allow a phenomenon to give itself as it may—to give itself by itself without any regulations imposed on the phenomenon by the human subject.[13] Building on the principles of phenomenology as set forth by Edmund Husserl, Marion asserts: "so much reduction, so much givenness."[14] The more the phenomenon is reduced to its pure giving, the more access is granted to the peculiar elements of the phenomenon as it gives them to be perceived. Let us provide an illustration of this process. I go for a walk in the woods on a sunny afternoon. If I perceive everything around me according to the common natural attitude, I most likely will remain unimpressed by what I see, hear, smell, etc. For instance, I may think: "Yes, there are many trees, the sun, little critters scurrying about in search of food, birds chirping, the stream flowing, and mud on my boots. There's nothing new under the sun. I've been here before and nothing will surprise me, just like nothing surprised me yesterday or the day before." The same walk through the woods with an intentional bracketing of the natural attitude will be a quite different experience. For example, I may think "Wow! So many sensations, so many bedazzling impressions of beauty. What is this I hear? A bird singing a brilliant melody? I wonder, what kind of bird is this? Why such a song of joy and exuberance? What is this I see? Rays of sunlight dancing on the rustling leaves. Spectacular! What is this I smell? Sweet nectar of flowers bursting with life and limitless contours of color." Can you tell the difference between these two distinct experiences informed by two contrasting attitudes from the outset? When the phenomenological reduction is exerted without abatement, there is no shortage of givenness to perceive.

In fact, as Marion has pointed out time and time again, through the reduction, consciousness is saturated with a host of perceptions and meanings. Awe-filled silence is the typical response to saturating phenomena in particular, and to every experience in general, when the natural attitude is bracketed and set aside. Marion contends that "only the reduction grants access to absolute givenness, and it has no other goal but this."[15] Absolute givenness is impossible to encounter outside of the reduction. Conversion

12. For further discussion on the phenomenological reduction, especially as developed in the work of Marion, see Horner, *Jean-Luc Marion*, 26–27, 106, 135–46.

13. For more on what is meant by "the natural attitude," see Husserl, *Ideas Pertaining to a Pure Phenomenology*, 51–62 (§§27–32), and Jean-Yves Lacoste's essay "Appearing and the Irreducible" in Benson and Wirzba, *Words of Life*, 42–67.

14. Marion, *Reduction and Givenness*, 203. Cf. Marion, *Being Given*, 14: "the more reduction, the more givenness."

15. Marion, *Being Given*, 14.

of outlook and attitude is necessary for open receptivity to givenness. In the example of walking through the woods, notice how the second experience turns to poetry in order to express its saturating content. In the face of saturation, poetry, music, art, dance, tears, laughter, play, and reverent silence become the most appropriate modes of response. Moreover, the one who experiences such goodness and beauty in truth is compelled to exclaim, "*Merci!*, Thank you!" Gratitude floods the soul to the degree that phenomena flood consciousness. In a word, this response is called prayer.[16] Prayer is the response of the finite to the call of the eternal. All phenomenological givenness testifies to the boundless givenness of givenness. Beginning with the reduction, givenness ascends to the heights of contemplation. Perhaps a new formula for phenomenology should be introduced: so much givenness, so much contemplation.

IV. Merleau-Ponty and the Perception of the Child

For all its merits, Marion's phenomenology of givenness still lacks a comprehensive depiction of the human beneficiary of givenness, *l'adonné*. Marion's language privileges manifestation and vision, though at times it attends to the phenomenality of the flesh. Yet his is an adult phenomenology, thought through an adult perspective according to adult concepts and categories. His descriptions are in need of augmentation by attending to the full phenomenality of perception vis-à-vis the lived experience, *Erlebnis*, of the child.

This is precisely where the work of Maurice Merleau-Ponty can be of help. Above all, Merleau-Ponty is known for his signature turn toward embodied perception within his studies at the intersection of phenomenology and psychology, especially within the realm of child psychology. For Merleau-Ponty, perception signifies all five senses perceiving the world in an integrated and intersensorial way. In her 2013 book, *The Child as Natural Phenomenologist*, Talia Welsh writes that "the child is engaged in her world. . . . Children first perceive 'wholes' . . . childhood perception precedes intellectual distinctions such as objective and subjective. . . . For the child, there is nothing but perception, nothing other than perception. Therefore, the child

---

16. See Thérèse of Lisieux, *Story of a Soul*, 242 [Manuscript C, 25r° ff] (italics original): "How great is the power of *Prayer*! One could call it a Queen who has at each instant free access to the King and who is able to obtain whatever she asks. . . . I do like children who do not know how to read, I say very simply to God what I wish to say, without composing beautiful sentences, and He always understands me. For me, *prayer* is an aspiration of the heart, it is a simple glance directed to heaven, it is a cry of gratitude and love in the midst of trial as well as joy; finally, it is something great, supernatural, which expands my soul and unites me to Jesus."

senses no 'lack,' no deficiency in her perceptions."[17] In other words, a child does not dissect her perceptions into superficial component parts. Instead, the child exercises the perfection of the phenomenological posture in a state of constancy. The natural attitude is bracketed perfectly because it has not yet emerged in the life of the young child. There is nothing to bracket because enculturation has not transpired with its tragic baggage and boundaries for possibility. "For children, experience is not something that is had; it is something that is. . . . The senses originally *lack* distinction."[18] In his Sorbonne lectures on child psychology and pedagogy, Merleau-Ponty relates that "'it is a question of a *totality* of given sensations experienced through the intermediary of the *whole* body. The child makes use of his body as a totality and does not distinguish between what is given by the eyes, the ears, and so forth' (CPP 145)."[19] As phenomenologist par excellence, the child does not break up the flow of givenness through abstract partitioning of its modes. What gives, gives as an intersensorial unity of givenness and saturates perception always to some degree. The child, as embodied perceiver and receiver, lives as a sponge immersed in the ocean of perception.

As a phenomenologist interested in child psychology, Merleau-Ponty critiques the typical empirical observation methods of psychology in which the hermeneutic optic is narrowed according to the dualistic assumptions of the adult world that are superimposed on that of the child. One of the major aporias for child psychology is the attempt of the adult to interpret experiences of the child through the language, categories, abstraction, and analytics of the adult. Phenomenology is necessary to expand the truncated hermeneutic of psychology that interprets only through those predetermined categories of meaning and association as formulated by lettered adults. Merleau-Ponty raises an objection to the standard approach of child psychology: "Do we have the right to comprehend the time, the space of the child as an undifferentiation of *our* time, of *our* space, etc. . . . ? This is to reduce the child's experience to our own, at the very moment one is trying to respect the phenomena. For it is to think it as the *negation* of *our* differentiations. It would be necessary to go all the way to thinking it *positively*, unto phenomenology."[20] Phenomenology prevents us from reducing the child's experience to our own adult experience by exacting the phenomenological reduction on the tacit "scientific" reductionism that otherwise

17. Welsh, *Child as Natural Phenomenologist*, 11.

18. Welsh, *Child as Natural Phenomenologist*, 54, 56 (italics original).

19. Merleau-Ponty, as quoted in Welsh, *Child as Natural Phenomenologist*, 56–57 (italics original).

20. Merleau-Ponty, *Visible and the Invisible*, 203–4 (italics original).

would prevail. Phenomenology prevents the psychologist from interpreting the child's experience as just another adult experience in miniature.

In her two insightful essays on this point, "The Infant's Experience of the World: Stern, Merleau-Ponty and the Phenomenology of the Preverbal Self," and "The Countryside of Childhood: A Hermeneutic Phenomenological Approach to Developmental Psychology," Eva-Maria Simms corroborates Merleau-Ponty's insistence of expanding psychological hermeneutics by phenomenology. Even though within the adult's interpretation of the child's experience "a degree of circularity is unavoidable," nevertheless we are called "to conceive of a primordial, interpersonal and meaningful relationship with the world that grounds our adult conceptions in an innocent and direct engagement of body and world."[21] In spite of the natural tendency of the adult to interpret the subjective experience of the child only with reference to his or her own subjective experience, there remains the possibility of reentering the life-world of the child through empathic participation. What is necessary, in the words of Jean Laplanche, is "a philosopher [or psychologist] who is willing to observe."[22] When the adult takes time, care and the posture of listener in observing the life-experiences/adventures (*Erlebnisse*) of the child, several characteristics are revealed:

1. "'For the child, the visual space (of the image) and the kinesthetic space (where his body resides) are not comparable. There is no true duality for the child; this notion belongs to the adult's thought. Thus, no reduction takes place permitting the convergence of two givens into one via some sort of intellectual effort.'"[23]

21. Simms, "Infant's Experience of the World," 17, 39. Cf. Merleau-Ponty, *Visible and the Invisible*, 204: "When I perceive the child, he is given precisely in a certain divergence (*écart*) (*originating presentation of the unpresentable*)."

22. As quoted in Welsh, *Child as Natural Phenomenologist*, xi, xvi.

23. Welsh, *Child as Natural Phenomenologist*, 64 (quoting from Merleau-Ponty's *Child Psychology and Pedagogy*, 424). Cf. Welsh, *Child as Natural Phenomenologist*, 64: "The original world is one of a meaningful background experience devoid of sharp demarcations and representations. The child thus relates through relationships and connections and not through acquiring new judgments about persons, things, or herself"; Merleau-Ponty, *Child Psychology and Pedagogy*, 141 (italics original): "The direct experience of the child: an experience not yet systematized by language and thought. The distinction between lived experience and rationalization marks the limit of the interrogative method of investigating children's experience. . . . In the first part of his work, *The Child's Conception of the World*, Piaget shows that the child's thought is essentially characterized by 'egocentrism.' Egocentrism (as a mode of thought and sensation) allows the child to overlook the external world. . . . For Piaget, the child is *singularly* directed toward the outer world with no trace of introversion. Contrary to the subjectivist prejudice, Piaget affirms that the child is caught up in an excessive realism which renders him incapable of taking a critical perspective on things. The child

2. "The child's body is not a part of the world but is, rather, the very invisible nexus of the world."[24]

3. "One of the essential differences between the child and the adult involves the fact that everything has an obvious meaning for the child and in such a way that no room for doubt exists."[25]

does not yet discern the limitations of the place of the personal in experience and, thus, assumes his ego [*moi*] is the essence of objective reality. In the child, a state of indifference exists between the external world and the ego"; Simms, "Infant's Experience of the World," 28: "Phenomenological thinkers have always challenged the very dualism of subject and object—and the natural scientific method that accompanies it"; and Simms, "Countryside of Childhood," 301, 307: "Young children's experience is marked by the absence of Cartesian dualisms . . . We have to make an attempt to unearth the country-side of childhood from the debris of a geography of human development which we have constructed in the last century." For Simms, the analytic discourse of the adult observer and the preverbal "naïve discourse" of the child are "two kinds of discourse at odds with each other" (Simms, "Countryside of Childhood," 306).

24. Welsh, *Child as Natural Phenomenologist*, 68. Cf. Merleau-Ponty, *Visible and the Invisible*, 263: "Speech does indeed have to enter the child as silence—break through to him through silence and as silence (i.e. as a thing simply perceived—difference between the word *Sinnvoll* [i.e. "the meaningful"] and the word-perceived)—Silence = absence of the word due. It is this fecund negative that is instituted by the flesh, by its dehiscence—the negative, nothingness, is the doubled-up, the two leaves of my body, the inside and the outside articulated over one another—Nothingness is rather the difference between the identicals—"; Bindeman, "Merleau-Ponty's Embodied Silence," 58: "Silence serves as the foundation for discourse just as the world is the foundation for objects."

25. Merleau-Ponty, *Child Psychology and Pedagogy*, 186. Cf. Merleau-Ponty, *Child Psychology and Pedagogy*, 186 (italics original): "We characterize the child as radically different insofar as we crystallize the child's experience into a 'representation of the world' which seems absolutely alien to that of the adult, a form of experience grounded in a totally different logic. It is perhaps on the condition that we do not speak of the child's 'representation of the world' that we will succeed in becoming aware of this *adherence to given situations* which might be the essential character of the child's thought"; Merleau-Ponty, *Child Psychology and Pedagogy*, 176, 241–42 (italics original): "For the child, perception is a *means of conduct* by which the child engages himself in a veritable commerce with things. . . . Perception and relationships of causality grasped by the child are not a reflection of external phenomena, nor are they a simple ordering of environmental givens. They are a 'structuring' [*mise en forme*] of the child's experience . . . the child's perception and knowledge are supported by a more profound function: a linear connection with affectivity . . . [for the child,] knowledge is more an effect than a cause"; Welsh, *Child as Natural Phenomenologist*, 14, 16, 17, 33 (italics original): "Normal structuration means a harmonious interaction, or dialectic, between the individual, naturally perceiving subject and the symbolic, intersubjective social order. Since the perceiving infant is always-already within this dialectic, she is always-already participating in a structure. . . . Childhood development is a progressive incorporation of new experiences into the symbolic order. . . . Childhood perception is the ur-Gestalt of all perceptual experience. . . . How we structure our early experience is admittedly prelinguistic as well as prescientific. . . . In Gestalt theory, a general, unthematic

According to the first point, the adult observer must bracket all dualistic thinking when approaching the lived experience of the child to access this "world which precedes knowledge."[26] Of this necessity we must re-mind ourselves lest "the scientifically pat answer (keep us) from looking any further."[27] Instead, we must allow the dualism to collapse before the saturating power of the "large common unit of subjective experience, the episode," or "the pure event" (Rilke, *Duino Elegies*).[28] Especially for the preverbal infant, lived experience occurs through "amodal perception" and "vitality affects."[29] There is not a sharp demarcation among the five senses as to which of the five is sensing in any given moment. Rather, all senses blend together as one in the episodic movement of perception. The child is affected not by percepts wedded with their respective concepts, but by the sheer magnitude of life as lived within an organic and symbiotic communion of sensation.[30] Here is where the child's "wild thinking" coincides

---

background underlies discrete and new experiences. Gestalt psychology teaches us that infantile perception is structured from the outset. The infant experiences a sensible world, not an incoherent set of random visual givens . . . 'the infant's experience does not begin as a chaos, but as a *world already underway [un monde déjà]*' (CPP 148)"; and Merleau-Ponty, *Phenomenology of Perception*, 407: "My first perception, along with the horizons which surrounded it, is an ever-present event, an unforgettable tradition; even as a thinking subject, I still am that first perception, the continuation of that same life inaugurated by it."

26. Simms, "Countryside of Childhood," 307.

27. Simms, "Countryside of Childhood," 302. Cf. Welsh, *Child as Natural Phenomenologist*, 110: "Merleau-Ponty's view is that children are natural phenomenologists in that they remain connected to experience and do not require a resolution in a theory. Such a perspective is limiting when one is considering ideal and not natural objects, but it is less likely to sacrifice experience on the altar of consistency. Children explore the world rather than analyze the world. Unlike adults, children do not tend to take objects out of their context, or take themselves out of context. . . . The child's reality has a solidity that while not static, can appear to be rigid to adults who are indoctrinated in certain philosophical and scientific interpretations."

28. Stern, *Interpersonal World of the Infant*, 110.

29. Simms, "Infant's Experience of the World," 33–34. Cf. Simms, "Infant's Experience of the World," 34, 36: "'Like dance for the adult, the social world experienced by the infant is primarily one of vitality affects before it is a world of formal acts' [Stern 57]. . . . The child's conception of the world, which is a world shot through with vectors of meaning, rather than built up out of the elements of conceptual thought"; and Simms, "Countryside of Childhood," 316: "Young children have no interiority, but there is also no mere exteriority to the world they experience."

30. See Welsh, *Child as Natural Phenomenologist*, 57 (italics original): "Perception's primordial status is not disorganized, although it is intersensorial. 'We claimed that *perception* does not commence through multiple, disjointed experiences, but rather through some very nebulous *global structures* that undergo a progressive differentiation. Prior to judgment, a more fundamental unity exists' (CPP 146)."

with Merleau-Ponty's concept of "wild being": "Here is the common tissue of which we are made. The wild Being. And the perception of this perception (the phenomenological 'reflection') is the inventory of this originating departure whose documents we carry within ourselves."[31] Moreover, the experience of the child is revealed as "the initial experience of a communal self, the *vie a plusieurs*"—"a shared situation" in which "the smiling infant lives in the face of the other."[32] The life of the child is intrinsically communal due to the radical dependence of the child on her adult caretakers. Interpersonal relationality is formed as a vital foundation for the edifice of individual and communal history in the earliest stages of human development. Within this schema of a loving and trustworthy *communio personarum*, the adult notion of understanding is revised: "To the extent that I understand, I no longer know who is speaking and who is listening."[33]

In reference to the second point above, that the child's body is the very invisible nexus of the world, Welsh writes that "the totality of the child's experience includes her sense of embodiment . . . their experience is a unity: body, world, and perception are parts of a meaningful whole. A type of schema of being exists in the child, but not yet a world of discrete objects. . . . It is the primal base of changing, living experience that makes our later abstractions from the world possible."[34] This is to say that the lived experience of the child cannot be interpreted without taking into careful account the place of the body within the unity of lived experience. For Merleau-Ponty, the beautifully saturating dehiscence of the world is experienced through the chiasm,

31. Merleau-Ponty, *Visible and the Invisible*, 204. Cf. Simms, "Countryside of Childhood," 313; Welsh, *Child as Natural Phenomenologist*, 18: "In everyday perception, the child experiences a sense of absoluteness, a kind of perspective-free perception. The child appears egocentric because she does not understand there are points of view at all"; Allefeld, "Hollow of Being," 6–7: "But if Being is supposed to appear it needs a medium, especially the sensible, which 'is Being's unique way of manifesting itself without ceasing to be ambiguous and transcendent' . . . the notion of wild Being as a fundamental unity, relative to which the difference of subject and object has to be considered as something subordinate"; and Merleau-Ponty, *Visible and the Invisible*, 200: "The order of brute or wild being which, ontologically, is primary."

32. Simms, "Infant's Experience of the World," 37; and Simms, "Countryside of Childhood," 317, 319. Simms regards the child subject as "multi-perspectival" and refers to a similar concept of Henri Wallon: the "syncretism of the child" (Simms, "Countryside of Childhood," 313, 317). Cf. Welsh, *Child as Natural Phenomenologist*, 48: "Children have an inherent intersubjective bond with others that allows for our later, mature relations to develop. It is this primal connection to others that allows us to not be overwhelmed by our mature alienation from each other."

33. Merleau-Ponty, *Prose of the World*, 143–44.

34. Welsh, *Child as Natural Phenomenologist*, 34. Cf. Allefeld, "Hollow of Being," 11: "The flesh is the tissue of the world itself, it forms the 'connective tissue of exterior and interior horizons.'"

or entwinement, between the unified flesh of body and world.[35] And it is
the child who exhibits this chiasm to the highest degree because the natural
attitude has not yet overcome it. The child's is a consciousness embodied
rather than disembodied. Upon epidermis, retina, saliva, membranes, ossi-
cles, and follicles, the world is born anew with each and every sensate event.
Genuß and *jouissance*—sheer pleasure and delight—describe the originary
life-world of the child. Any unpleasant or painful experience serves only to
testify to that which is more originary and more decidedly final: receptivity to a fleshly world of givenness that gives itself once and for all, that is,
always.[36] Just as evil is merely a deprivation of goodness—the goodness that
otherwise would be without the evil that detracts from it—pain, abuse, and
trauma are merely deprivations of the holistic order of givenness that attests
to the meaning of life as gift. It is the child who attests, in the first place, to
the meaning of life as gift in and through her self-attested givenness to the
world and her experience of the world as precious gift. Innocence is bound
up in the ripe naïveté of receptivity to gift as gift.

The third point above follows the second in that the intuitive exigency
of the child is ever open to the obvious meanings of what gives itself to
perception, so much so that there remains no room for casting doubt upon
what gives itself by itself. A child's perception, beginning with those most

35. See Merleau-Ponty, *Visible and the Invisible*, chapter 4, entitled "The Intertwin-
ing–The Chiasm." Cf. Simms, "Infant's Experience of the World," 36: "Merleau-Ponty's
notion of the 'lived body' implies that we experience our bodies not as anatomical,
scientific, outside shells to our psyches, but as powers that interact with the environment." The word "dehiscence" is derived from the Latin verb, *dehiscere*, which means
"to part, divide, gape, yawn; to develop a crack; to split open and reveal," in a word,
"to burst open." Cf. Merleau-Ponty, *Phenomenology of Perception*, xiv: "In order to see
the world and grasp it as paradoxical, we must break with our familiar acceptance of it
and, also, from the fact that from this break we can learn nothing but the unmotivated
upsurge of the world."

36. The tragic within human experience enters in a gradual way as a detraction from
the originary goodness and wholeness of interpersonal givenness. See Simms, "Infant's
Experience of the World," 38–39: "The infant's first questioning glances at the other as
other become necessary when the pattern of their dual, unreflected involvement in a
situation is broken . . . the appearance of the linguistic-symbolic self brings with it the
possibility of alienation and psychopathology. . . . The lived, 'amodal' version of an
experience goes underground and becomes accessible only under special conditions,
such as moments of contemplation, emotional states and certain experiences of works
of art that try to evoke the global, preconceptual, lived experience." Herein emerges the
vocation to recuperate the amodal perception and vital affectivity of the child within
the compromised and calloused life-world of the adult. Cf. Welsh's introduction in
Merleau-Ponty, *Child Psychology and Pedagogy*, xvi: "Merleau-Ponty repeatedly asserts
that in certain ways, children are more directly in contact with their environment because children do not have as many cultural tools to separate themselves. They have not
yet fully acquired social norms, including preferred styles of expression."

tender stages of infancy, inaugurates an entwined and dialectical relationship with the world. A perpetual process of structuring (*mise en forme*) commences by which the infantile ur-Gestalt remains the unbroken point of reference. As Merleau-Ponty suggests, because the infant experiences "the *world already underway* [*un monde déjà*]," rather than a sheer chaos of sensate stimuli, the perceptual world of the infant/child-becoming-adult must be regarded as exceptionally formative and foundational for all subsequent life-experiences.[37] Similar to the way Paul of Tarsus understands the irreversible inception of the Christian gospel—"for no one can lay a foundation other than the one that is there, namely, Jesus Christ"—so too the nascent experiences of the infant lay the foundation for a field of experience that will unfold over the course of time.[38] Those originary obvious meanings of experience abide as enduring witnesses to the exorbitant flow of givenness, even if they become progressively latent as the natural attitude accrues in proportion to the entropic demands of economics and social convention. This is why it is necessary that the child serve as prophetic witness to the one who has "come of age." For instance, when peace no longer seems possible in a world ravaged by war and haunted by a history of malfeasance, the possibility stands that "a little child shall lead them."[39] Perhaps in many, if not most, situations, taking cues from the child is the wisest thing to do. Talia Welsh puts this idea eloquently as she writes:

> Merleau-Ponty's descriptions not only want to evoke this early element of human existence, but also want to "praise" childhood insofar as it reveals our true immersion in the world. What divorces us from our underlying syncretic nature could be nothing else but the social-cultural-linguistic world we become increasingly enmeshed with as we mature. Pregnant women, children, artists, and poets bring us back to our real connection with the world, from where all diversity of culture and history spring. At face value, it appears to be a repetition of the classic themes of the romantic ethos—children, poets, and women are more "in contact" with reality since they are not immersed in civilization. Poets, painters, and musicians will be our salvation from the constraining, unnatural effects of our modern society.[40]

To return to the natural order of things, before all of the cultural distortions that unnaturalize nature, one must become attentive to the prophets

---

37. Merleau-Ponty, *Child Psychology and Pedagogy*, 148 (italics original).

38. 1 Cor 3:11 (NAB).

39. Isa 11:6 (RSV).

40. Welsh, *Child as Natural Phenomenologist*, 147.

of the natural syncretic way of being-in-the-world. Prior to its mechanized and technologized dissection, the natural world gives itself as itself by itself. The first romance concerns the dehiscent givenness of creation and its conscious uptake by personal, spiritual, and embodied souls. Psychology, after all, originates in the "science (*logos*) of the soul (*psyche*)" and thereby is summoned back to ruminate on the chiasm between embodied conscious life and the life-world that gives itself to this spiritual "zero point of orientation."[41] A conversion is necessary to discover nature once again as nature: the conversion of the natural attitude of the adult into the chiastic and receptive perception of the child. For this conversion to take place, the child will lead the way if there be any way at all.

So Merleau-Ponty has welcomed us back to rediscover the philosophical genius of the child as perceiver par excellence of the nearness of world and flesh. In a non-dualistic, embodied, and maturely naïve aperture of immanent perception—an immanence that awakens transcendence to the degree of sacramental intimacy between flesh and world—Merleau-Ponty elevates the child as master of mondial mystery, unlocking a world of wonder to the one who won what was thought to be the prize of the rite of passage, only to find the passageway to an enchanted world barred from entry. Yet we can proceed one step farther whereupon the experience of transcendent immanence becomes all the more transcendent and all the more immanent. This step, one that Merleau-Ponty seemed hesitant to take, is a theological one, and, moreover, a mystical one. We must turn to a discourse beyond the point at which philosophical discourse reached its maximum limit. In addition to the testimony of the child herself, we must look to those adults who became children once again as the apogee of their paradoxical maturity. In these testimonies we find a love that has reasons of which reason knows nothing about.[42] The next step in the order of argument will demonstrate the immeasurable potential of the natural attitude's conversion to dehiscent givenness and unbounded perception: mystical contemplation.

V. Givenness, Ubiquitous Perception, and the Ascent of Mount Carmel

If givenness as reawakened by the child surely leads to contemplation, what better than the tradition of Carmelite spirituality—especially the reformed Discalced Order of Teresa of Ávila—to pick up where philosophy and psychology leave off? First, let us recall some of the outstanding

41. See Stein, *On the Problem of Empathy*, 43.
42. See Pascal, *Pensées*, 146–47 (277); translation my own.

personalities within the Order of Discalced Carmelites: Teresa of Ávila, John of the Cross, Thérèse of Lisieux, Teresa of the Andes, Elizabeth of the Trinity, Raphael Kalinowski, Teresa Benedicta of the Cross, and so many more. In her work counseling her fellow Carmelite nuns on the vocation of contemplative prayer, *The Way of Perfection*, Teresa of Ávila defines contemplation as the kind of prayer in which "we can do nothing; His Majesty is the one who does everything, for it is His work and above our nature."[43] Teresa's words strike a chord with the itinerary of a phenomenology of givenness and the primacy of perception. Her way of prayer begins with quieting the noisy customary way of approaching life. It requires a disposition of humility and docility before what gives. It is self-aware to the measure that it is other-aware. Subjectivity is pronounced in proportion to alterity. The phenomenon which captivates Teresa's attention is divinity, which is at once the highest degree of possibility and the most fertile soil of givenness. Teresa immediately recognizes the non-object character of the phenomenon with which she is dealing: limitless love and personal relationality.[44] To receive such saturating givenness extending from the revelation of personal divinity, one must become completely passive. All intentional attempts to control, manage, convert, or even interpret what gives itself by itself must subside. Radical passivity—that of the small child, the infant in fact—must be in force precisely by attempting to enforce nothing. The phenomenon of divinity, whose saturating character is perceived in mystical experience, is received to the measure that it remains untamed by finite demands to calculate and manipulate.

Such a phenomenon recalls Stephen Lewis's observation of "phenomenology's extrication of the concept of givenness from thingification and objectification."[45] Non-object phenomena, such as that of divinity, cannot be measured, commodified, or predetermined according to any previous experience. They are to be received with absolute openness and passivity. Ryan Coyne, in his article entitled "A Difficult Proximity," mentions the paradoxical nature of the soul's relation to God as he writes that "the soul can cling

---

43. Teresa of Ávila, *Collected Works of Saint Teresa of Avila*, 2:132. Cf. John of the Cross, *Collected Works of St. John of the Cross*, 429 [*The Dark Night*, 2.14.1]: "All natural ability is insufficient to produce the supernatural good that God alone infuses in the soul passively, secretly, and in silence. All the faculties must receive this infusion, and in order to do so they must be passive and not interfere through their own lowly activity and vile inclinations."

44. Cf. John of the Cross, *Collected Works of St. John of the Cross*, 382 [*The Dark Night*, 1.10.6]: "For contemplation is nothing else than a secret and peaceful and loving inflow of God, which, if not hampered, fires the soul in the spirit of love."

45. Stephen E. Lewis's introduction in Marion, *Reason of the Gift*, 8.

to God . . . only by chastely fearing God."[46] Chaste fear before the divine is, paradoxically, the attitude which turns the key to open intimate relationship with God. The phenomenon of divinity gives itself with perfect autonomy and "auto-manifestation" to the humble soul who lives in obedient reverence before God.[47] Christina Gschwandtner, in her book, *Degrees of Givenness*, writes that "to speak of a saturated phenomenon is an illuminating way to interpret dramatic cases of conversion in response to the divine gaze."[48] Given this warrant by Gschwandtner, I am suggesting the correlation between Teresa's experience of divinity and the saturated phenomenon, as well as that between interior conversion and the phenomenological reduction. Reducing a phenomenon to its sui generis modes of givenness demands an intellectual conversion in order to perceive anew. Is this not precisely what is meant in the Christian gospel by the term *metanoia*?[49] *Metanoia* signifies a change of heart or mind, resulting in a radically new way of living, and, above all, a radically new way of loving. *Metanoia* begins with the gift and act of faith in the goodness of that which provokes the conversion. This implies an aspersion of will before what gives—a vulnerable surrender of will to the ethical adumbrations of personal givenness.

In his 2010 book, *Interpreting Excess*, Shane Mackinlay points to the fundamental attitude of faith which underlies every experience of an ultimate or transcendent reality: "faith as openness to receiving Revelation, as acceptance of the claims made in Revelation, as trust in what is given, and as preparedness to make a personal commitment in response."[50] Mackinlay underscores the fact that access to givenness is determined largely according to the preparedness of its recipient. A willful vulnerability of the self transpires in the form of surrender before ultimate and transcendent givenness, similar to the form of maternity as "the vulnerability of being-for-the-other" as expressed in the work of Emmanuel Levinas and observed by Jennifer Rosato in her 2012 article, "Woman as Vulnerable Self."[51] With the conver-

---

46. Coyne, "Difficult Proximity," 385.

47. Marion, *Being Given*, 219.

48. Gschwandtner, *Degrees of Givenness*, 162. Similarly, see David Tracy's afterword in Kessler and Sheppard, *Mystics*, 242: "The category of The Impossible can relate mystical awareness to postmodern discussions of death and dying, innocent suffering, limit experiences, radical alterity, and, positively, the Good beyond Being. And the God beyond Being as analyzed by Jean-Luc Marion as well as his category of the saturated phenomenon have also proved fruitful to think through a mystical awareness related to the category of the Impossible."

49. See, for example, Mark 1:15: "'This is the time of fulfillment. The kingdom of God is at hand. Repent (μετανοέω), and believe in the gospel'" (NAB).

50. Mackinlay, *Interpreting Excess*, 194.

51. See Rosato, "Woman as Vulnerable Self."

sion to givenness and, in particular, divine revelation, comes a reorientation of being: from being-for-oneself to being-for-the-other. Givenness inspires the self to be turned inside-out. Just as givenness demonstrates a giving without remainder, so does it compel the self to become a gift of self without exception. This is exactly what we find in the testimony of Teresa of Ávila and in the other Carmelite saints: given over to God and to the other to the point of abandonment *in imitatio Christi.*

It is no wonder that the Christian Scriptures speak so frequently of the child and, specifically, call the faithful "children of God."[52] The radical passivity of perception exhibited by the child serves as a model for adults to peel themselves away from the natural attitude, or better, to let themselves be peeled away from it by the unrelenting flow of givenness that floods perception. Carmelite spirituality, as inspired by this biblical motif of the child's genius, facilitates the conversion of the natural attitude through the purifying process of detachment from inhibiting appetites and inclinations. A return to perceptive (and moral) innocence is enabled by the purgation of the natural attitude according to the penitential spiritual itinerary of the Carmelite monastic tradition. Contemplation is the prize to be won by fighting in the form of *fiat*: "let it be done unto me according to thy word."[53]

VI. Toward a Theology of Childhood

To conclude this reflection on the rapprochement between givenness, perception, and contemplation, I want to suggest that Marion's and Merleau-Ponty's work can be classified under the rubric of a theology of childhood. To begin with Marion, many scholars have laid claim to the relevance of Marion's phenomenology within the domain of theology.[54] Peter Joseph Fritz is one of them, and in his 2009 article, entitled "Black Holes and Revelations," he claims that "Marion's philosophy . . . within . . . its prevailing momentum, can help us to open up theology to the plentitude of God's saving works (*erga*), both visible and invisible."[55] Theology thrives on the pursuit of the plentitude of divine mystery and Marion's phenomenology of givenness certainly contributes to the investigation of infinite possibility. By setting aside what would obstruct divine activity, for example, callousness,

---

52. See, for instance, Matt 5:9; John 1:12; Rom 8:16; Gal 3:26; Eph 5:1; 1 John 3:1–2.

53. Luke 1:38.

54. In particular, see Steinbock, *Phenomenology and Mysticism,* and J. Aaron Simmons's essay, "Continuing to Look for God in France: On the Relationship Between Phenomenology and Theology," in Benson and Wirzba, *Words of Life,* 15–29.

55. Fritz, "Black Holes and Revelations," 435.

self-interest, disbelief, and hubris, human perception is liberated from the bondage of self-conceit and cynicism. Instead of fashioning God according to our own silhouette of finitude, we lay down our arms and yield to the rhythms of eternal Love. Givenness is neither too near nor too abstract for subjective manipulation. Similarly, Antonio Calcagno, in his 1998 paper entitled "God and the Caducity of Being," with both appreciation for and critique of Marion via Edith Stein, writes that "the tendencies to either anthropomorphize or make God too 'other worldly' must be kept in check."[56] While Calcagno raises the objection of moving *au-delà de l'être* too quickly, he affirms Marion's intuition to think God as love through interface with the icon. In identifying Marion's work as a theology of childhood on the whole, reference is made to the fact that his work extends into theological application in its attunement to the phenomenality of speechless and awe-filled manifestation. By no means does the expression "theology of childhood" infer that Marion's work is "childish" or "child's play." To the contrary, it suggests a redoubled post-naïveté in which the paradigmatic contemplative is the child. Why? Because it is the child who approaches the world with a disposition of unobstructed openness. Since the child has been sheltered from the marching of time toward the calloused natural attitude, she inherently inclines toward possibility and surprise: the true and transparent state of affairs for the playing field of pure givenness.

Even though during his lifetime Merleau-Ponty was reluctant to draw a positive and explicit correlation between the child's perception and the concept of divinity, it is not without warrant that I suggest such a close correspondence here. If any perceptive disposition is suited to encounter at least the remote possibility of the divine, it is that of the child. Due to the credulous chiastic structure of the child's perception, no limits are set on possibility. No phenomenon must pay obeisance to premade categories and mandates of a certain fabricated field of scientific investigation. Is this not the implicit contradiction of virtually all arguments in favor of atheism—that belief in the divine is not granted unless the divine comply with my feebly constructed parameters of reality? As if I bear the right of jurisdiction upon the eternal since I am blissfully (and therefore ignorantly) synonymous with it? Rather, the child suggests a much more humble posture before the perpetuity of possibility. For who is insolent and impudent enough to cast doubt on the possible and, moreover, on the divine? Here is where metaphysics meets phenomenology in interpreting possibility not just as that which might occur in the future, but regarding possibility as that which may occur because it already has occurred, just as we see the

---

56. Calcagno, "God and the Caducity of Being," para. 14.

light of stars from Earth some four hundred light-years after the actuality of its emittance. The possible is possible because it has been actualized as such from eternity. The child refuses to eliminate that which is ineliminable because such an amputation to possibility does not occur to her. She is convinced of the contradiction of eliminating possibility inasmuch as the impossibility of impossibility is possibility. The shadow of the impossible does not even come on the scene of her experience because the possibility of impossibility is still possibility, just as a shadow appears inasmuch as a light is shining. The impossibility of possibility is simply impossible insofar as the alleged negation of possibility only attends to the perpetual givenness of possibility in the first and last place.

Running complementary to the philosophical work of Marion and Merleau-Ponty, twentieth-century biblical theologian and catechetical pioneer Sofia Cavalletti has developed an entire method of Christian catechesis based on the religious genius of the child. In her 1979 book, *The Religious Potential of the Child*, Cavalletti speaks of the thirst for the infinite and the virgin dynamism of the child: "Experience (*esperienza*) offers a basis for this message: a field that has already been tilled—and sometimes ruined—by the life one has already lived and that is, in any event, limited. However an exigence (*esigenza*) is like a hunger waiting to be assuaged; it is like a coiled spring ready to burst forth and, as opposed to experience, presents itself as a virgin dynamism."[57] Cavalletti admits that accumulated experience naturally can restrict our perceptive capacity for possibility. With more experience comes more presupposed limitation of the possible, more skepticism, and more cynicism. The yearning for love and transcendence of the child is instructive for adults whose hunger for possibility has dissipated over the course of time. Children exhibit a virgin dynamism toward life, toward beauty, toward mystery. Children set the pace for encountering the possible: it is slow, quiet, vulnerable, and uncanny. A child's world is the space where the only expectation is to be surprised. Cavalletti talks about the unrelenting need to "strip ourselves of these superfluous elements, and seek to go always closer to the vital nucleus of things. . . . The child himself will be our teacher of essentiality, if we know how to observe him."[58] Does not Cavalletti's notion of the vital nucleus of things form a unity with the phenomenological concept of givenness and open perception? How does one learn the art of phenomenology by enacting the reduction to access the unlimited storehouse of givenness? Is it not by observing those master artists of perception who have not written books that outlaw various figures of possibility and therefore

57. Cavalletti, *Religious Potential of the Child*, 25.
58. Cavalletti, *Religious Potential of the Child*, 48.

clutter up the shelves of true learning that instead should be ordered according to a Montessorian cosmic pedagogy?

Is my suggestion that Marion's and Merleau-Ponty's work can be
characterized as a theology of childhood so far-fetched? Perhaps the following passage from *Prolegomena to Charity* will confirm my hypothesis
even further. In discussing the art of apologetics, Marion writes that "love
opens the eyes. Opens the eyes: not in the way violence opens the eyes of
the disabused, but as a child opens his eyes to the world, or a sleeper opens
his eyes to the morning."[59] Marion's depiction of the child opening his eyes
to the world, reminiscent of Merleau-Ponty's insights into child psychology, implies the unassuming disposition through which the child perceives.
There are no presuppositions about what could give itself when, where, or
how. The purity of the child's gaze is not tarnished by false expectations of
banality and nothing but banality. Instead, the child opens to the universe
in loving self-surrender inasmuch as "surrendered" is the given status of
the child's self in relation to the womb of the world.[60] Situating Marion's
oeuvre as a theology of childhood—in effect signifying love at once as possibility, gift, and receptivity—is corroborated by Kevin Hart's claim that
"we see Marion in sharpest focus when we perceive that he can be grasped
in his totality as a philosopher of love."[61] Marion never tires of regarding
love as the most fascinating and inspiring phenomenon for philosophical
reflection. Just as a child humbly approaches a world of wonder, so does the
philosopher of love approach phenomena according to the unpretentious
hermeneutic of givenness. Thérèse of the Child Jesus of the Holy Face, the
"little flower," relates this humble way of approaching all things according
to her "little doctrine of love": "The science of Love, ah, yes, this word resounds sweetly in the ear of my soul, and I desire only this science."[62] Can it

59. Marion, *Prolegomena to Charity*, 69.

60. See Stein, *Potency and Act*, 258 (including footnote 220) (italics original): "The
child is surely unaware of the blissful aura issuing from its pure soul. But is its unaware-
ness the unconsciousness of dull sensation, let alone of 'lifeless' things? The child does
not *know* what it is nor what it is like inwardly. It is given over wholly to its actual living,
radiates itself therein without restraint, and this is precisely why the aura it gives off is
so strong. . . . Children differ greatly, however, in how much their 'depth' is involved in
their actual living; we should sharply distinguish this involvement or non-involvement
from the kind we are reflexively aware of. I daresay, though, that on average children
also live 'with their whole soul' more than adults do."

61. From the introduction of Hart, *Counter-Experiences*, 3.

62. Thérèse of Lisieux, *Story of a Soul*, 187–88 (Manuscript B, 1r° ff). Cf. Thérèse of
Lisieux, *Story of a Soul*, 189 (italics original): "You asked me, dear Sister, to write to you
my dream and '*my little* doctrine' as you call it"; and John of the Cross, *Collected Works
of St. John of the Cross*, 437–38 [2.27.4, 6]: "Since the wisdom of this contemplation is
the language of God to the soul, of Pure Spirit to pure spirit, all that is less than spirit,

be the case that this "science of love" describes the heights of the phenomenological reduction in light of the amorous exigencies of the child? Cavalletti writes that "we believe that the child, more than any other, has need of love because the child himself is rich in love. The child's need to be loved depends not so much on a lack that requires filling, but on a richness that seeks something that corresponds to it."[63] Cavalletti observes that children show natural aptitude not only for possibility, but for the highest in possibility, love. Love connotes the highest in possibility because it involves the least discrimination and discretion. It does not pass judgment before the appointed time. Further, the highest degree of love is unconditional love because it is unfastened to any conditions for its free exercise. In a similar way, the aim of the phenomenological reduction is to free the human subject from any conditions which would render a given phenomenon contingent on the self's predeterminations and requirements.

Marion's phenomenology of givenness, and Merleau-Ponty's phenomenology of embodied perception, appropriately can be called a theology of childhood because together they are tethered to the possible as revealed in limitless givenness. Theology implies the utmost in possibility and childhood signifies the highest degree of receptivity to possibility. Just as the questions of the child are without limit, so are the answers theology supplies, both in its kataphatic and apophatic forms denominating and predicating divinity. In the final analysis, as John Panteleimon Manoussakis suggests in his book, *God After Metaphysics*, theological language about God is liturgical language above all.[64] Carmelite spirituality, imbued as it is with the charism of contemplation and childlike simplicity, humility, and passivity, is a certain vector to conversion of gaze and receptivity before gift. Liturgical contemplation begins at the end of every experience, for every end is a new beginning in the face of givenness and its unpredictability: *arrivage*.[65] May it land according to its pleasure and may we reconsider the

---

such as the sensory, fails to perceive it. Consequently this wisdom is secret to the senses; they have neither the knowledge nor the ability to speak of it, nor do they even desire to do so because it is beyond words . . . Souls are so elevated and exalted by this abyss of wisdom, which leads them into the heart of the science of love, that they realize that all the conditions of creatures in relation to this supreme knowing and divine experience are very base, and they perceive the lowliness, deficiency, and inadequacy of all the terms and words used in this life to deal with divine things."

63. Cavalletti, *Religious Potential of the Child*, 44.

64. See Manoussakis, *God after Metaphysics*, 82.

65. See Marion, *Being Given*, 131–39, for example, 132 (including endnote 13) (italics original): "*To arrive* must here be understood in the most literal sense: not of a continuous and uniform arrival, delivering identical and foreseeable items, but of discontinuous, unforeseen, and entirely dissimilar arrivals. Sometimes phenomena

precocious sapiential comportment of the child, contemplative par excellence, who never ceases to behold and create something mysterious, for "the kingdom of heaven belongs to such as these."[66]

To close, it is fitting to reference two of Karl Rahner's essays that are quite apropos to the topic at hand: "Ideas for a Theology of Childhood" and "Christmas, the Festival of Eternal Youth." In the former essay, Rahner insists that childhood is not a time of life to outgrow or to let fade into a forgotten past. Instead, he writes that "we do not lose childhood as that which recedes ever further into our past, that which remains behind as we advance forward in time, but rather we go towards it as that which has been achieved in time and redeemed forever in time. We only *become* the children whom we *were* because we gather up in time—and in this our childhood too—into our eternity."[67] Rahner's claim about the dual maturation toward both adulthood and childhood resonates with the Hebrew notion of eternity—עוֹלָם (*olam*)—that connotes at once futurity and antiquity. This is the paradoxical nature of time as revealed in the Jewish theological tradition. It is multidirectional, multidimensional. Liturgical tempo encompasses all time in such a comprehensive way that to move in one direction is to move in all directions.[68] The season of childhood is indispensable for the liturgical actor. Childhood is destined to be reinvigorated at every moment to ensure immunity from the sway of the natural attitude.

Like Merleau-Ponty, Rahner perceives the history of one's personal childhood to form the bedrock of all ensuing life-experience: "(Childhood) is important in itself also, as a stage of man's personal history in which that takes place which can only take place in childhood itself, a field which bears fair flowers and ripe fruits such as can only grow in *this* field and in no other, and which will themselves be carried into the storehouses of eternity.

---

arrive, sometimes they do not, and each time, differently. They differ by not resembling one another; they differ especially by delaying (or accelerating) their arisings. Rather than of arrivals, we must therefore speak of the unpredictable landings [*arrivage*] of phenomena, according to discontinuous rhythms, in fits and starts, unexpectedly, by surprise, detached each from the other, in bursts, aleatory. They make us wait, desire them, before seeing them. In these mountings of visibility (as one speaks of mounting vigor, fever, desire, or anger), we—the *I/me*—no longer decide the visibility of the phenomenon. Our initiative is limited to remaining ready to receive the shock of its anamorphosis, ready to take a beating from its unpredictable landing. This powerlessness to stage the phenomenon, which compels us to await it and be vigilant, can be understood as our abandoning the decisive role in appearing to the phenomenon itself."

66. Matt 19:14 (NAB).

67. See "Ideas for a Theology of Childhood" in Rahner, *Further Theology of the Spiritual Life*, 2:36 (italics original).

68. See Wallenfang, *Dialectical Anatomy of the Eucharist*, 173–76.

... *This* morning does not derive its life simply from the afternoon which follows."[69] The sui generis character of childhood preserves its dawn of meaning throughout the course of life—a course anchored in the eternal morning of redemption, the greatest possibility. To begin to experience this twilight of redemption in the here and now demands infinite openness to possibility—above all, openness to the possibility of forgiveness, reconciliation, healing, and transfiguration: "Childhood is openness. Human childhood is infinite openness. The mature childhood of the adult is the attitude in which we bravely and trustfully maintain an infinite openness in all circumstances and despite the experiences of life which seem to invite us to close ourselves."[70] This radical openness of which Rahner speaks is an appeal to the phenomenological attitude that overcomes, by way of daily conversion, the concupiscent force of the natural attitude. And for Christian theology, this victory is won by a child-king who ushers in the reign of the possible once and for all: "(The Christ) child is one in whom the eternal youth of God breaks in upon this world definitively and victoriously; into this world, which seems only able to go on living in that the death of one of its inhabitants makes way for another to be born."[71] Grace is the word used to describe this unmatchable process wherein the eternal youth of God commingles with one's own. Death is overcome by its own death, resulting in eternal life, just as impossibility is rendered impossible by possibility's power to cancel cancelation. In the manifestation of the eternal life of God in the Christ-child, death is revealed as a temporary interruption to the perpetual flow of life from eternity. Givenness attests to this eternal life as gift and is perceived as such by the chiastic structure of the child's perception. As masterful contemplative, the child invites us to reenter the dialectical dance of mystical hermeneutics where "the one who is least (μικρότερος) among all of you is the one who is the greatest (μέγας)."[72]

69. Rahner, *Further Theology of the Spiritual Life*, 2:36 (italics original).

70. Rahner, *Further Theology of the Spiritual Life*, 2:48. Cf. Rahner, *Further Theology of the Spiritual Life*, 2:50: "In the child a man begins who must undergo the wonderful adventure of remaining a child forever, becoming a child to an ever-increasing extent, making his childhood of God real and effective in this childhood of his, for this is the task of his maturity."

71. See "Christmas, the Festival of Eternal Youth" in Rahner, *Further Theology of the Spiritual Life*, 1:121. See Luke 1:37: "For nothing will be impossible (οὐκ ἀδυνατήσει) for God" (NAB).

72. Luke 9:48 (NAB).

CHAPTER 7

LEVINAS AND MOUNT CARMEL

רְעֵה עַמְּךָ בְשִׁבְטֶךָ צֹאן נַחֲלָתֶךָ
שֹׁכְנִי לְבָדָד יַעַר בְּתוֹךְ כַּרְמֶל
יִרְעוּ בָשָׁן וְגִלְעָד כִּימֵי עוֹלָם

Shepherd your people with your staff, the flock of your heritage,
that lives apart in a woodland, in the midst of Carmel.
Let them feed in Bashan and Gilead, as in the days of eternity.

—Micah 7:14

WHEREAS THIS BOOK BEGAN with chapter 1, entitled "Levinas and Mount Zion," articulating the ethical anthropology of Judaism and the primary philosophical points of emphasis within Levinas's writings, the final chapter of this book, "Levinas and Mount Carmel," will attempt a careful and original response to Levinas's essay "A Man-God?"[1] Throughout this book, I have set the ethical phenomenology of Levinas against the contemplative phenomenology of Marion, suggesting the dialectical complementarity between the two.[2] In this chapter, I hope to show, once again, this pivotal relationship between the ethical face of Mount Zion and the contemplative face of Mount Carmel. I want to ask: What does Levinas have to do with Carmelite spirituality? As a Secular Discalced Carmelite, I would like to find both points of similarity and points of dissimilarity between Levinasian ethics and Carmelite ethical contemplation. It is with great trepidation that I write this chapter, given the post-Holocaust world in which I live as a Catholic today. Who am I to furnish any word of critique

1. See "A Man-God?" in Levinas, *Entre Nous*, 53–60.
2. See also my 2017 book, *Dialectical Anatomy of the Eucharist: An Étude in Phenomenology*, for the most thorough presentation of this dialectic and my analysis of the evolution of the phenomenological method.

in the direction of Levinas and all of the "useless suffering" he experienced in his life? The most appropriate response I could have is one of reverent silence. This, indeed, is my initial and long-lasting response. It is only appropriate to sit *shiva* alongside Levinas and his Jewish family in the wake of the Shoah.[3] Yet, in addition to the necessity of sitting *shiva*, I suspect that Levinas would welcome a kind of rabbinic counterpoint to his own ideas, not as a zero-sum game in which the winner takes all, but simply as an ongoing dialogue full of respect and intellectual sincerity.

I. Humiliation and Substitution

My aim here is to summarize the main points Levinas makes in his short essay delivered at the Week of Catholic Intellectuals Paris meeting in April of 1968, one month before the May protests, strikes, and riots would generate a major political upheaval in France. Levinas was invited by this group of intellectuals to deliver an address, and he set as his goals (1) "to reflect on two of the multiple meanings suggested by the notion of Man-God," namely, "the idea of a self-inflicted humiliation on the part of the Supreme Being, of a descent of the Creator to the level of the Creature . . . an absorption of the most active activity into the most passive passivity . . . [and] the Passion, the idea of expiation for others, that is, of substitution" and (2) "to ask to what extent these ideas . . . have philosophical value, and to what extent they can appear in phenomenology."[4] Those already familiar with Levinas's work know that he would find great value in the second of these general notions, namely, the idea of "expiation for others." However, these same students of Levinas might wonder what he might say about the first of these ideas. Let us now summarize Levinas's argument and, in turn, give a response.

As it turns out, Levinas speaks positively about the application of both of these ideas—the humility of God and substitution—as very valuable for philosophy inasmuch as they promote divine transcendence and better comprehension of human subjectivity. They escort us beyond the naïve conflations of divinity with finite beings, such as in the doctrines and practices of pantheism, polytheism, and so many ahistorical mythologies that reduce the affairs of the gods to the affairs of men. Levinas believes that the idea of divine humility allows theology to refuse the reductionism of transcendence to immanence, and aids philosophy to reject the reductionism of the world to the Absolute, as in German Idealism. The uncanniness of God, at once revealed and concealed in divine humility as a persecuted

3. See Job 2:11–13.
4. Levinas, *Entre Nous*, 53–54.

truth, prevents immanence from always winning out over transcendence: "To present oneself in this poverty of the exile is to interrupt the coherence of the universe. To pierce immanence without thereby taking one's place in it."[5] It is clear, and no surprise, that Levinas's concern is to defend transcendence against the pretensions of immanence that always seem to attempt to reduce transcendence to one of immanence's own modes of manifestation by way of its own logic of participation and presence. In a world in which everything is nearby and reducible to an object, why not reduce God to yet another object—the Object par excellence? Why not hyper-immanentize God as a household deity, a talisman, the most sublime instance of immanence that assumes the perfect malleability for human subjectivity, thereby treating God as a toy or plaything? Why not reenact the original sin and make ourselves gods all over again, taking the place of God, since divine transcendence has been converted completely into divine immanence? Look no further than the self to find God!

For Levinas, divine transcendence is revealed through divine humility assuredly, not through a Man-God but through the trace of the Infinite in the proximity of the face of the other who approaches me, "the destitution and poverty of absence that constitutes the proximity of God—the trace."[6] Through the trace, encountered in the face of the other, transcendence is left alone, untouched, unmasterable, irreducible to the legion modalities of immanence. The vocation of responsibility for the other renews the otherness of transcendence insofar as I am never finished with my tasks of responsibility vis-à-vis the other who faces me. Further, I never could reduce the other to more of the same. The face of the other ever transcends my attempts to reduce it to an object of manipulation, a prerogative of the self, an obstacle to be annihilated to promote my own miserable self-preservation. In "a world which cannot accommodate Him . . . [the Infinite] solicits through a face. A Thou is inserted between the I and the absolute He. It is not history's present that is the enigmatic interval of a humiliated and transcendent God, but the face of the Other."[7] For Levinas, it is more fitting for the Infinite, according to the glory of his transcendence, to perpetually conceal himself as such, while hinting at his non-immanent presence only through the traceable presence of his absence. It is not that the Infinite reveals himself through the presence or manifestation of the face of the other, but rather through its deflection of the attempt of the self to reduce the proximity of the other to just another event of manifestation or just another birth of being.

5. Levinas, *Entre Nous*, 55–56.
6. Levinas, *Entre Nous*, 57.
7. Levinas, *Entre Nous*, 57–58.

Concerning the second primary idea stemming from the general concept of a Man-God, that is, substituting oneself for the other, Levinas affirms that this is the very signification of human subjectivity: "the *self* ... the accusative that is not preceded by any nominative ... subjectivity as substitution ... that incessant event of substitution, the fact for being of emptying itself of *its* being."[8] This, too, is the concept of the Messiah—the anointed one, the appointed one, the chosen one—the one responsible for the world, the one responsible for all. The meaning of Messiah is to have been ordained for the mission of greatest responsibility—substituting oneself, one-for-the-other. For Levinas, the meaning of Messiah is the meaning of human subjectivity writ large: "To be me is always to have one more responsibility. ... The *I* is the one who, before all decision, is elected to bear all the responsibility for the World. Messianism is that apogee in Being—a reversal of being 'persevering in his being'—which begins in me."[9] Levinas would not be willing to concede this personal responsibility and reassign it to another man—to another figure other than the self. For to be a self is to be responsible for the other, to be responsible for all. The mystery of the Messiah: it is me.

Overall, on Levinas's view, the idea of an actual Man-God seems to result in two problems in light of his two affirmations derived from the Christian concept as mentioned above. First, the incarnation of God would somehow compromise divine transcendence, forcing the transcendent into another presentation of presence alongside the rest in the world of immanence. Not only would transcendence be emptied and converted into immanence, transcendence would be lost in the process, and so would the incommunicability of the face of the other that attests to the direct inaccessibility of transcendence as a trace of its immemorial and diachronic passing. If "the saying" were entirely exhaustible into "a said," what would become of "the saying?" What happens to the uncanny glory of transcendence when it is subjugated as an appanage beneath the familiarity of immanence? In this case, transcendence disappears precisely because it appears. Rather, as Levinas argues, divine transcendence truly reveals itself to creatures through divine humility in which the face of the other mediates the invisible countenance of divinity as a trace of infinite illeity. The divine He as indirect referent of the human Thou. Even more, the heights of divine glory are revealed as unlimited responsibility for the other as the universal vocation of personal subjectivity, always articulated in the first-person: "Here I am!" If transcendence betrays itself through incarnate immanence, perhaps this perennial summons to

8. Levinas, *Entre Nous*, 58–59 (italics original).
9. Levinas, *Entre Nous*, 60 (italics original).

responsibility would cease for the human subject because it could be trans-
ferred to a God who has come to save the day in the flesh.

And this leads us to the second problem inferred by Levinas in relation to the idea of substitution. Levinas agrees with identifying the Messiah
as the one who is responsible for all. However, for Levinas, the Messiah
is subjectivity itself, again in the first-person: "Here I am!" To locate the
Messiah and the messianic vocation outside of the self is to forfeit the very
essence of being human: to be responsible for the other who faces me. If I
claim that a divine Messiah bears the weight of responsibility for the world,
then, it seems to follow, that I do not bear this weight. It seems, then, that I
am relieved of responsibility to the degree that I can "pass the buck" of responsibility to the incarnate Savior and thereby be discharged of my duties.
And if I fail morally in any way, I can be forgiven that same day through
a procedure that absorbs my moral negligence through the soteriological
scapegoat, namely, the procedure of sacramental confession wherein the
priest acts *in persona Christi*, once again establishing the fact that there is
a Messiah and I am not him. Because the divine Messiah has come in the
flesh, I am permitted to persevere in my being while claiming to be responsible for myself alone, if my responsibility must extend that far. Whether or
not it does is up to me. In the name of "self-care," I may care about myself
to the nth degree or to no degree whatsoever, all the while leaving it to
my neighbor to go about the business of his own "self-care." For Levinas,
responsibility unravels to the measure that I can exercise responsibility
through a surrogate exactly by exercising no responsibility at all.

Levinas's argument is haunting and riveting for Christianity, especially since its truth has played itself out in lived human history, including
the unspeakable horrors of recent human history: 6 million Jewish men,
women, and children murdered in the Holocaust. And who is to bear the
weight of responsibility for their lives? Who should have been bearing the
weight of responsibility for their lives so that they would have been prevented from being murdered systematically like herded cattle shuffled to
the slaughter? How could so many men and women, in the name of self-
preservation of their own being, fail to live in solidarity with their Jewish
brothers and sisters, saying, "Here I am!?" As it turns out, grace may be
the most inexcusable theological concept in human history. How could a
concept, accompanied by so many alibis, appeals, apologies, palliations,
and excuses, function as the crux of all redemption? How could Christianity, with its central concept of grace, predispose a people to fall under the
spell of mythological racial supremacy, exclusionary nationalism, fascist
totalitarianism, and a fatal eugenic program? There really is no sufficient

answer to these questions, unless Christianity and such a concept of grace alone are not to blame for these irrational atrocities.

II. A Man-God or a God-Man?

Can I study the life and works of Emmanuel Levinas, as well as reflect on the Holocaust, and still choose to be a Catholic Christian? After all this, can I still believe that Jesus of Nazareth and his church constitute the fullness of divine revelation, rooted as they are in Judaism? Yes, I can. Why? How? I must say that I credit Emmanuel Levinas for helping me to become much more a Catholic Christian by reintroducing me to my Jewish roots of faith and the undeniable Jewish character of Christianity. Christianity, after all, is first a reform movement within Judaism. Jesus, as a point of fact, is Jewish, and so are his mother, his adoptive father, and the twelve apostles. They never for a second denied their Jewish roots or identity. Christianity is meant to be an extension of Judaism and not a cancellation of it. What have I learned from Emmanuel Levinas? To be a human being is to live in responsibility for the other. This is the heart of it all. What Levinas acknowledges in his essay "A Man-God?" is that Christianity contributes to the ideas of divine humility and substitution, one-for-the-other. The concept of divine incarnation implies divine condescension and humiliation, while the concept of the suffering and death of Jesus signifies a lived-out responsibility for the other to the most radical point of substitution and abandonment. Not a Man-God but a God-Man. The eucharistic giving of Jesus—"This is my body given up for you. . . . This is my blood shed for you"—speaks the language of substitution and is fulfilled to the end in and through his tortured and crucified flesh. And this, above all, is why I remain a Catholic Christian in complete solidarity with my Jewish brothers and sisters and all humanity. There is no revelation more divine than this: that the LORD God, the Creator of the heavens and the earth, would become one of us in order to save us. Is this not the impossible for God, accomplished perfectly in the name of possibility, of making the impossible possible, namely, my salvation and yours?

For me, this is the most divine concept: that the LORD God, the Creator of the heavens and the earth, would plunge himself into the fray of personal embodied creation in order to redeem the cosmos. For how else would it be redeemed? Moreover, in Jesus Christ is manifest and proclaimed not only responsibility for the other lived to the end, but also love that loves in face and name. God's revelation in Jesus envelops the dynamisms of both manifestation and proclamation, not one or the other.[10] Christianity

10. See Wallenfang, *Dialectical Anatomy of the Eucharist*, for a full account of this dialectical divine revelation.

encompasses contemplation and ethics, sacrament and word, gift and witness, showing and telling, flesh and speech, givenness and hermeneutics. My
reverent rejoinder to Levinas's argument in "A Man-God?" is to ask if there
is not an otherwise to the otherness of transcendence? Not a Man-God but
a God-Man. And does this otherwise than the otherness of transcendence
not go by the name of immanence? Is not immanence the radical other in
relation to transcendence? Perhaps transcendence would lose its heights
of glory without earth-bound immanence, without a location of nearness
from which to transcend? Could we not invoke Albert Einstein's theory of
relativity in this sense as well? Are not both distance and proximity relative
to one another? Maybe, in the end, the transcendence of transcendence is
immanence, and the immanence of immanence is transcendence? Is God
transcendent to God? Is God immanent to God? Could it be that the nature
of divinity includes both otherness and unity in Godselves?

It seems to me that Levinas's work must be filled out by an other in
relation to the otherness about which he never tires of speaking. And what
might be the other in relation to the transcendent otherness of which Levinas
attests? Immanence. Divine immanence. The humiliation of transcendence
is immanence. Divine proximity to his beloved creatures. Not a Man-God
but a God-Man. Divine nearness to created persons who had drifted far from
God: "But now in Christ Jesus you who once were far off have become near
by the blood of Christ" (Eph 2:13).[11] There is no enmity between us and God
because God is Emmanuel, "God with us" (Isa 7:14; Matt 1:23). A God who
bleeds. A God who bleeds with us and for us. A God whose blood dries up
the hemophilia of human history: "By his wounds we were healed" (Isa 53:5;
1 Pet 2:24). "According to the law almost everything is purified by blood,
and without the shedding of blood there is no forgiveness" (Heb 9:22). For
Judaism, blood is the seat of life.[12] It is God who gave us life. It is God who
makes blood flow through our veins. It is God who wills to give us eternal
life with him. And he does this by restoring our hemorrhaged and exsangui-
nated state to one of abundant life: "I came so that they might have life and
have it more abundantly" (John 10:10). If God had never left his hidden transcendent throne to come and save us, would he really be a God who saves us
from useless suffering? If God had not entered into our misery and suffered
alongside us, could he really be the one to relieve us of such bondage? If God
had not united to himself a human face and name, could we call upon him

11. Cf. John 6:55–59; Acts 20:28; Rom 3:24–25; 5:9; Col 1:20; Eph 1:7; Heb 9:14;
10:19; 13:12; 1 Pet 1:18–19; 1 John 1:7; Rev 1:5; 7:14; 12:11.

12. See Lev 17:11: "The life of the flesh is in the blood, and I have given it to you to
make atonement on the altar for yourselves, because it is the blood as life that makes
atonement."

so intimately as we can call upon Jesus? If God had not come to save us in the flesh, would we not still be making the futile attempt to save ourselves? Cannot divine responsibility go so much further than my responsibility for my fellowman, even working in and through me? "Which of you by worrying can add one cubit to his stature?" (Matt 6:27). Does my anxious existence serve to save my brother, or at times add to his own anxiety? Why would I claim to be the Messiah if I am not in fact him?[13]

Perhaps the pattern of divine humility revealed in Jesus should be our model? "Though he was in the form of God, Jesus did not regard equality with God something to be grasped. Rather, he emptied himself, taking the form of a slave, coming in human likeness, and found human in appearance, he humbled himself, becoming obedient to death, even death on a cross" (Phil 2:6–8). If God remains so distant as not to be permitted to act directly, decisively, and immediately in our history, do we not usurp the rightful place of God by our own "just deeds that are like polluted rags" (Isa 64:5)? If "the ambiguity of transcendence—and consequently the alternation of the soul moving from atheism to belief and from belief to atheism" simply remains ambiguous, and, therefore, more atheistic than theistic, has divine revelation thereby been sharpened enough to the point of cutting through our calloused history in order to redeem it?[14] Do I not, once again, take the place of God when I leave God nothing left to do among us? Am I not left with a vague and empty atheism when I prohibit the possibility of divine transcendence from turning against itself as its most impossible impossibility: divine immanence—Emmanuel, "God with us?"[15] Do we not run the risk of saying

13. See John 1:19–34; 3:22–30. For example, John 3:27–30: "John answered and said, 'No one can receive anything except what has been given him from heaven. You yourselves can testify that I said that I am not the Messiah, but that I was sent before him. The one who has the bride is the bridegroom; the best man, who stands and listens to him, rejoices greatly at the bridegroom's voice. So this joy of mine has been made complete. He must increase; I must decrease."

14. Levinas, *Entre Nous*, 56. Cf. Heb 4:12–13: "Indeed, the word of God is living and effective, sharper than any two-edged sword, penetrating even between soul and spirit, joints and marrow, and able to discern reflections and thoughts of the heart. No creature is concealed from him, but everything is naked and exposed to the eyes of him to whom we must render an account."

15. See Benedict XVI, *Deus caritas est*, paras. 10, 12. "God's passionate love for his people—for humanity—is at the same time a forgiving love. It is so great that it turns God against himself, his love against his justice. Here Christians can see a dim prefigurement of the mystery of the Cross: so great is God's love for man that by becoming man he follows him even to death, and so reconciles justice and love.... His death on the Cross is the culmination of that turning of God against himself in which he gives himself in order to raise man up and save him. This is love in its most radical form. By contemplating the pierced side of Christ . . . it is there that this truth [namely, that "God is love"] can be contemplated. It is from there that our definition of love must begin. In

nothing at all about God when we are afraid of saying too much about him, especially by not letting him say all that he wants to say, both in the call of the other who faces me and also in the Word made flesh? What, after all, is there to be proclaimed if nothing has been made manifest in the flesh?

III. The Transcendent Immanence of Mount Carmel

And this is Mount Carmel: contemplating the Crucified One so as to channel his precious blood to give life to the world. From the beating of the sacred heart of Jesus flows the blood of the new and everlasting covenant that was shed for us. For what could heal and redeem my bleeding heart if not the bleeding heart of Jesus, the bleeding heart of God, the bleeding heart of Emmanuel, "God with us?" Mount Carmel is the holy territory of ethical contemplation, and the model contemplative is the prophet Elijah atop Mount Carmel, "crouched down to the earth with his head between his knees" (1 Kgs 18:42). And the rains came because the prophet prayed. Elijah exercises his responsibility for the other who faces him according to his zeal for the LORD, the God of hosts, conducted through intercessory prayer. It was not Elijah who filled the widow of Zarephath's jars with oil, or resuscitated her son back to life, but YHWH.[16] "But we hold this treasure in earthen vessels, that the surpassing power may be of God and not from us ... always carrying about in the body the dying of Jesus, so that the life of Jesus may also be manifested in our body. For we who live are constantly being given up to death for the sake of Jesus, so that the life of Jesus may be manifested in our mortal flesh" (2 Cor 4:7, 10–11). The surpassing power is from God and not from us. This is the secret of the Messiah. Yes, I have a share in his messianic mission and ministry, but I say with Saint John the Baptist, "I am not him." I am not the Messiah. I am not the Savior of the world. The power to redeem does not come from me. Only YHWH God "gives the increase" (1 Cor 3:7). Only YHWH God gives life and raises from the dead. And YHWH-saves, Jesus, has come in the flesh to do just that absolutely. In the forge ("Zarephath") of his great love and responsibility for us, Jesus tests our own work in relation to his: "No one can lay a foundation other than the one that is there, namely, Jesus Christ. If anyone builds on this foundation with gold, silver, precious stones, wood, hay, or straw, the work of each will come to light, for the Day will disclose it. It will be revealed with fire, and the fire itself will test the quality of each one's work ... the person will be saved,

this contemplation the Christian discovers the path along which his life and love must move."

16. See 1 Kgs 17:7–24.

but only as through fire" (1 Cor 3:11–13, 15). It is the fire of divine love that abides as the scarlet standard of moral acts.

All of these things being said, the self is not exonerated from its vocation to responsibility for the other simply because it is not identical to the cosmic Messiah. Instead, the self is intertwined all the more with the mission of the Messiah if the self remains united to the Messiah as to a vine: "Remain in me, as I remain in you. Just as a branch cannot bear fruit on its own unless it remains on the vine, so neither can you unless you remain in me. I am the vine, you are the branches. Whoever remains in me and I in him will bear much fruit, because without me you can do nothing" (John 15:4–5). The disciples of Jesus are truly his followers only if they live as he lives: in radical responsibility for the other. Like its elder brother, Judaism, Christianity is not a cultural phenomenon, but an ethical summons. Yet, when Jesus compares himself to a vine, he is claiming that no one can live as he lives without him, without his power, namely, God the Holy Spirit, at work in the soul of his disciple. I can desire to be responsible for the other all I want, but if I lack the power to carry out this desire all the way, what good am I to the other? But if I serve to connect the other to the source of all empowerment, healing, and restoration, then I fulfill my greatest responsibility: to be witness and mediator between the other and the actual Messiah who alone is worthy of the name. Mount Carmel is the very place of personal intercession and mediation. Mount Carmel faces Mount Zion as contemplative annex and satellite. Mount Carmel stands witness to the metamorphosis of the Jerusalem temple into the temple of the soul, God's heaven on earth. It is through my soul in its union with the soul of the Messiah that sacrificial atonement is consummated.

Without complete dependence on the actual Messiah, who alone can bear the weight of the world, my attempt to lift the world out of my responsibility, alone, even with the help of fulcrum and lever (Archimedes), is entirely overwhelming and futile. Saint Thérèse of Lisieux writes that

> what Archimedes was not able to obtain, for his request was not directed by God and was only made from a material viewpoint, the saints have obtained in all its fullness. The Almighty has given them as *fulcrum: himself alone*; as *lever: prayer* which burns with a fire of love. And it is in this way that they have *lifted the world*; it is in this way that the saints still militant lift it, and that, until the end of time, the saints to come will lift it.[17]

I sense that what the other needs most I cannot give: God. Only God speaks well of God, and only God can give God to souls who thirst for him. Further,

17. Thérèse of Lisieux, *Story of a Soul*, Manuscript C, 36r°–36v° (italics original).

I must confess that my soul thirsts for him as well, and, the face of the other, for all of the glorious traces of divinity that signify therewith, does not in itself deliver the fullness of divine glory to my weary soul.[18] I yearn for God within—in the interior chambers of my soul!—and only God can manifest himself and speak to me therein. This is the redoubled humility of divine immanence. It certainly is not that God is conflated with the self. No, God remains entirely distinct from and other than the self. However, a genuine unity obtains between the soul and God in and through this irreducible otherness of spirit. The face of the human other is not God, and neither am I God. What I need most is God. What the other needs most is God. This is why evangelization might be the greatest task of responsibility imaginable: "Peter said, 'I have neither silver nor gold, but what I do have I give you: in the name of Jesus Christ the Nazorean, rise and walk.' Then Peter took him by the hand and raised him up, and immediately his feet and ankles grew strong. He leaped up, stood, and walked around, and went into the temple with them, walking and jumping and praising God" (Acts 3:6–8). Notice how this scene ends with the healed man entering the temple to praise God. And that was the point all along, that this man would encounter the living God in all of his self-revealed power and goodness.

Without divine grace, Levinasian ethics is simply impossible. Without Jesus the Messiah, Levinasian ethics is a messianic dream. Without God the Holy Spirit at work within us, Levinasian responsibility amounts to an impossible weight that I cannot lift on my own, a crushing anxiety that paralyzes my most hopeful intentionalities, and an insurmountable scrupulosity that suffocates any ounce of self-esteem. Without divine grace, Levinasian ethics can breed an overly judgmental attitude toward oneself, and, inevitably toward other people too. There becomes the danger of "straining out the gnat while swallowing the camel" (Matt 23:24). If "the world in which pardon is all-powerful becomes inhuman" and "the possibility of infinite pardon tempts us to infinite evil," a world without the almighty potencies of pardon is one in which no one is allowed to say, "I am sorry." Rabbi Jonathan Sacks has made a similar observation: a culture without forgiveness makes it impossible to say, "I am sorry." A culture without forgiveness is a culture without contrition and admission of guilt. A culture without forgiveness prohibits the possibility of owning up to my own wrongdoing because no one would forgive me anyway. A world without the almighty potencies of pardon is one which disqualifies the merciful power

18. See 2 Cor 3:16–18: "Whenever a person turns to the Lord the veil is removed. Now the Lord is the Spirit, and where the Spirit of the Lord is, there is freedom. All of us, gazing with unveiled face on the glory of the Lord, are being transformed into the same image from glory to glory, as from the Lord who is the Spirit."

of forgiveness. As an *abuela* said to Pope Francis upon coming to him to confess her sins, "If the Lord didn't forgive everything our world would not exist."[19] And unlimited forgiveness need not cancel out the vocation to responsibility. Could it be that my responsibility for the other goes that far—to forgive the other everything since I am responsible for his responsibility? "Then Peter approaching asked Jesus, 'Lord, if my brother sins against me, how often must I forgive him? As many as seven times?' Jesus answered, 'I say to you, not seven times but seventy-seven times'" (Matt 18:21–22). Human responsibility without divine grace and the exercise of forgiveness is Pelagianism writ large, as if our own virtuous actions originated with ourselves and could save the world by themselves.

Mount Carmel is the elevation at which I raise my white flag and cry out, "I surrender!" And it is this place of utmost surrender and powerful passivity that all divine activity is unleashed into the world. The battle is won to the degree that the arms of Moses remain uplifted and outstretched, with his companions supporting them.[20] The rains of blessing come to the degree that Elijah remains crouched down to the earth with his head between his knees, with his servant keeping watch over the sea and King Ahab descending Mount Carmel by chariot.[21] The paradox of loving and contemplative responsibility: divinity acts to the measure that humanity yields to this divine activity in an active passivity of soul. "The LORD will fight for you; you have only to keep still" (Exod 14:14). I fulfill my greatest responsibility when I invite God to act, when I leave something for God to do. The thirst of my neighbor is not for me, but for him. The point is not Saint John the Baptist, but the waters of baptism. That is why he points to the Point that is the Messiah that he himself is not: "he must increase; I must decrease" (John 3:30). The most responsible hero is the most relaxed and restful contemplative: "Unless the LORD build the house, they labor in vain who build. Unless the LORD guard the city, in vain does the guard keep watch. It is vain for you to rise early and put off your rest at night, to eat the bread earned by hard toil—all this God gives to his beloved in sleep" (Ps 127:1–2). If Levinasian ethics be coopted by the ideological left, it results in a communist world order in which "responsibility" is finalized since everyone has enough material bread but no temple on earth at which to worship God in spirit and truth. If Levinasian ethics be coopted by the ideological right, it amounts to a capitalist world order in which the economic elite fulfill their "responsibilities" by flooding the faceless throng of disenfranchised and marginalized with tokens of their self-congratulating

19. Francis, *Name of God Is Mercy*, 25.
20. See Exod 17:8–13.
21. See 1 Kgs 18:41–45.

beneficence in the name of "god." In either case, when the human vocation is reduced to political activism, God is eclipsed because he has nothing left to do. On the other hand, when the human vocation is reduced to worship only, with no ethical activism, God still has nothing to do among us because I am doing nothing for the other who faces me. Dialectical theology prevents the ideological collapse of truth into just a few of its many parts. If we are true to truth, its whole always will be greater than the sum of its many innumerable parts. When Mount Carmel meets Mount Zion, solitude meets solicitude. When Mount Carmel meets Mount Zion, contemplation meets ethics. When Mount Carmel meets Mount Zion, manifestation meets proclamation. When Mount Carmel meets Mount Zion, immanence meets transcendence. When Mount Carmel meets Mount Zion, heart meets hand.

Levinas has much to teach Christianity, and this book hopes to witness to this happy exchange. At the same time, Christianity, and especially the Carmelite charism of contemplation, has something to add to Levinasian ethics. So much contemplation, so much ethical action. No ethics without contemplation, and no contemplation without ethics. Mount Zion and Mount Carmel have everything to do with one another. The Christian claim that Jesus is the Messiah affirms all that Levinas has to say about the universal human vocation to responsibility for the other. What Jesus adds to this vocation is the real potential to accomplish it actually, for he is Actuality in the flesh. As a follower of Jesus, I readily admit my frailty, weakness, and caducity of being. However, as Jesus said to Saint Paul, he also says to me, "My grace is sufficient for you, for power is made perfect in weakness" (2 Cor 12:9). And, to say with Saint Paul, "for when I am weak, then I am strong" (2 Cor 12:10). This is the truth about me and the Messiah: I am not him, but because he is Jesus, and Jesus is God in the flesh, I can participate in his redemptive mission and ministry in the world. Through the sacramental life of the church, I remain in the Vine and he remains in me. Mount Carmel signifies the messianic perichoresis of responsibility, one-for-the-other. Without the divine Wind, the sail of the soul is to no avail. So much rogation, so much responsibility. So much responsibility, so much rogation.

BIBLIOGRAPHY

Allefeld, Carsten. "The Hollow of Being: What Can We Learn from Maurice Merleau-Ponty's Ontology for a Science of Consciousness?" *Mind and Matter* 6.2 (2008) 235–56. http://www.carsten-allefeld.de/pub/hollow.pdf.

Allen, Sarah. *The Philosophical Sense of Transcendence: Levinas and Plato on Loving Beyond Being*. Pittsburgh: Duquesne University Press, 2009.

Almog, Meirav. "Transforming the Problem of the Other: Rethinking Merleau-Ponty's Itinerary." *The Southern Journal of Philosophy* 54.3 (2016) 293–311.

Aronowicz, Annette. "Introducing 'The Temptation of Temptation': Levinas and Europe." *The Journal of Scriptural Reasoning* 11.2 (2012). http://jsr.shanti.virginia. edu/back-issues/volume-11-no-2-december-2012-levinas-and-philosophy/ introducing-the-temptation-of-temptation-levinas-and-europe/.

Bahler, Brock. "Merleau-Ponty on Children and Childhood." *Childhood & Philosophy* 11.22 (2015) 203–21.

Bataille, Georges. "The Use Value of D. A. F. de Sade." In *Visions of Excess: Selected Writings, 1927–1939*, edited by Allan Stoekl, 94–102. Minneapolis: University of Minnesota Press, 1986.

Beach, Bradley, and Matthew Powell. *Interpreting Abraham: Journeys to Moriah.* Minneapolis: Fortress, 2014.

Beals, Corey. *Levinas and the Wisdom of Love: The Question of Invisibility.* Waco, TX: Baylor University Press, 2007.

Becker, Brian, et al. "Introduction to the Special Section: A Relational-Existential Psychology: Ethics and Embodiment." *The Humanistic Psychologist* 43.2 (2015) 121–27.

Benedict XVI, Pope. *Deus caritas est.* http://www.vatican.va/content/benedict-xvi/en/ encyclicals/documents/hf_ben-xvi_enc_20051225_deus-caritas-est.html.

Benson, Bruce Ellis, and Norman Wirzba, eds. *Words of Life: New Theological Turns in French Phenomenology.* New York: Fordham University Press, 2010.

Bernasconi, Robert, and Simon Critchley, eds. *Re-Reading Levinas.* Bloomington, IN: Indiana University Press, 1991.

Bindeman, Steven L. "Merleau-Ponty's Embodied Silence." In *Silence in Philosophy, Literature, and Art*, edited by Steven L. Bindeman, 57–72. Leiden: Brill-Rodopi, 2017.

Bindeman, Steven L., ed. *Silence in Philosophy, Literature, and Art*. Leiden: Brill-Rodopi, 2017.

Bloechl, Jeffrey, ed. *Christianity and Secular Reason: Classical Themes and Modern Developments*. Notre Dame, IN: University of Notre Dame Press, 2012.

———, ed. *The Face of the Other and the Trace of God: Essays on the Philosophy of Emmanuel Levinas*. New York: Fordham University Press, 2000.

———. *Liturgy of the Neighbor: Emmanuel Levinas and the Religion of Responsibility*. Pittsburgh: Duquesne University Press, 2000.

———, ed. *Religious Experience and the End of Metaphysics*. Bloomington: Indiana University Press, 2003.

Brooks, Neil, and Josh Toth, eds. *The Mourning After: Attending the Wake of Postmodernism*. New York: Rodopi, 2007.

Bruckner, Pascal. *The Temptation of Innocence: Living in the Age of Entitlement*. New York: Algora, 2000.

Burggraeve, Roger, ed. *The Awakening to the Other: A Provocative Dialogue with Emmanuel Levinas*. Leuven: Peeters, 2008.

———. "Dialogue of Transcendence: A Levinasian Perspective on the Anthropological-Ethical Conditions for Interreligious Dialogue." *Journal of Communication and Religion* 37.1 (2014) 2–28.

———. "Violence and the Vulnerable Face of the Other: The Vision of Emmanuel Levinas on Moral Evil and Our Responsibility." *Journal of Social Philosophy* 30.1 (1999) 29–45.

Calcagno, Antonio. "God and the Caducity of Being: Jean-Luc Marion and Edith Stein on Thinking God." Paper delivered at the Twentieth World Congress of Philosophy in Boston, Massachusetts, from August 10–15, 1998. https://www.bu.edu/wcp/Papers/Reli/ReliCalc.htm.

Caputo, John D., and Michael J. Scanlon, eds. *God, the Gift, and Postmodernism*. Bloomington: Indiana University Press, 1999.

Cavalletti, Sophia. *The Religious Potential of the Child: Experiencing Scripture and Liturgy with Young Children*. Translated by Patricia M. Coulter and Julie M. Coulter. Chicago: Liturgy Training, 1992.

Chanter, Tina, ed. *Feminist Interpretations of Emmanuel Levinas*. University Park: Pennsylvania State University Press, 2001.

Charlier, Catherine. *Figures du féminin*. Paris: La Nuit surveillée, 1982.

Chouraqui, Frank. "*Circulus Vitiosus Deus*: Merleau-Ponty's Ontology of Ontology." *Studia Phænomenologica* 16 (2016) 469–87.

Ciocan, Cristian, and Georges Hansel. *Levinas Concordance*. Dordrecht: Springer, 2005.

Cohen, Richard A., ed. *Face to Face with Levinas*. Albany: State University of New York Press, 1986.

———. "Judaism and Philosophy." *Common Ground Journal* 12.2 (2015) 64–76.

Coyne, Ryan. "A Difficult Proximity: The Figure of Augustine in Heidegger's Path." *Journal of Religion* 91.3 (2011) 365–96.

Crisp, Oliver D., and Michael C. Rea, eds. *Analytic Theology: New Essays in the Philosophy of Theology*. New York: Oxford University Press, 2009.

Critchley, Simon, and Peter Dews, eds. *Deconstructive Subjectivities*. Albany: State University of New York Press, 1996.

Crowther, Paul. "The Poetry of 'Flesh' or the Reality of Perception? Merleau-Ponty's Fundamental Error." *International Journal of Philosophical Studies* 23.2 (2015) 255–78.

Dalton, Drew M. *Longing for the Other: Levinas and Metaphysical Desire*. Pittsburgh: Duquesne University Press, 2009.

Davis, Colin. *Levinas: An Introduction*. Cambridge, MA: Polity, 1996.

Derrida, Jacques. *Adieu to Emmanuel Levinas*. Translated by Pascale-Ane Brault and Michael Naas. Stanford: Stanford University Press, 1999.

Diamond, Cora. *Wittgenstein's Lectures on the Foundations of Mathematics: Cambridge, 1939: From the Notes of R. G. Bosanquet, Norman Malcolm, Rush Rhees, and Yorick Smythies*. Ithaca, NY: Cornell University Press, 1976.

Dillon, M. C. *Merleau-Ponty Vivant*. Albany: State University of New York Press, 1991.

Douglas, Mark. "Theologies of Childhood and the Children of War." *Journal of Childhood and Religion* 3.2 (2012) 1–29.

Dupont, Christian Y. "Jean Héring and the Introdution of Husserl's Phenomenology to France." *Studia Phænomenologica* 15 (2015) 129–53.

Edgar, Orion. *Things Seen and Unseen: The Logic of Incarnation in Merleau-Ponty's Metaphysics of Flesh*. Eugene, OR: Cascade, 2016.

Fleming, Daniel J. "Primordial Moral Awareness: Levinas, Conscience, and the Unavoidable Call to Responsibility." *The Heythrop Journal* 56.4 (2015) 604–18.

Francis, Pope. *The Name of God Is Mercy: A Conversation with Andrea Tornielli*. Translated by Oonagh Stransky. New York: Random House, 2016.

Fritz, Peter Joseph. "Black Holes and Revelations: Michel Henry and Jean-Luc Marion on the Aesthetics of the Invisible." *Modern Theology* 25.3 (July 2009) 415–40.

Gibbs, Robert. "Enigmatic Authority: Levinas and the Personal Effacement." *Modern Theology* 16.3 (2000) 325–34.

Grondin, Jean. *Introduction to Metaphysics: From Parmenides to Levinas*. Translated by Lukas Soderstrom. New York: Columbia University Press, 2012.

Gschwandtner, Christina M. "À Dieu or from the Logos? Emmanuel Levinas and Jean-Luc Marion—Prophets of the Infinite." *Philosophy and Theology* 22.1/2 (2010) 177–203.

———. *Degrees of Givenness: On Saturation in Jean-Luc Marion*. Bloomington: Indiana University Press, 2014.

———. "Ethics, Eros, or Caritas? Levinas and Marion on Individuation of the Other." *Philosophy Today* 49.1 (2005) 70–87.

———. "The Neighbor and the Infinite: Marion and Levinas on the Encounter between Self, Human Other, and God." *Continental Philosophy Review* 40.3 (2007) 231–49.

Guenther, Lisa. *The Gift of the Other: Levinas and the Politics of Reproduction*. Albany: State University of New York Press, 2006.

Hallett, Garth. *Wittgenstein's Definition of Meaning as Use*. New York: Fordham University Press, 1967.

Hand, Seán. *Emmanuel Levinas*. New York: Routledge, 2009.

Hansel, Joëlle. "Beyond Phenomenology: Levinas's Early Jewish Writings." *Levinas Studies* 5 (2010) 5–17.

———, ed. *Levinas in Jerusalem: Phenomenology, Ethics, Politics, Aesthetics*. Dordrecht: Springer, 2009.

Hart, Kevin, ed. *Counter-Experiences: Reading Jean-Luc Marion*. Notre Dame, IN: University of Notre Dame Press, 2007.

Hart, Kevin, and Michael A. Signer, eds. *The Exorbitant: Emmanuel Levinas between Jews and Christians*. New York: Fordham University Press, 2010.

Heidegger, Martin. *Being and Time*. Translated by John Macquarrie and Edward Robinson. San Francisco: HarperCollins, 1962.

Herzog, Annabel. "Levinas and Derrida on Translation and Conversion." *Prooftexts* 34.2 (2014) 127–46.

Horner, Robyn. *Jean-Luc Marion: A Theo-logical Introduction.* Burlington, VT: Ashgate, 2005.

———. *Rethinking God as Gift: Marion, Derrida, and the Limits of Phenomenology.* New York: Fordham University Press, 2001.

Husserl, Edmund. *Ideas Pertaining to a Pure Phenomenology and to Phenomenological Philosophy, First Book: General Introduction to a Pure Phenomenology.* Translated by F. Kersten. The Hague: Martinus Nijhoff, 1982.

Hyde, Brendan, ed. *The Search for a Theology of Childhood: Essays by Jerome W. Berryman from 1978–2009.* Ballarat, VIC: Modotti, 2013.

Ignatius of Loyola. *Ignatius of Loyola: The Spiritual Exercises and Selected Works.* Edited by George E. Ganss. New York: Paulist, 1991.

John of the Cross, Saint. *The Collected Works of St. John of the Cross.* Translated by Kieran Kavanaugh and Otilio Rodriguez. Washington, DC: ICS, 1991.

John Paul II, Pope. *Mulieris dignitatem.* http://www.vatican.va/content/john-paul-ii/en/apost_letters/1988/documents/hf_jp-ii_apl_19880815_mulieris-dignitatem.html.

———. *Veritatis splendor.* http://www.vatican.va/content/john-paul-ii/en/encyclicals/documents/hf_jp-ii_enc_06081993_veritatis-splendor.html.

Jones, Tamsin. *A Genealogy of Jean-Luc Marion's Philosophy of Religion: Apparent Darkness.* Bloomington: Indiana University Press, 2011.

Kaplan, Lawrence. "Israel under the Mountain: Emmanuel Levinas on Freedom and Constraint in the Revalation of the Torah." *Modern Judaism* 18.1 (1998) 35–46.

Katz, Claire Elise. "'Before the Face of God One Must Not Go with Empty Hands': Transcendence and Levinas's Prophetic Consciousness." *Philosophy Today* 50.1 (2006) 58–68.

———. "'For Love Is as Strong as Death': Taking Another Look at Levinas on Love." *Philosophy Today* 45 (2001) 124–32.

———. *Levinas and the Crisis of Humanism.* Bloomington: Indiana University Press, 2013.

———. *Levinas, Judaism, and the Feminine: The Silent Footsteps of Rebecca.* Bloomington: Indiana University Press, 2003.

———. "Lisa Guenther's 'The Gift of the Other': Levinas and the Politics of Reproduction." *Symposium* 11.2 (2007) 447–54.

———. "Raising Cain: The Problem of Evil and the Question of Responsibility." *Cross Currents* 55.2 (2005) 215–33.

———. "The Significance of Childhood." *International Studies in Philosophy* 34.4 (2002) 77–101.

Katz, Claire Elise, and Lara Trout, eds. *Levinas and the History of Philosophy.* Vol. 2, *Emmanuel Levinas: Critical Assessments of Leading Philosophers.* 12 vols. New York: Routledge, 2005.

Kavka, Martin. "Is There a Warrant for Levinas's Talmudic Readings?" *Journal of Jewish Thought and Philosophy* 14.1/2 (2006) 153–73.

Kearney, Richard. *Debates in Continental Philosophy: Conversations with Contemporary Thinkers.* New York: Fordham University Press, 2004.

Keenan, Dennis King. *Death and Responsibility: The "Work" of Levinas.* Albany: State University of New York Press, 1999.

Kessler, Michael, and Christian Sheppard, eds. *Mystics: Presence and Aporia*. Chicago: University of Chicago Press, 2003.

Kosky, Jeffrey L. "Contemplative Recovery: The Artwork of James Turrell." *Cross Currents* 63.1 (March 2013) 44–61.

———. *Levinas and the Philosophy of Religion*. Bloomington: Indiana University Press, 2001.

Leask, Ian, and Eoin Cassidy, eds. *Givenness and God: Questions of Jean-Luc Marion*. New York: Fordham University Press, 2005.

Levinas, Emmanuel. *Alterity and Transcendence*. Translated by Michael B. Smith. New York: Columbia University Press, 1999.

———. *Beyond the Verse: Talmudic Readings and Lectures*. Translated by Gary D. Mole. Bloomington: Indiana University Press, 1994.

———. *Collected Philosophical Papers*. Translated by Alphonso Lingis. Dordrecht: Martinus Nijhoff, 1987.

———. *Difficult Freedom*. Translated by Seán Hand. Baltimore: Johns Hopkins University Press, 1990.

———. *Discovering Existence with Husserl*. Translated by Richard A. Cohen and Michael B. Smith. Evanston, IL: Northwestern University Press, 1998.

———. *Emmanuel Levinas: Basic Philosophical Writings*. 2nd edition. Edited by Adriaan T. Peperzak et al. Bloomington: Indiana University Press, 2008.

———. *En découvrant l'existence avec Husserl et Heidegger*. Paris: Librairie Philosophique J. Vrin, 1967.

———. *Entre Nous: On Thinking of the Other*. Translated by Michael B. Smith and Barbara Harshav. New York: Columbia University Press, 1998.

———. *Ethics and Infinity: Conversations with Philippe Nemo*. Translated by Richard A. Cohen. Pittsburgh: Duquesne University Press, 1985.

———. *Existence and Existents*. Translated by Alphonso Lingis. Pittsburgh: Duquesne University Press, 2001.

———. *God, Death, and Time*. Translated by Bettina Bergo. Stanford: Stanford University Press, 2000.

———. *Humanism of the Other*. Translated by Nidra Poller. Chicago: University of Illinois Press, 2003.

———. *In the Time of the Nations*. Translated by Michael B. Smith. Bloomington: Indiana University Press, 1994.

———. *The Levinas Reader*. Edited by Seán Hand. Cambridge, MA: Basil Blackwell, 1989.

———. *New Talmudic Readings*. Translated by Richard A. Cohen. Pittsburgh: Duquesne University Press, 1999.

———. *Nine Talmudic Readings*. Translated by Annette Aronowicz. Bloomington: Indiana University Press, 1990.

———. *Of God Who Comes to Mind*. Translated by Bettina Bergo. Stanford: Stanford University Press, 1998.

———. *On Escape*. Translated by Bettina Bergo. Stanford: Stanford University Press, 2003.

———. *Otherwise than Being or Beyond Essence*. Translated by Alphonso Lingis. Pittsburgh: Duquesne University Press, 1981.

———. *Outside the Subject*. Translated by Michael B. Smith. London: Athlone, 1993.

———. *Positivité et transcendance*. Paris: Presses Universitaires de France, 2000.

————. *Proper Names.* Translated by Michael B. Smith. Stanford: Stanford University Press, 1996.

————. "Reflections on the Philosophy of Hitlerism." *Critical Inquiry* 17.1 (1990) 62–71.

————. *The Theory of Intuition in Husserl's Phenomenology.* 2nd ed. Translated by Andre Orianne. Evanston, IL: Northwestern University Press, 1995.

————. *Time and the Other.* Translated by Richard A. Cohen. Pittsburgh: Duquesne University Press, 1987.

————. *Totality and Infinity: An Essay on Exteriority.* Translated by Alphonso Lingis. Pittsburgh: Duquesne University Press, 1969.

————. *Unforeseen History.* Translated by Nidra Poller. Chicago: University of Illinois Press, 2004.

Louth, Andrew. *The Origins of the Christian Mystical Tradition: From Plato to Denys.* New York: Oxford University Press, 2007.

Mackinlay, Shane. *Interpreting Excess: Jean-Luc Marion, Saturated Phenomena, and Hermeneutics.* New York: Fordham University Press, 2010.

Malka, Salomon. *Emmanuel Levinas: His Life and Legacy.* Translated by Michael Kigel and Sonja M. Embree. Pittsburgh: Duquesne University Press, 2006.

Manoussakis, John Panteleimon. *God after Metaphysics: A Theological Aesthetic.* Bloomington: Indiana University Press, 2007.

Marion, Jean-Luc. *Being Given: Toward a Phenomenology of Givenness.* Translated by Jeffrey L. Kosky. Stanford: Stanford University Press, 2002.

————. *Cartesian Questions: Method and Metaphysics.* Translated by Jeffrey L. Kosky et al. Chicago: University of Chicago Press, 1999.

————. *Certitudes negatives.* Paris: Grasset, 2010.

————. *The Crossing of the Visible.* Stanford: Stanford University Press, 2004.

————. *Dieu sans l'être.* Paris: Quadrige, 2002.

————. *The Erotic Phenomenon.* Chicago: University of Chicago Press, 2007.

————. *The Essential Writings.* Edited by Kevin Hart. New York: Fordham University Press, 2013.

————. *Givenness and Hermeneutics.* Translated by Jean-Pierre Lafouge. Milwaukee: Marquette University Press, 2013.

————. *Givenness and Revelation.* Translated by Stephen E. Lewis. New York: Oxford University Press, 2016.

————. *God without Being: Hors-Texte.* Translated by Thomas A. Carlson. Chicago: University of Chicago Press, 1991.

————. *The Idol and Distance: Five Studies.* Translated by Thomas A. Carlson. New York: Fordham University Press, 2001.

————. *In Excess: Studies of Saturated Phenomena.* Translated by Robyn Horner and Vincent Berraud. New York: Fordham University Press, 2002.

————. *In the Self's Place: The Approach of Saint Augustine.* Translated by Jeffrey L. Kosky. Stanford: Stanford University Press, 2012.

————. "The Invisibility of the Saint." Translated by Christina M. Gschwandtner. *Critical Inquiry* 35.3 (2009) 703–10.

————. "La phénoménalité du sacrement: être et donation." *Communio* 26.5 (2001) 59–75.

————. *Le croire pour le voir: réflections diverses sur la rationalité de la révélation et l'irrationalité de quelques croyants.* Paris: Parole et Silence, 2010.

————. *L'idole et la distance: cinq etudes.* Paris: Grasset, 1977.

————. *Negative Certainties.* Translated by Stephen E. Lewis. Chicago: University of Chicago Press, 2015.

————. *On Descartes' Metaphysical Prism: The Constitution and the Limits of Onto-theology in Cartesian Thought.* Translated by Jeffrey L. Kosky. Chicago: University of Chicago Press, 1999.

————. *On the Ego and on God: Further Cartesian Questions.* Translated by Christina M. Gschwandtner. New York: Fordham University Press, 2007.

————. *Prolegomena to Charity.* Translated by Stephen E. Lewis. New York: Fordham University Press, 2002.

————. "The Question of the Unconditioned." Translated by Christina M. Gschwandtner. *The Journal of Religion* 93.1 (2013) 1–24.

————. *The Reason of the Gift.* Translated by Stephen E. Lewis. Charlottesville: University of Virginia Press, 2011.

————. *Reduction and Givenness: Investigations of Husserl, Heidegger, and Phenomenology.* Translated by Thomas A. Carlson. Evanston, IL: Northwestern University Press, 1998.

————. *Réduction et donation: recherches sur Husserl, Heidegger et la phenomenologie.* Paris: Presses Universitaires de France, 1989.

————. *The Visible and the Revealed.* Translated by Christina M. Gschwandtner et al. New York: Fordham University Press, 2008.

Martinich, A. P., and David Sosa, eds. *Analytic Philosophy: An Anthology.* West Sussex: Wiley-Blackwell, 2012.

McGinn, Bernard. *The Foundations of Mysticism: Origins to the Fifth Century.* The Presence of God: A History of Western Christian Mysticism 1. New York: Crossroad, 1991.

Merleau-Ponty, Maurice. *Adventures of the Dialectic.* Translated by Joseph Bien. Evanston, IL: Northwestern University Press, 1973.

————. *Child Psychology and Pedagogy: The Sorbonne Lectures, 1949–1952.* Translated by Talia Welsh. Evanston, IL: Northwestern University Press, 2010.

————. *Consciousness and the Acquisition of Language.* Translated by Hugh J. Silverman. Evanston, IL: Northwestern University Press, 1973.

————. *Maurice Merleau-Ponty: Basic Writings.* Edited by Thomas Baldwin. New York: Routledge, 2004.

————. *Phenomenology of Perception.* Translated by Colin Smith. London: Routledge and Kegan Paul, 1981.

————. *The Primacy of Perception.* Edited by James M. Edie. Evanston, IL: Northwestern University Press, 1964.

————. *The Prose of the World.* Translated by Claude Lefort. Evanston, IL: Northwestern University Press, 1973.

————. *Sense and Non-sense.* Translated by Hubert L. Dreyfus and Patricia Allen Dreyfus. Evanston, IL: Northwestern University Press, 1964.

————. *Signs.* Translated by Richard C. McCleary. Evanston, IL: Northwestern University Press, 1964.

————. *Themes from the Lectures at the Collège de France, 1952–1960.* Translated by John O'Neill Evanston, IL: Northwestern University Press, 1970.

————. *The Visible and the Invisible.* Edited by Claude Lefort. Translated by Alphonso Lingis Evanston, IL: Northwestern University Press, 1968.

Moore, G. E. *Ethics*. New York: Oxford University Press, 1977.

———. *Principia Ethica*. Cambridge, MA: Cambridge University Press, 1966.

———. *Some Main Problems of Philosophy*. New York: Humanities, 1978.

Morgan, Michael L. *The Cambridge Introduction to Emmanuel Levinas*. New York: Cambridge University Press, 2011.

———. *Discovering Levinas*. New York: Cambridge University Press, 2007.

Mumford, James. *Ethics at the Beginning of Life: A Phenomenological Critique*. Oxford: Oxford University Press, 2013.

Nelson, Eric Sean, et al., eds. *Addressing Levinas*. Evanston, IL: Northwestern University Press, 2005.

Panikkar, Raimon. *The Rhythm of Being: The Gifford Lectures*. Maryknoll, NY: Orbis, 2010.

Pascal, Blaise. *Pensées*. Paris: Garnier, 1964.

Peperzak, Adriaan Theodoor. *Beyond: The Philosophy of Emmanuel Levinas*. Evanston, IL: Northwestern University Press, 1997.

———, ed. *Ethics as First Philosophy: The Significance of Emmanuel Levinas for Philosophy, Literature and Religion*. New York: Routledge, 1995.

———. *To the Other: An Introduction to the Philosophy of Emmanuel Levinas*. West Lafayette, IN: Purdue University Press, 1993.

Pinardi, Sandra. "Expresión y Desnudez: Un Acercamiento a la Noción de Justicia en el Pensamiento de Emmanuel Lévinas." *Eidos* 21 (2014) 104–26.

Pinckaers, Servais. *Morality: The Catholic View*. Translated by Michael Sherwin. South Bend, IN: St. Augustine's Press, 2001.

———. *The Sources of Christian Ethics*. Translated by Mary Thomas Noble. Washington, DC: Catholic University of America Press, 1995.

Plato. *Plato: Complete Works*. Edited by John M. Cooper. Indianapolis: Hackett, 1997.

Pseudo-Dionysius. *Pseudo-Dionysius: The Complete Works*. Translated by Colm Lubheid. New York: Paulist, 1987.

Purcell, Michael. "An *Agape* of Eating: The Eucharist as Substitution (Levinas)." *Bijdragen* 57 (1996) 318–36.

———. *Levinas and Theology*. New York: Cambridge University Press, 2006.

Rahner, Karl. *Further Theology of the Spiritual Life 1*. Vol. 7 of *Theological Investigations*. 23 vols. Translated by David Bourke. New York: Herder & Herder, 1971.

———. *Further Theology of the Spiritual Life 2*. Vol. 8 of *Theological Investigations*. 23 vols. Translated by David Bourke. New York: Herder & Herder, 1971.

Ratzinger, Joseph. *The Spirit of the Liturgy*. Translated by John Saward. San Francisco: Ignatius, 2000.

———. *Truth and Tolerance: Christian Belief and World Religions*. Translated by Henry Taylor. San Francisco: Ignatius, 2004.

Rawnsley, Andrew. "Practice and Givenness: The Problem of 'Reduction' in the Work of Jean-Luc Marion." *New Blackfriars* 88.1018 (2007) 690–708.

Rea, Michael C. "Introduction." In *Analytic Theology: New Essays in the Philosophy of Theology*, edited by Oliver D. Crisp and Michael C. Rea, 1–30. New York: Oxford University Press, 2009.

Ricoeur, Paul. "Biblical Hermeneutics." *Semeia* 4 (1975) 29–148.

———. *The Conflict of Interpretations: Essays in Hermeneutics*. Translated by Evanston, IL: Northwestern University Press, 1974.

———. *The Course of Recognition*. Translated by David Pellauer. Cambridge, MA: Harvard University Press, 2005.

———. *Essays on Biblical Interpretation*. Edited by Lewis S. Mudge. Philadelphia: Fortress, 1980.

———. *Fallible Man*. Translated by Charles A. Kelbley. New York: Fordham University Press, 1986.

———. *Figuring the Sacred: Religion, Narrative, and Imagination*. Edited by Mark I. Wallace. Minneapolis: Fortress, 1995.

———. *Freedom and Nature: The Voluntary and the Involuntary*, Translated by Erazim V. Kohák. Evanston, IL: Northwestern University Press, 2007.

———. *Freud and Philosophy: An Essay on Interpretation*. Translated by Denis Savage. New Haven: Yale University Press, 1970.

———. *From Text to Action: Essays in Hermeneutics, II*. Translated by Kathleen Blamey and John B. Thompson. Evanston, IL: Northwestern University Press, 1991.

———. *Hermeneutics and the Human Sciences: Essays on Language, Action and Interpretation*. Translated by John B. Thompson. New York: Cambridge University Press, 1993.

———. *History and Truth*. Translated by Charles A. Kelbley. Evanston, IL: Northwestern University Press, 1965.

———. *Husserl: An Analysis of His Phenomenology*. Translated by Edward G. Ballard and Lester E. Embree. Evanston, IL: Northwestern University Press, 1967.

———. *Interpretation Theory: Discourse and the Surplus of Meaning*. Fort Worth: Texas Christian University Press, 1976.

———. *The Just*. Translated by David Pellauer. Chicago: University of Chicago Press, 2000.

———. *A Key to Husserl's Ideas I*. Translated by Bond Harris and Jacqueline Bouchard. Milwaukee: Marquette University Press, 1996.

———. *Main Trends in Philosophy*. New York: Holmes & Meier, 1979.

———. "Manifestation and Proclamation." *The Journal of the Blaisdell Institute* 12 (1978) 13–35.

———. *Memory, History, Forgetting*. Translated by David Pellauer and Kathleen Blamey. Chicago: University of Chicago Press, 2004.

———. *Oneself as Another*. Translated by Kathleen Blamey. Chicago: University of Chicago Press, 1994.

———. "Philosophy and Religious Language." *The Journal of Religion* 54.1 (1974) 71–85.

———. *Reflections on The Just*. Translated by David Pellauer. Chicago: University of Chicago Press, 2007.

———. *The Rule of Metaphor: The Creation of Meaning in Language*. Translated by Robert Czerny et al. New York: Routledge, 2003.

———. *The Symbolism of Evil*. Translated by Emerson Buchanan. New York: Harper & Row, 1967.

———. *Thinking Biblically: Exegetical and Hermeneutical Studies*. Translated by David Pellauer. Chicago: University of Chicago Press, 1998.

———. *Time and Narrative, Vol 1*. Translated by Kathleen McLaughlin and David Pellauer. Chicago: University of Chicago Press, 1984.

———. *Time and Narrative, Vol 2*. Translated by Kathleen McLaughlin and David Pellauer. Chicago: University of Chicago Press, 1985.

————. *Time and Narrative, Vol 3*. Translated by Kathleen Blamey and David Pellauer. Chicago: University of Chicago Press, 1988.

Robbins, Jill, ed. *Is It Righteous to Be? Interviews with Emmanuel Levinas*. Stanford: Stanford University Press, 2001.

Rogers, Brian. "Traces of Reduction: Marion and Heidegger on the Phenomenon of Religion." *Southern Journal of Philosophy* 52.2 (2014) 184–205.

Rosato, Jennifer. "Woman as Vulnerable Self: The Trope of Maternity in Levinas's *Otherwise Than Being*." *Hypatia* 27.2 (2012) 348–65.

Russell, Bertrand. *The Art of Philosophizing and Other Essays*. Totowa, NJ: Rowman & Allanheld, 1974.

————. *An Inquiry into Meaning and Truth*. London: Allen & Unwin, 1966.

————. *Logic and Knowledge: Essays, 1901–1950*. London: Allen & Unwin, 1977.

————. *Mysticism and Logic and Other Essays*. London: Longmans, Green, 1918.

————. *Our Knowledge of the External World as a Field for Scientific Method in Philosophy*. New York: Routledge, 2006.

————. *An Outline of Philosophy*. Cleveland: Meridian, 1964.

————. *Sceptical Essays*. New York: Routledge, 2005.

————. *Why I Am Not a Christian and Other Essays on Religion and Related Subjects*. Edited by Paul Edwards. New York: Simon & Schuster, 1957.

Sailakumar, Silpa, and K. P. Naachimuthu. "A Phenomenological Approach to Understand the Nature Based Experiences and Its Influence on Holistic Development." *Indian Journal of Positive Psychology* 8.2 (2017) 186–95.

Schrijvers, Joeri. *An Introduction to Jean-Yves Lacoste*. Burlington, VT: Ashgate, 2012.

————. "Ontotheological Turnings? Marion, Lacoste and Levinas on the Decentering of Modern Subjectivity." *Modern Theology* 22.2 (2006) 221–53.

Simms, Eva-Maria. "The Countryside of Childhood: A Hermeneutic Phenomenological Approach to Developmental Psychology." *The Humanist Psychologist* 27.3 (1999) 301–27.

————. "The Infant's Experience of the World: Stern, Merleau-Ponty and the Phenomenology of the Preverbal Self." *The Humanistic Psychologist* 21.1 (1993) 26–40.

————. "Milk and Flesh: A Phenomenological Reflection on Infancy and Coexistence." *Journal of Phenomenological Psychology* 32.1 (2001) 22–40.

————. "Phenomenology of Child Development and the Postmodern Self: Continuing the Dialogue with Johnson." *The Humanistic Psychologist* 22.2 (1994) 228–35.

Simpson, Christopher Ben. *Merleau-Ponty and Theology*. New York: T. & T. Clark, 2014.

Smith, Michael B. *Toward the Outside: Concepts and Themes in Emmanuel Levinas*. Pittsburgh: Duquesne University Press, 2005.

Stein, Edith. *Essays on Woman*. Translated by Freda Mary Oben. Washington, DC: ICS, 1996.

————. *The Hidden Life: Essays, Meditations, Spiritual Texts*. Translated by Waltraut Stein. Washington, DC: ICS, 1992.

————. *On the Problem of Empathy*. Translated by Waltraut Stein. Washington, DC: ICS, 1989.

————. *Potency and Act: Studies Toward a Philosophy of Being*. Translated by Walter Redmond. Washington, DC: ICS, 2009.

Steinbock, Anthony J. *Phenomenology and Mysticism: The Verticality of Religious Experience*. Bloomington: Indiana University Press, 2009.

Stern, Daniel N. *The Interpersonal World of the Infant: A View from Psychoanalysis and Developmental Psychology*. New York: Basic, 2000.

Sweeney, Conor. *Sacramental Presence after Heidegger: Onto-theology, Sacraments, and the Mother's Smile*. Eugene, OR: Cascade, 2015.

Teresa of Ávila. *The Collected Works of Saint Teresa of Avila, Vol. 2*. 3 vols. Translated by Kieran Kavanaugh and Otilio Rodriguez. Washington, DC: ICS, 1980.

Thatcher, Adrian. "Theology and Children: Towards a Theology of Childhood." *Transformation* 23.4 (2006) 194–99.

Thérèse of Lisieux. *Story of a Soul: The Autobiography of St. Thérèse of Lisieux*. Translated by John Clarke. Washington, DC: ICS, 1996.

Tirosh-Samuelson, Hava, ed. *Women and Gender in Jewish Philosophy*. Bloomington: Indiana University Press, 2004.

Tracy, David. *The Analogical Imagination: Christian Theology and the Culture of Pluralism*. New York: Crossroad, 1981.

———. *Dialogue with the Other: The Inter-religious Dialogue*. Louvain: Peeters, 1990.

———. *Plurality and Ambiguity: Hermeneutics, Religion, Hope*. Chicago: University of Chicago Press, 1987.

Vieira, Emanuel Meireles. "Ethics and the Person-centered Approach: A Dialogue with Radical Alterity." *Theory & Psychology* 25.6 (2015) 798–813.

Wall, John. *Ethics in Light of Childhood*. Washington, DC: Georgetown University Press, 2010.

Wallenfang, Donald L. "Aperture of Absence: Jean-Luc Marion on the God Who 'Is Not.'" In *Models of God and Alternative Ultimate Realities*, edited by Jeanine Diller and Asa Kasher, 861–73. New York: Springer, 2013.

———. *Dialectical Anatomy of the Eucharist: An Étude in Phenomenology*. Eugene, OR: Cascade, 2017.

———. "Dialectical Truth between Augustine and Pelagius: Levinas and the Challenge of Responsibility to Superabundant Grace." In *Global Perspectives on the New Evangelization: Evangelization as Interreligious Dialogue*, edited by John C. Cavadini and Donald Wallenfang, 2:122–39. 5 vols. Eugene, OR: Pickwick, 2019.

———. "Face Off for Interreligious Dialogue: A Theology of Childhood in Jean-Luc Marion versus a Theology of Adulthood in Emmanuel Levinas." *Listening* 50.2 (2015) 106–16.

———. "Figures and Forms of Ultimacy: Manifestation and Proclamation as Paradigms of the Sacred." *The International Journal of Religion in Spirituality and Society* 1.3 (2011) 109–14.

———. *Human and Divine Being: A Study on the Theological Anthropology of Edith Stein*. Eugene, OR: Cascade, 2016.

———. "Introduction." In *Global Perspectives on the New Evangelization: Evangelization as Interreligious Dialogue*, edited by John C. Cavadini and Donald Wallenfang, 2:xv–xl. 5 vols. Eugene, OR: Pickwick, 2019.

———. "Introduction." In *Global Perspectives on the New Evangelization: Pope Francis and the Event of Encounter*, edited by John C. Cavadini and Donald Wallenfang, 1:xv–xxv. 5 vols. Eugene, OR: Pickwick, 2018.

———. "Levinas and Marion on Law and Freedom: Toward a New Dialectical Theology of Justice." *Pacifica* 29.1 (2017) 71–98.

———. *Metaphysics: A Basic Introduction in a Christian Key*. Eugene, OR: Cascade, 2019.

———. *Phenomenology: A Basic Introduction in the Light of Jesus Christ.* Eugene, OR: Cascade, 2019.

———. "Pope Francis and His Phenomenology of *Encuentro.*" In *Global Perspectives on the New Evangelization: Pope Francis and the Event of Encounter,* edited by John C. Cavadini and Donald Wallenfang, 1:57–71. 5 vols. Eugene, OR: Pickwick, 2018.

———. "Sacramental Givenness: The Notion of Givenness in Husserl, Heidegger, and Marion, and Its Import for Interpreting the Phenomenality of the Eucharist." *Philosophy and Theology* 22.1/2 (2010) 131–54.

———. *Trilectic of Testimony: A Phenomenological Construal of the Eucharist as Manifestation-Proclamation-Attestation.* Ann Arbor, MI: ProQuest, 2011.

———. "Virtual Counterfeit of the Infinite: Emmanuel Levinas and the Temptation of Temptation." In *The Html of Cruciform Love: Toward a Theology of the Internet,* edited by Eric Lewellen and John Frederick, 132–50. Eugene, OR: Pickwick, 2019.

Wallenfang, Donald L., and Megan Wallenfang. *Shoeless: Carmelite Spirituality in a Disquieted World.* Eugene, OR: Wipf & Stock, 2021.

Welsh, Talia. *The Child as Natural Phenomenologist: Primal and Primary Experience in Merleau-Ponty's Psychology.* Evanston, IL: Northwestern University Press, 2013.

Westphal, Merold. *Levinas and Kierkegaard in Dialogue.* Bloomington: Indiana University Press, 2008.

———. "Vision and Voice: Phenomenology and Theology in the Work of Jean-Luc Marion." *International Journal for Philosophy of Religion* 60.1–3 (2006) 117–37.

Whitehead, Alfred North. *Science and the Modern World: Lowell Lectures, 1925.* New York: Macmillan, 1967.

Whitehead, Alfred North, and Bertrand Russell. *Principia Mathematica Vol. 1.* 2 vols. Cambridge, MA: Cambridge University Press, 1910.

Wittgenstein, Ludwig. *The Blue and the Black Books: Preliminary Studies for "The Philosophical Investigations."* Oxford: Blackwell, 1969.

———. *Culture and Value.* Edited by G. H. von Wright. Translated by Peter Winch. Chicago: University of Chicago Press, 1980.

———. *Letters to Russell, Keynes and Moore.* Edited by G. H. von Wright. Ithaca, NY: Cornell University Press, 1974.

———. *Notebooks: 1914–1916.* Edited by G. H. von Wright and G. E. M. Anscombe. Chicago: University of Chicago Press, 1979.

———. *On Certainty.* Edited by G. E. M. Anscombe and G. H. von Wright. New York: Harper & Row, 1969.

———. *Philosophical Investigations.* Translated by G. E. M. Anscombe et al. West Sussex: Wiley-Blackwell, 2009.

———. *Tractatus Logico-Philosophicus.* Translated by D. F. Pears and B. F. McGuinness. London: Routledge & Kegan Paul, 1966.

———. *Zettel.* Edited by G. E. M. Anscombe and G. H. Wright. Berkeley: University of California Press, 1967.

Wynn, Francine. "The Embodied Chiasmic Relationship of Mother and Infant." *Human Studies* 19 (1997) 253–70.

Wyschogrod, Edith. *Emmanuel Levinas: The Problem of Ethical Metaphysics.* New York: Fordham University Press, 2002.

Zhao, Guoping. "Freedom Reconsidered: Heteronomy, Open Subjectivity, and the 'Gift of Teaching.'" *Studies in Philosophy and Education* 33.5 (2014) 513–25.

Zimmermann, Nigel. *Facing the Other: John Paul II, Levinas, and the Body.* Eugene, OR: Cascade, 2015.

INDEX